D0207876

WEALTH AND POWER
IN TUDOR ENGLAND

WITHDRAWN

Wealth and Power in Tudor England

Essays presented to

S. T. BINDOFF

edited by

E. W. IVES

R. J. KNECHT

J. J. SCARISBRICK

UNIVERSITY OF LONDON

THE ATHLONE PRESS

1978

Published by
THE ATHLONE PRESS
UNIVERSITY OF LONDON
at 4 Gower Street London WC1

Distributed by Tiptree Book Services Ltd
Tiptree, Essex

USA and Canada
Humanities Press Inc
New Jersey

© *University of London* 1978

British Library Cataloguing in Publication Data
Wealth and power in Tudor England.
  1. Great Britain—Economic conditions—
Addresses, essays, lectures
I. Ives, Eric William II. Knecht, Robert
Jean III. Scarisbrick, John Joseph
IV. Bindoff, Stanley Thomas
330.9'42'05   HC254.3

ISBN 0 485 11176 4

HC
254.4
.W4

Printed in Great Britain by
WESTERN PRINTING SERVICES LTD
BRISTOL

Foreword

This Festschrift has been a labour of love; and it is offered to the man whom it honours as a token of gratitude and admiration, as well as affection.

Professor S. T. Bindoff's scholarly achievement consists above all in having done much to enlarge and modernise the study of the sixteenth and seventeenth centuries and our understanding of them. The main reasons for this are not hard to find. First, he has had a keen eye for the realities which lie below the surface and for the interdependence of the socio-economic and political. Secondly, he has shown a special sensitivity to the interplay of ideas and action, to the role of groups and classes and to the ways in which the local can illumine the national. Next, though delighting in the challenge of particular problems (the more complex and technical the better) and a master at teasing out the knottiest of them, he has never lost sight of the larger world beyond the boundaries of England—in Europe, and particularly the Netherlands. Finally, he has cultivated a catholicity of mind which gives due weight to every kind of historical enquiry, whether it concerns kings or peasants, grand theory or single text, religious allegiance or commercial practice, institutions such as parliament, the common law and the City of London or bricks and mortar.

To have done full justice to him would have required a much larger volume than this one. Alas, the stringencies of the times have forced us to restrict the scope of this work almost exclusively to sixteenth-century England and to limit the list of contributors severely. There were not a few others who were eager to contribute (indeed, some of them had even prepared their essays) and would certainly have done so in less harsh times. We hope that this collection nonetheless shows some of the ways in which Professor Bindoff has encouraged us to study the past, and reflects some of the range and high standards of scholarship, literacy and readability which he himself has rigorously taught and practised.

We wish to express our gratitude to Miss Norah Fuidge for compiling the bibliography of S. T. Bindoff's historical writings and the index, and to Professors R. F. Leslie and A. G. Dickens for their biographical memoirs. We also acknowledge most gratefully the financial support for this volume provided by The Twenty-Seven Foundation.

E. W. I.
R. J. K.
J. J. S.

Contributors

GINA ALEXANDER,
PH.D.
H. M. I.

B. DIETZ, PH.D.
Senior Lecturer in History,
University of Glasgow

A. G. DICKENS, D.LIT.,
F.B.A.
Emeritus Professor of History and
formerly Director of the Institute of
Historical Research, University of
London

G. R. ELTON, LITT.D., F.B.A.
Professor of English Constitutional
History, University of Cambridge

NORAH FUIDGE, M.A.
Research Assistant, History of
Parliament Trust

J. J. GORING, M.A., PH.D.
Principal Lecturer in History, Gold-
smiths' College, University of London

PHYLLIS HEMBRY,
PH.D.
formerly Head of the History
Department, The Cheltenham
Ladies' College

E. W. IVES, PH.D.
Senior Lecturer in Modern History,
University of Birmingham

R. J. KNECHT, M.A.
Senior Lecturer in Modern History,
University of Birmingham

R. F. LESLIE, PH.D.
Professor of History, Queen Mary
College, University of London

HELEN MILLER, M.A.
Senior Lecturer in History,
University College of North Wales,
Bangor

M. J. POWER, PH.D.
Lecturer in Modern History,
University of Liverpool

J. J. SCARISBRICK, M.A.,
PH.D.
Professor of History, University of
Warwick

R. VIRGOE, PH.D.
Senior Lecturer in English History,
University of East Anglia

Contents

     of Trade in the 1560s   186
     B. DIETZ

xi   Wealden Ironmasters in the Age of Elizabeth   204
     J. J. GORING

     The Historical Writings of S. T. Bindoff   228

     Index   233

Maps

Abbreviations

APC	*Acts of the Privy Council of England*, ed. J. Dasent (1890–1907)
BIHR	*Bulletin of the Institute of Historical Research*
BL	British Library (formerly British Museum)
CCR	*Calendar of the Close Rolls*
CFR	*Calendar of the Fine Rolls*
CJ	*Journals of the House of Commons*
Complete Peerage	G. E. Cokayne, *Complete Peerage of England, Scotland Ireland, etc.*, ed. V. Gibbs *et al.* (1910–49)
CPR	*Calendar of the Patent Rolls*
CS	Camden Society
CSP Dom.	*Calendar of State Papers Domestic*
CSP Scot.	*Calendar of State Papers relating to Scotland*, ed. J. Bain *et al.* (in progress)
CSP Span.	*Calendar of State Papers relating to the Negotiations between England and Spain*
CSP Ven.	*Calendar of State Papers relating to English Affairs existing in the Archives of Venice*
DNB	*Dictionary of National Biography*
EcHR	*Economic History Review*
EETS	Early English Text Society
EHR	*English Historical Review*
HMC	Historical Manuscripts Commission
LP	*Letters and Papers, Foreign and Domestic, of the Reign of Henry VIII*, ed. J. S. Brewer *et al.* (1862–1932)
LJ	*Journals of the House of Lords*
PCC	Prerogative Court of Canterbury (now at the Public Record Office, class PROB)
RP	*Rotuli Parliamentorum* (1783)
SAC	*Sussex Archaeological Collections*

SR	*Statutes of the Realm*, ed. A. Luders *et al.* (1810–28)
STC	*Short Title Catalogue of Books printed in England, Scotland and Ireland, and of English Books printed abroad, 1475–1640*, ed. A. W. Pollard and G. R. Redgrave (1926)
StP	*State Papers King Henry VIII* (1830–52)
TRHS	*Transactions of the Royal Historical Society*
VCH	Victoria County History
Tudor Procs.	*Tudor Royal Proclamations*, ed. P. L. Hughes and J. F. Larkin (1964–69)
YB	*Les Reports de Cases*, ed. J. Maynard (1678–80)

Manuscripts at the Public Record Office, London, are quoted by the call number only, according to the following key:

C1	Early Chancery Proceedings
C3	Chancery Proceedings, Series II
C43	Placita in Cancellaria, Rolls Chapel Series
C47	Chancery Miscellanea
C54	Close Rolls
C66	Patent Rolls
C67	Patent Rolls (Supplementary)
C78	Chancery Decree Rolls
C82	Warrants for the Great Seal, Series II
C142	Inquisitions post Mortem (Chancery), Series II
C219	Writs and Returns of Members to Parliament
C244	Chancery, Files, Corpus cum Causa
E23	Exchequer, Treasury of Receipt, Royal Wills
E36	Exchequer, Treasury of Receipt, Books
E122	Exchequer, King's Remembrancer, Customs Accounts
E135	Exchequer, King's Remembrancer, Ecclesiastical Documents
E159	Exchequer, King's Remembrancer, Memoranda Roll
E164	Exchequer, King's Remembrancer, Miscellaneous Books, Series I
E179	Exchequer, King's Remembrancer, Subsidy Rolls
E190	Exchequer, King's Remembrancer, Port Books
E305	Exchequer, Augmentations, Deeds of Purchase and Exchange
E317	Exchequer, Augmentations, Parliamentary Surveys
E318	Exchequer, Augmentations, Particulars for Grants of Crown Lands

E334	Exchequer, First Fruits and Tenths, Composition Books
E337	Exchequer, First Fruits and Tenths, Plea Rolls
E356	Exchequer, Pipe Office, Enrolled Accounts
E368	Exchequer, Lord Treasurer's Remembrancer, Memoranda Rolls
KB9	King's Bench, Ancient Indictments
KB27	Coram Rege Rolls
CP40	De Banco Rolls
REQ2	Court of Requests, Proceedings
STAC1	Star Chamber, Proceedings, Henry VII
STAC2	Star Chamber, Proceedings, Henry VIII
STAC5	Star Chamber, Proceedings, Elizabeth I
HCA31	High Court of Admiralty, Examinations
DL42	Duchy of Lancaster, Miscellaneous Books
SC6	Special Collections, Ministers' and Receivers' Accounts
SP1	State Papers, Henry VIII, General Series
SP4	State Papers, Signatures by Stamp
SP10	State Papers Domestic, Edward VI
SP12	State Papers Domestic, Elizabeth I
SP46	State Papers (Supplementary)
PC2	Privy Council Registers
PSO2	Warrants for the Privy Seal, Series II
PROB 11	Prerogative Court of Canterbury. Probate Registers

S. T. Bindoff
An appreciation

(i) R. F. LESLIE

It is difficult in any appreciation of Professor S. T. Bindoff to divorce the historian from the man. Bindoff arrived at University College London in 1926 with the advantage of having been taught at Brighton Grammar School by Dr A. E. Wilson, himself a historian and antiquary of distinction who remained a life-long friend.

Unusually tall, Bindoff was a sportsman of great prowess, but his contemporaries recall also his impressively wide knowledge of music, architecture, the fine arts and literature. He wished to obtain an academic post, but, in spite of enjoying the high regard of Professor A. F. Pollard, Professor Pieter Geyl and Sir Charles Webster, his advancement was delayed by the bleak economic circumstances of the 1930s. The research assistant at the Institute of Historical Research could have resisted the temptations of a possible career beyond the university only if his love for his subject had been more than compensation for the meagre part-time salaries which the Institute could then offer. He had graduated in 1929 and in 1934 submitted a thesis for the degree of M.A., which not only earned a mark of Distinction, but was published in 1945 with the aid of a subvention from the government of the Netherlands to become the authoritative account of the Scheldt Question. In 1935 he was awarded the Alexander Prize by the Royal Historical Society and in that year obtained a post in the Department of History at University College, where in 1945 he was to become a Reader.

The London School of History provided Bindoff with an umbrella to cover activities extending beyond the formal duties of his teaching. Today it is often forgotten that forty years ago tuberculosis and other dangerous diseases afflicted students in particular. At University College he was a stout supporter of the creation of a student health service. He may be justly proud of the fact that not only was a service provided at his own college, but that now similar provision is made in all the other London colleges. A lesser-known aspect of his activity has been his solicitude for sick colleagues and students, whom he invariably visited when they fell ill, or whom, in the event of dire need, he took into his own home for care.

In 1951 he was translated from his Readership at University College to the Chair of History at Queen Mary College, the first university Chair of History tenable at that college. The Department of History was then small, but it had Dr Helena M. Chew as one of its teachers, for whose welfare Bindoff did much during the long illness which afflicted her almost immediately upon her retirement in 1963. The Department at that time consisted of only four teachers, whereas today it has two established Chairs and two established Readerships, together with nine other members of staff. This expansion took place under Bindoff's leadership. His burden as Head of Department was not lightened by the additional tasks which he was always ready to undertake. He became Chairman of the Board of Examiners, then Chairman of the Board of Studies in History at the University of London. In this capacity he presided over the first stages of reform of the syllabus in the post-war period, a problem so fraught with possible conflict that only a chairman of his ability, seeking consciously to capture the sense of the Board, could have achieved reform at all. Having served his terms of office as Dean of the Faculty of Arts (1955–58) and Governor of Queen Mary College (1958–61), he was called upon in 1966 to become a member of the Senate of the University of London to which he brought the wide practical experience of a man who knew the work of the university in all its aspects.

His progression through the often tiresome tasks of college and university office meant no slackening of his efforts as a teacher and director of research. His love of London, comparable to that of Dr Samuel Johnson, included a love of East London. He was instrumental in forming the East London History Group and promoting the publication of *East London Papers*, the activities of which have now been continued in *The London Journal*, in the foundation of which Bindoff played a prominent part. Much as he has loved London Bindoff has loved the countryside no less, as many a student conducted on long walks will know. He served for sixteen years as a member of the committee of the *Victoria County History* and acted as its chairman in the years from 1969 to 1971, during which time he helped to secure a uniformity of conditions of employment for the editorial staff and successfully negotiated the beginning of work on several counties which had hitherto been untouched.

Bindoff has had an uncanny faculty for supporting the projects of others. Promoters of a good cause often found that it became the subject of informal discussions at dinner in the Reform Club. The London Record Society undoubtedly owes much to the loyal support which he gave it in the early days of its formation. His work for the History of Parliament Trust will bring to fruition the Tudor section of that vast enterprise. In a wider field Bindoff, acting as the representative of the University of London, did much to serve the cause of multi-racial education in the University College of Rhodesia, now the University of Rhodesia, both as an adviser and as an examiner. In 1958, Bindoff received recognition for his contribution to the welfare of the community by his election as a Fellow of University College.

Proof of Bindoff's popularity as a teacher and a man came in the warm receptions given to him by his colleagues and students on the occasion of his retirement in 1975. This volume of essays, presented to him on his seventieth birthday, is further evidence of our respect and affection. In his lifetime Bindoff has done many good deeds, the most impressive of which have been those which we have discovered by accident. He has given his university the example of a dedicated scholar and a devoted teacher, which is the best memorial a man can leave behind him at the end of his years of formal service. In retirement he has remained a sage counsellor and firm friend in the troubles which daily confront us. There is no man with whom his colleagues would be happier to be compared.

(ii) A. G. DICKENS

S. T. Bindoff first became known to me in the year 1950, when I read his *Pelican* on Tudor England, and recognised the hand of a master. Already displaying many of the 'new' dimensions of post-war historiography, the work has worn wonderfully well, and after a quarter of a century it still caters for large and important groups of readers. It was one of those books which made several of us see the vital necessity of *haute vulgarisation*, and inspired us to try our own hands in that genre. By the time he wrote it, Bindoff had already enjoyed a stimulating and versatile early career. Both socially and intellectually he had been a leading spirit among the undergraduates of University College London; and then during the early thirties among postgraduates at the Institute of Historical Research, still a small but select body. He belonged to a regular discussion-group which included Walter Adams, later Director of the London School of Economics, A. T. Milne, subsequently Secretary and Librarian of the Institute, Olwen Kendall, the future Lady Brogan, and A. F. Pollard's research assistant Marjorie Blatcher, whom Bindoff himself was to marry in 1936. In this last gracious alliance he proved singularly fortunate, and he has on many occasions acknowledged the magnitude of his debt, both personal and professional.

At first Bindoff specialised in eighteenth- and nineteenth-century diplomatic history, attending the seminars of Pieter Geyl and Charles Webster. He took a major share in compiling the *List of British Diplomatic Representatives, 1789–1852* (Royal Historical Society, Camden Series, 1934), while his thesis ultimately became a standard monograph. In those years the holders of junior appointments at the Institute badly needed to supplement their stipends, since even then £100 a year did not go far. Among the temporary sidelines pursued by Bindoff was the private coaching of the teenager destined to become King Farouk of Egypt. I hope they paid him well, since I know he did not find the task intellectually rewarding and was often sorely tempted to commit *lèse-majesté*. Even so, by 1935 his foot was firmly on the academic ladder with his appointment to an assistant lectureship at University College.

At the outbreak of war, the Bindoffs helped to evacuate the history department of University College to North Wales, after which he spent three years with the Naval Intelligence Division of the Admiralty. From his time in North Wales, if not earlier, his main interest shifted to the Tudor and early Stuart periods. Already in 1942 he published in *History* an article on the Jacobean traitor Thomas Douglas, while not long after the war he wrote his pamphlet *Ket's Rebellion, 1549*, still the best guide to that episode. It was done for the Historical Association, in which he remained active and influential for some twenty years after the war, serving on the Council and, for a long period, as chairman of its highly productive Publications Committee. In 1966 he was appointed honorary vice-president for life of the Association.

As I have said, he was one of the pioneer students in the newly-founded Institute of Historical Research. When he joined, A. F. Pollard's ambitious plan to create in London a major centre of historical scholarship had got no further than some ex-army huts in Russell Square, containing the nucleus of a first-class research library and a handful of students—among whom Bindoff and his future wife were conspicuous—sufficiently dedicated to go out into highways and byways to give lectures and then donate their fees to Institute funds. This was in the mid-1930s. After the war, when Bindoff resumed his close association with the Institute, he naturally joined Neale's Tudor seminar, but his own powerful influence as a director of studies led him to break away from that august empire and to start his own classes. For a quarter of a century his seminars in English social and economic history of the sixteenth and early seventeenth centuries remained a major feature in the life of the Institute; and all who took part in those tough weekly sessions will know how much their scholarly formation owes to them. Bindoff was an outstanding director of postgraduate work thanks, above all, to three special qualities: a remarkable capacity for clearing his powerful mind of his own preoccupations, however pressing, in order to give himself to his students'; an elephantine memory for bibliographical detail; a most generous concern for the academic and material well-being of all who found themselves under his large and reassuring wing. Nobody ever sought his help in vain. Indeed, he always tempered zeal with humanity and knew enough Greek to be able to translate *Symposium*: many a consultation began in the Institute but ended up in the extramural amenities of the *University Arms* or the *Rising Sun*.

In 1951 Bindoff went to the Chair of History at Queen Mary College. During the subsequent two decades his high standards and diplomacy did much to create a large and successful Department: like so many others during that now fabulous age of expansion, he accomplished all this at heavy cost to his personal researches. Obscuring its marvellous opportunities by such ponderous loads of teaching, thesis-reading and committee-work, London has always exposed its best sons to the torments of Tantalus. Outside the University, Bindoff's influence spread abroad. At the invitation of the Foreign Office he twice toured German universities and he remained a welcome figure among old friends at Anglo-Dutch conferences. Between 1961 and 1973 he paid four visits to the United States, where even his very Englishness endeared him to students and large audiences alike at Harvard, Columbia, Swarthmore, Wellesley and other leading places. I myself vividly remember the occasion when he came to Hull and gave my Department a lecture on a dramatic episode in the history of the Marian House of Commons. With the aid of a blackboard diagram he made it a brilliant experiment in audience-participation, and amid the final applause I could not doubt that all my own students would gladly have migrated to Queen Mary College.

In the event I migrated to London myself, and from 1962 to 1967 taught along with Bindoff, Hurstfield, Dugmore and Collinson in the Tudor England Special Subject seminar held at King's College. These should have been remarkable years for the third-year students exposed to this concentrated bombardment. Certainly they were a golden period for me, then in the last stage of a general book on the English Reformation and needing all the stimulus these distinguished colleagues could give. When in 1967 I was summoned from King's to the Institute, Bindoff had already been a pillar of the latter for over thirty years, yet he welcomed and helped me with a fine mixture of generosity and restraint. The advice he gave me was usually conservative, but in the event always 'right'; the more so since the constrictions of finance and space would soon have made nonsense of my own innovatory leanings. Throughout his long period as a member of the Committee of Management and the Committee of the *Victoria County History*, Bindoff's contribution to the Institute has not been excelled by that of any other person, including the successive Directors themselves.

Meanwhile in that independent yet related activity, the *History of Parliament*, the full extent of his contribution has yet to be revealed, and will in due course appear with the publication of the important volume on the earlier Tudor parliaments and their members. This battle has been prolonged by the inevitably diffused character of his later interests, but it also illustrates the general dilemma facing so many senior scholars of our generation. Despite occasional glib assurances to the contrary, society has wanted us to mass-produce graduates, not to make significant additions to knowledge. But in Bindoff's case it was employing a perfectionist who in the last resort preferred delays to slapdash and provisional answers. Indeed, he let this restraint grow with the years, unlike those of us who with less caution tend to abandon it as we hear the winged chariot steadily gaining ground. After preliminary work with junior assistants, he finally assumed in person the gigantic task of rewriting hundreds of the biographies in his volume of the *History*. A sceptic might well ask whether one with so clear a gift for large-scale exposition should have buried it among the nuts and bolts of Namierization. The final result will doubtless justify the choice, but meanwhile from time to time Bindoff has himself indicated some of the alternatives which might otherwise have come our way: in 1973, for example, by his attractive Neale Lecture, *The Fame of Sir Thomas Gresham*.

To conclude: this is a career marked by an unusual selflessness and an equally unusual versatility. Perhaps the effort to chronicle even the most basic facts has already brought me too near to writing a premature *Times* obituary! If so, I can safely deny the implication, for nowadays life commonly begins at seventy. Released from some of the almost intolerable burdens he has borne for almost half a century, the Emeritus Bindoff will in future years surely do more than tie up the loose ends of middle life.

I

The Recovery of the Howards in East Anglia, 1485-1529

R. VIRGOE

When in his tennis-court in Norwich, asserted Thomas Howard, 4th duke of Norfolk, he thought himself 'in a manner equal with some kings'.[1] More than a hundred years previously his predecessor in the title, John, the third Mowbray duke, proclaimed in similar, if significantly less arrogant terms, that 'next the kyng our soverayn Lord, be his good grace and lycence, we woll have the principall rewle and governance throwh all the schir of whishe we ber our name whyle that we be lyvyng, as ferre as reson and lawe requyrith'.[2] Earls and dukes of Norfolk—Bigods, Mowbrays and Howards—did indeed possess from the twelfth century until the reign of Elizabeth I sufficient lands, vassals and retainers in East Anglia to give them for long periods 'principal rule' in the region.[3] It was not, however, a consistent supremacy; the accident of personality, early deaths and long minorities, long-lived dowagers and the fluctuating fortunes of their political activities brought long periods when they played a lesser role. The Howard dynasty suffered three major catastrophes, in 1485, 1546 and 1572: from the first two they recovered but the last ended for ever their paramount position in East Anglia.[4] This essay tries to show by what means and to what extent the Howards regained, after the first of these catastrophes, the pre-eminence in East Anglia which their predecessors had felt to be theirs of right for nearly four hundred years. It is not intended to deal, save in passing, with the careers of the second and third Howard dukes in national politics, though these, of course, greatly affected their

1. N. Williams, *Thomas Howard, Fourth Duke of Norfolk* (1964), p. 159.
2. *The Paston Letters*, ed. J. Gairdner (1904), ii, 258–60.
3. *Complete Peerage*, ix, 568–624.   4. Williams, op. cit., pp. 258–9.

regional authority, but to concentrate upon their relations with the other magnates and gentry of East Anglia from 1485 until the late 1520s, when a new political era was to bring the family new opportunities for increasing its authority in the country at large and for extending its lands and power in East Anglia.[5]

The basis of regional authority with all it implies—the ability to nominate local officials, interfere in local politics and justice, raise troops and attract clients—was landed wealth. Influence at court or high office under the crown could override this landed position at times but unless these were accompanied by the acquisition of a large territorial base they had only a temporary impact. The Howard dependence upon royal favour has often been commented upon but for them, too, a great landed estate was essential to secure their authority in the region, and when this was established it inevitably became, as the career of the fourth duke shows, to some extent independent of royal favour.

Thus a study of the landed position of the magnates in East Anglia is essential to any attempt to describe and understand their changing political fortunes. The Howard lands in this period have already had some attention, but further material does exist, though inadequate, for a more detailed study.[6] It is difficult to use this material—mostly scattered estate records—to estimate the actual income the lands provided and even more difficult to find direct evidence of the political influence which this landed wealth gave to the Howards and other magnates. Even for the later sixteenth century there is comparatively little evidence for the way in which patronage and influence were brought to bear upon appointments to offices and commissions, the election of members of parliament and the obtaining of royal grants for clients.[7] Most of what direct evidence does survive comes from private correspondence and this is very scanty for the period 1485 to 1530 when the Paston Letters peter out and other surviving family collections have hardly begun. For other periods, earlier and

5. The careers of the second and third dukes are considered in M. Tucker, *The Life of Thomas Howard, Earl of Surrey and 2nd Duke of Norfolk, 1443–1524* (The Hague, 1964), and F. R. Grace, 'The Life and Career of Thomas Howard, third duke of Norfolk, (1473–1554)' (Nottingham Univ. M.A. thesis, 1961). There is a useful study of the first duke by Anne Crawford, 'The Career of John Howard, duke of Norfolk, 1420–85' (London Univ. M.Phil. thesis, 1975).

6. J. R. Lander, 'Attainder and forfeiture, 1453–1509', *Historical Journ.* 4 (1961), 136–8.

7. Cf. A. Hassell Smith, *County and Court* (Oxford, 1974).

later, it is possible to go some way towards assessing influence by correlating known servants and clients of magnates with membership of parliaments, offices and commissions, but for the early Tudor period the method is less effective partly because of the absence of parliamentary returns where influence can be most often discerned, and partly because of the shortage of private correspondence, household accounts and indentures of service.[8] The sorts of connection between magnates and gentry that can readily be established, such as kinship and the employment of legal counsel, do not always imply a very close bond. Even where a connection between a magnate and a local official or commissioner can be established, as in the case of the earl of Oxford whose will provides a full list of servants, retainers and friends at the end of his life, it is, of course not certain that the appointment was owed to the magnate.[9] Other undiscovered connections may have existed and in any case a variety of other factors may account for such appointments at this or any other time. But all this said, it is possible to illustrate, if not to analyse, relations between the landed position of the Howards and their rivals in this period and to assess the extent of their clientage.

The core of the Howard lands in the sixteenth century lay in the estates inherited from the Mowbrays, which on the death of the last Mowbray duke in 1476 comprised over one hundred manors and numerous other lands, advowsons, parks and forests, as well as franchises, feudal lordships and knight's fees.[10] The lands extended into twenty-eight English counties and into Wales, Ireland and Calais, but were particularly extensive in four areas: (1) East Anglia, predominantly in north-east Suffolk and south Norfolk, the centre of the earldom of Norfolk since the twelfth century; (2) Sussex, together with the lordship of Reigate in Surrey; (3) the north Midlands, particularly Leicester-

8. See e.g. ibid., pp. 21–44; J. S. Roskell, *The Commons in the Parliament of 1422* (Manchester, 1954).

9. PCC 11 Fetiplace [printed in W. H. St John Hope, 'The last testament and inventory of John de Veer, thirteenth earl of Oxford', *Archaeologia*, 66 (1914–15), 275–348].

10. Calculated from the lands mentioned in the acts of 1478 and 1489, from the lists of Duchess Katharine's lands, and from the valuation of the lands left by the third duke in 1461 [*RP*, vi, 168–70, 411–12; *CCR, 1429–35*, pp. 204–5, 208–14; BL, Add. Ch. 16558].

shire and Derbyshire; and (4) Yorkshire. Until 1468 there had
been a fifth important group of lands in South Wales and the
Marches, but in that year the duke had been induced to grant his
lordships of Gower and Chepstow to the earl of Pembroke and,
though he retained lands in North Wales, he had ceased to be a
Marcher lord. In return for this alienation, the earl of Pembroke
had persuaded, perhaps forced, Thomas Charles of Kettleburgh to
grant the duke two manors in East Anglia, and the king had made
to him an unusual grant of franchisal rights over a large part of
his East Anglian and Sussex and Surrey lands, thus creating 'the
liberty of the duke of Norfolk'.[11] This liberty comprised some of
the most important of Norfolk's estates—though it did not
include Framlingham—but it is important to remember that in
the fifteenth century Mowbray interests were national rather
than regional and they had castles, lands and clients in many parts
of England.

In 1476, however, the duke did not leave the estates un-
encumbered. A considerable proportion had been for forty
years in the possession of the Dowager Duchess Katharine, who
had outlived four husbands and until 1483 was to hold nearly all
the Bedfordshire lands, most of those in Yorkshire and Leicestershire, four valuable Norfolk manors and scattered lands and
rights in other counties.[12] The dower lands of the fourth duke's
mother had reverted to him on her death in 1474, but his own
death necessitated the provision of a substantial dower for his
widow, Elizabeth.[13] She was persuaded to settle for less than her
legal due but in the event was to hold her dower, provided
largely from the East Anglian estates, with lands in Derbyshire and
Leicestershire and Sussex, for thirty years.[14] At the same time
Framlingham and other manors were in the hands of the duke's
feoffees for the fulfilment of his will.[15]

The rest of the duke's estates, perhaps half of the total Mow-

11. *Glamorgan County History*, iii: The Middle Ages, ed. T. B. Pugh (Cardiff,
1971), pp. 257–62; *RP*, vi, 292–4, 478–9; *CPR, 1467–77*, pp. 110–11, 163; *CCR,
1468–76*, 67, 142; *Cal. Charter Rolls, 1427–1516*, pp. 223–5.

12. *RP*, vi, 168–9; *CCR, 1429–35*, pp. 204, 208–14.

13. *CPR, 1467–77*, pp. 191, 488.

14. *RP*, vi, 169–70. Pembroke College Cambridge, Ms. L. 1 is a detailed
valuation of her dower drawn up in 1478. It shows that the lands provided her
with a clear income of around £1200, but this was considerably burdened by
annuities, fees to stewards etc.

15. *RP*, vi, 169–70; BL, Add. Ch. 26598.

bray inheritance, together with the reversion of the rest, went to his daughter and heir, Anne, and her young husband, Richard duke of York, and by act of parliament these were settled on Richard for life even if, as happened, Anne died without issue.[16] The bulk of the lands that were to come to the young couple immediately were not in East Anglia but in Sussex. As the crown could certainly have controlled the choice of lands for Duchess Elizabeth's dower, it seems that the king was not primarily concerned at this time with adding an East Anglian appanage to the lands his son already possessed in the Midlands: perhaps, he preferred to leave East Anglia as the sphere of influence of his brothers-in-law, the duke of Suffolk and Earl Rivers, and of his trusted servant, Lord Howard.

Howard was legally one of the co-heirs of the young duchess on her death in 1481, but there is no evidence that he deeply resented his exclusion from the inheritance, and he remained in favour at court. An act of 1482 vested the rights of the other co-heir, Lord Berkeley, in the young duke of York and his heirs, with remainder to the king in tail male, but York continued to hold the Howard share for life only, so there was no permanent disinheritance.[17] Nevertheless, Richard III's usurpation could only benefit Howard and, though there is no evidence that he played a major part in bringing it about, from early in the new reign he was heaped with offices, honours and lands.[18] Although the act of 1482 was never repealed, York was treated as dead by the end of June when the Mowbray inheritance was allowed to revert to the co-heirs. During the summer of 1483 Howard and Lord Berkeley partitioned the inheritance, Howard taking the East Anglian and the bulk of the Sussex lands with manors in Essex, Bedfordshire etc.[19] Most of the East Anglian lands were for the moment held by the dowagers, but Framlingham and the other lands held by feoffees came to Howard at once and his share of the lands of Duchess Katharine on her death in the later summer

16. *RP*, vi, 168–9, 205–7.   17. Ibid., vi, 205–7.
18. Crawford, op. cit., pp. 182–200, discusses the implications of these grants for the date of death of the young princes and Howard's role in the affair.
19. *RP*, vi, 411–12. Berkeley took most of the lands in the North and Midlands and some in Essex, Sussex etc., but he granted these to the king in 1484 in return for an annuity. The complicated later history of the Berkeley share is not the concern of this paper [*CCR, 1476–85*, 1225, 1363; John Smyth, *The Berkeley MSS*, ed. J. Maclean (Gloucester, 1883–85), ii].

of 1483.[20] Howard's new wealth and status were recognised by his creation as duke of Norfolk and earl marshal on 28 June 1483. His son was created earl of Surrey on the same day.[21]

The partition had given to Lord Berkeley the bulk of the midland and northern lands; the new duke's territories were largely confined to East Anglia and the south-east, and the extensive royal grants which followed on 28 July strengthened this emphasis. The first granted to Howard and his heirs male a large part of the lands of the earl of Oxford in Essex, Suffolk and Cornwall, together with a score of former Hungerford manors mainly in Wiltshire.[22] The second granted him virtually all the Scales lands of the late Lord Rivers.[23] This was a grant 'during the king's pleasure' and was not transformed into a tail male grant until February 1485, but its score of manors, mostly in west Norfolk, immediately helped to make him much the greatest landowner in East Anglia.[24] His receiver-general's accounts for 1483-4 show receipts from the Mowbray, De Vere and Scales lands totalling over £1000 and this excludes lands held before 1483 and estate outside East Anglia.[25] Howard thus had a secure landed basis for authority in the region, which was bolstered by his influence at court. The two other lords with large estates in East Anglia—the duke of Suffolk and Lord Fitzwalter—had neither the wealth nor the influence at court to rival his.

There is little direct evidence of the influence that Howard was able to exert in East Anglian politics. He was given very wide military powers in eastern England in July 1483, but the thousand armed men he had ready for the king's service in 1484 were drawn from his tenants and servants, a number of whom, such as Richard Southwell and James Hobart, the stewards of his estates, had been inherited by him from his Mowbray predecessor.[26] But

20. Katharine died before 28 September 1483, and Howard was certainly in possession of her lands as well as Framlingham and the enfeoffed lands by Michaelmas 1483 [BL, Harl., 433, f. 117v; Add. Ch. 16599].

21. CPR, 1476-85, p. 358; Cal. Charter Rolls, 1427-1516, p. 258.

22. CPR, 1476-85, p. 359.   23. Ibid., p. 365.

24. Ibid., p. 497. Other lands were added by the same grant. For an incomplete summary of lands granted to Howard in tail male see BL, Harl., 433, ff. 287-8.

25. BL, Add. Ch. 16559.

26. CPR, 1461-67, p. 45; 1476-85, p. 362; The Household Books of John Duke of Norfolk etc., ed. J. P. Collier (Roxburghe Club, 1844), pp. 480-92; BL, Add, Ch. 16559; I. H. Jeayes, Descriptive Catalogue of the Charters etc. at Berkeley Castle (Bristol, 1892), p. 190.

two surviving letters from Howard to John Paston show that in 1483 and 1485 he expected the armed support of leading Norfolk gentlemen and their servants, though it is uncertain how many followed him to Bosworth.[27] There is no clear evidence that he exerted great influence on local offices and commissions. The two sheriffs appointed in Richard's reign were associated with the royal household rather than with Howard, and only a few gentlemen definitely associated with Howard—James Hobart, Richard Southwell, John Wyndham, Thomas Jenney and perhaps Sir Henry Wentworth—sat on the commission of the peace.[28] But these few examples probably do not truly reflect Howard's position in the region which derived not only from his estates but also from his standing at court and from thirty years of political and social influence in East Anglia.

This wealth and power disappeared with the death of the duke at Bosworth and the attainder of his heir, the earl of Surrey. The lands granted them by Richard III reverted for the most part to their rightful heirs and the Mowbray estates escheated to the crown. During the first years of the new reign substantial parts of these lands were granted away. In particular Lord De la Warr was granted in tail male in March 1486 a large part of the Sussex lands, and in July 1486 the caput of the Mowbray estates, Framlingham, with other manors, was granted in tail male to the earl of Oxford.[29] In April of the same year the Mowbray dowager, Duchess Elizabeth, received a lease for life of the East Anglian manors formerly held by the Duchess Katharine.[30] She now held all the Mowbray lands in Norfolk and half of those in Suffolk; though charged with a number of annuities, rents and fees, her estates brought her in the early 1490s a gross income of over £1700 and net cash receipts of over £1100.[31]

The fall of the Howards did not, as in 1546 and 1572, leave the

27. *Paston Letters*, vi, 73, 85.

28. *CPR, 1476–85*, pp. 428, 566–7, 573–4; Roxburghe Club, op. cit., pp. 4, 10–11; *Paston Letters*, vi, 87–8; J. C. Wedgwood, *History of Parliament: Biographies* (1936), p. 690; PSO2/1. Membership of commissions of the peace here and elsewhere is taken from the lists in *CPR* and *LP*.

29. *CPR, 1485–94*, pp. 121, 128.   30. Ibid., p. 99.

31. Ibid., pp. 23, 150; *CCR, 1485–1500*, 565, 705, 939, 1209. The income is estimated from an incomplete account roll of the estates of the duchess for 1491–2 which was included in Phillipps Ms. 3840. This ms. is now in the possession of Mr B. Spencer of the London Museum, to whom I am much indebted for permission to consult it.

region leaderless. From 1485 John, 13th earl of Oxford, was the dominant figure in Norfolk and Suffolk, as well as in the neighbouring counties. His part in Henry's victory, and his military and political activities during the next decade brought him much influence at court and numerous honours, offices and other grants, including the offices of lord high admiral and constable of the Tower (in which posts he succeeded John Howard), great chamberlain of England and chief steward of the southern part of the duchy of Lancaster.[32] At the same time he built up a great landed estate in eastern England. The 1485 parliament reversed his attainder, thus restoring him to his patrimony, mainly in Essex and Suffolk, and at the same time annulled the grant made by his mother in 1474 to the duke of Gloucester, so putting him into possession of her large estates which were mainly in Norfolk.[33] He also succeeded to half of the Scales lands formerly held by Earl Rivers and subsequently by John Howard; his share consisted for the most part of manors in west Norfolk.[34] His influence in the same area was augmented by the stewardship of Castle Rising in September 1486 and in the same year he was granted in tail male a large number of manors in several counties, including Framlingham and other Mowbray lands, and the reversion of the stewardship of the honour of Clare; in March 1488 he received the custody of the lands of the lunatic, Viscount Beaumont.[35]

Oxford had other grants, of course, but it is clear that the effect of those just listed, when added to his large inheritance, was to make him not only the greatest land-owner in eastern England but to give him the opportunity of great political control there. A receiver-general's account of 1488–9 shows Oxford receiving a net income of over £1400 from lands, apart from fees and annuities, and this was increased, presumably by efficient administration, during the next few years to perhaps £1800 to £1900.[36] Although Lord Fitzwalter also gained from the change of dynasty

---

32. *Complete Peerage*, x, 239–44.

33. *RP*, vi, 282, 473–4; *CCR, 1468–76*, 1214.

34. *Complete Peerage*, xi, 507; *Cal. Inquisitions post Mortem, Henry VII*, i, 33–6; *Paston Letters*, vi, 124.

35. *CPR, 1486–94*, pp. 75, 121, 142, 222.

36. Essex R.O., D/D Pr. 139 [1488–9]; Norfolk R.O., 1615. The latter is incomplete and undated, but probably derives from the early 1490s; in virtually every case the clear value for each manor is substantially larger than in the account for 1488–9.

and until 1488–9 was lord steward of the household as well as steward of the duchy of Lancaster in Norfolk and Suffolk, neither he nor any other nobleman could rival Oxford's agglomeration of offices and lands.[37] Whether this was deliberate royal policy cannot be known for certain but it cannot have occurred without the king's consent and Oxford's position in the region in the early years of the reign seems similar to that enjoyed by other magnate families connected with the king by ties of old loyalty and recent support, such as the duke of Bedford in Wales, the Stanleys in the North-West and the earl of Northumberland in the far North.

The Paston Letters provide some welcome direct evidence of the earl's influence in East Anglia. There is some bias in the source as John Paston was undoubtedly Oxford's client and his brother the earl's household servant, but the correspondence shows Oxford extensively involved in local government and administration, arbitrating in gentry disputes, organising attendance at royal progresses, advising commissioners and leading the military forces of the counties.[38] He was on all the important commissions of the region during Henry's reign. In 1487 he had a special commission to lead the musters of the five eastern counties against Simnel and the earl of Lincoln. There seems to have been some doubt in Norfolk, perhaps inspired by Lord Fitzwalter, at whose house a number of leading gentlemen met in May 1487, as to whether they should accept Oxford's instructions for mustering, but the sheriff, Sir Edmund Bedingfeld, had no doubt that 'nexte the Kynge . . . I was bownde to do him service', and undoubtedly Paston and other gentlemen of the region felt the same. Many followed Oxford to the battle of Stoke where nine or ten were knighted, a number of them certainly clients of the earl. A month later Oxford was raising more troops to go to the North and there was again a large contribution from Essex and East Anglia, though not many Norfolk gentlemen went in person. Again in 1489 Oxford was organising the military forces of the region.[39]

37. *Complete Peerage*, v, 486–7.
38. *Paston Letters*, vi, 99–101, 111–16, 120–2, 138–9, 160.
39. *CPR, 1485–94*, pp. 179, 278; *Paston Letters*, vi, 99–101, 128–31, 187; Roxburghe Club, op. cit., pp. 493–502. The documents concerning the musters of 1487 in the latter, like the household accounts that follow them, clearly concern Oxford and not (*pace* the editor), Surrey.

Wealth and authority attracted clients who in turn brought more power. Francis Bacon's story of the fine imposed upon Oxford for retaining has no direct contemporary support but the evidence of his will makes it plausible.[40] A codicil names fifty-seven knights and gentlemen to whom he had granted annuities 'for such true and faithful service as they have done unto me'— these were to be continued for the retainers' lives. The will itself mentions a large number of servants, some of gentry status. Evidence from the early years of the reign of Henry VII suggests that his affinity was already large and included the heads of such important families as the Bedingfelds, Pastons, Drurys, Sheltons, Broughtons, Carews, Tyrells, FitzLewis, Heighams and Cloptons.[41] The powerful administrator and councillor, Sir Thomas Lovell, was described as 'my old friend' in Oxford's will and both he and the attorney-general, Sir James Hobart, a dominant figure in local government in the region, were among the earl's executors, as was Sir Robert Drury, speaker of the Commons in 1495 and another of Henry VIII's councillors. Hobart and Lovell were powerful men in their own right and there is no evidence that Oxford was responsible for their advancement. It is doubtful, for instance, whether it was the earl who secured their joint succession to Lord Fitzwalter as steward of the Duchy lands in East Anglia in 1489.[42] On the other hand a closer link with Drury is suggested by the latter's appointment as Oxford's deputy-steward of the southern parts of the Duchy by 1499.[43] Oxford's other important public office, that of lord admiral, also provided him with patronage for his servants and clients, while the management of his own estates gave fees and influence to such men as John Paston, Robert Drury, Thomas Heigham and Richard FitzLewis.[44]

Although direct evidence is lacking, Oxford seems to have had considerable influence during the first decade of the reign upon

40. Francis Bacon, *The History of the Reign of King Henry the Seventh*, ed. J. R. Lumby (Cambridge, 1885), p. 192; St John Hope, op. cit., pp. 310–20. For a comment on this 'fine' see S. R. Chrimes, *Henry VII* (1972), p. 190n.

41. Roxburghe Club, op. cit., pp. 493–4, 504–20; Essex R.O., D/D Pr.139, 135c; Norfolk R.O., 1615; *CCR, 1485–1500*, 177; *Paston Letters*, vi, 99–100, 128–9.

42. R. Somerville, *Duchy of Lancaster* (1953), i, 595.

43. By 1509 he was chief steward of the earl's Suffolk lands and was one of his active executors [ibid., i, 431; PCC 11 Fetiplace; Phillipps Ms. 3840, which includes the accounts of Oxford's executors].

44. *Paston Letters* vi, 115–16 etc.; *LP*, i 4,38 (2 m.20); and nn. 41, 42 above.

crown appointments to local offices. Of the early sheriffs of the reign the first two—Paston and Bedingfeld—were certainly closely associated with him, Ralph Shelton (1487–8) was witness with known servants of the earl to a grant made by him in 1494, Robert Lovell (1488–9) was certainly later a retainer and executor to the earl, Philip Lewes (1490–1) was his household servant, and William Carew (1493–4) made the earl overseer of his will in 1503. Among the few knights of the shire known for Suffolk— Robert Broughton, William Carew, Robert Drury, Simon Wiseman and William Waldegrave—all except, possibly, Wiseman were closely associated with him, though this is not so obviously true of the only two Norfolk knights known, Robert Brandon and Philip Calthorpe. The commission of the peace in each county was reduced considerably at the beginning of the new reign, though as duties were added and, no doubt, com- petition for places became keener, the numbers inexorably increased to a total of over thirty in each county by 1497. Those omitted in 1485 included the Howards and some of their followers (but not Hobart or Richard Southwell) and those associated with Richard's court. Those added were, for the most part, men who had been involved in opposition to the regime, such as Oxford himself, William Knyvett, Thomas Lovell, William and Robert Brandon and Sir John Wingfield. During the next few years a number of the earl's clients were appointed to the Suffolk bench, as to other commissions in the county; rather fewer in Norfolk, where it seems that his influence was less direct.[45]

The evidence, then, though circumstantial, suggests that for at least the first part of the reign the earl of Oxford held a position in East Anglia of great authority, resting upon a combination of landed wealth and influence at court. There is little evidence that such authority was resented as the rather similar pre-eminence of William, duke of Suffolk, had been fifty years before, though this may be because the Pastons, who at both periods provide the main evidence for 'public opinion' were this time among those who benefited from the regime. There is, of course, no likelihood that Henry VII would have permitted to Oxford the unre- stricted power that Henry VI allowed to his favourite minister.

45. See nn. 41, 42 above; Wedgwood, op. cit., *s.n.*; Broughton made his 'especiall and singler good lord', the earl of Oxford, overseer of his will in 1507 [PCC 29 Adeane].

Nor is there any evidence that Oxford sought such power, was overbearing to the knights and squires of the region or vindictive to its fallen magnates. Indeed Lady Surrey admitted in October 1485 that unlike Lord Fitzwalter, Oxford had been 'singuler very good and kynde lorde to myn lord and me' and it would seem that the relationship remained harmonious.[46] In spite of political conflict and the potential clash of interest over the Howard inheritance the Howards and De Veres appear to have remained on good terms throughout the turbulent third quarter of the century and the reversal of political fortunes does not seem to have changed this.[47]

It is in this context that the grant of Framlingham to the earl of Oxford in 1486 may be seen. Once it was decided after Bosworth not to execute the earl of Surrey, all precedent suggested that he would eventually recover much of his inheritance in spite of its dispersal during 1486.[48] Surrey's release was forecast as early as December 1485, and he received a partial pardon early in the following year but it was not until 1489 that he was finally released from the Tower and sent to the North.[49] In the parliament that sat later in that year he had two bills passed. The first repealed his attainder and invalidated the consequent forfeitures. It was only to apply, however, to the earldom, lands held in right of his wife, lands granted to the earl of Oxford or Lord Daubeney and those he might inherit other than through his father. In a petition which immediately follows this on the parliament roll Lord Berkeley had confirmed his rights to all the lands partitioned with Howard in 1483, perhaps in anticipation of Surrey's eventual recovery of his rights to the Mowbray estates. In the second session of the parliament after his successful pacification of the North, Surrey petitioned for the right to enter on all lands without suing out livery and to be granted all reversions and rents reserved on lands still held by the king. He expressly disclaimed, however, his rights to the reversion of the dower lands of the Duchess Elizabeth and to all lands granted away by the king, though he was to be permitted to buy them back from their present holders. Royal approval of this petition gave Surrey directly little more

46. *Paston Letters*, vi, 87–8.   47. Crawford, op. cit., pp. 26–30.

48. Attainted noble families were rarely permanently disinherited [J. R. Lander, op. cit., pp. 136–8; L. Stone, *Crisis of the Aristocracy* (Oxford, 1965), pp. 412–13].

49. *Materials for a History of the Reign of Henry VII*, ed. W. Campbell (Rolls ser., 1873), i, 199.

than the lands held by his father before 1476, some of which were held by his stepmother, but in the following parliament of 1491–2 he put in a very similar petition, this time, however, omitting the disclaimer of his rights to the lands held by the Duchess Elizabeth. This was of vital significance, as the implication of the king's approval of the bill was that Surrey would eventually gain the greater part of the Howard share of the Mowbray estates and would once again become a major landowner in East Anglia.[50]

Long before this occurred, however, Surrey, though domiciled and busy in the North, had gone some way towards recapturing his position in East Anglia. Before 1494 he had redeemed from the earl of Oxford, Framlingham and the other Mowbray manors granted away in 1486.[51] Part of the purchase price seems to have been in the form of a life-annuity of 100 marks secured to Oxford on these lands. During the early 1490s, too, he acquired much other property. In 1493 he and his wife were licensed to enter on the lands of her father, no doubt as part of a settlement.[52] In 1494 the death of his stepmother brought him Stoke Neyland and other Howard lands worth about £120 per annum.[53] In 1495 he bought from Lord De la Warr the Sussex lands which had been granted to him in 1486.[54] He acquired other Mowbray properties in these years and bought out a number of rent-charges and annuities levied on Mowbray lands.[55] By 1495 he was drawing a gross annual income of about £666 from his East Anglian lands, with net cash receipts of £560, and in the 1495 parliament he was in a sufficiently powerful position, cemented by his son's marriage to the queen's sister Anne in February of that year, to secure the repeal of an act of 1485 which invalidated the grant of Kettleburgh and Sisland manors to the 4th Mowbray duke in 1468; he seems to have come into possession of these properties soon after.[56]

50. *RP*, vi, 410–12, 426–8, 448–50.
51. Pembroke College Ms. B.4 is a receiver-general's account for 1494–5 for these and other lands.
52. *CPR, 1485–94*, p. 458. He was already drawing revenue from these dozen manors by 1491, and continued to hold them after his wife's death; they included dower from her first husband, Lord Berners [Arundel Castle Ms. G.1/4; Pembroke College Ms. B.4; *Cal. Inq. post Mort. Henry VII*, ii, 18–19].
53. *CFR, 1485–1509*, 500; PCC 16 Vox; Pembroke College Ms. B.4.
54. *CCR, 1485–1500*, 824.   55. Ibid., 781, 939, 1209.
56. Pembroke College Ms. B.4; *RP*, vi, 292–3, 478–89; *CPR, 1467–77*, p. 110; Norfolk R.O., P.182D.

In 1495 Surrey was able to entail upon his son and son's wife as jointure four manors and the reversion of some of the lands held by the Duchess Elizabeth.[57] In return he was granted by the king an annuity of £120 to hold until the death of the duchess. Two years later he settled Framlingham Castle and lands in Sussex on feoffees, probably in connection with his second marriage in November 1497 to Agnes Tilney, sister of his servant, Philip; she can have brought him little if any dowry and it is perhaps significant that he could by now afford to marry a girl without property.[58]

By 1500, when Surrey finally came south, he already held, then, substantial estates centred upon Framlingham where he was carrying out extensive repairs in these years. His East Anglian lands brought him a net income of perhaps £600 a year, not yet comparable with that of his predecessors but sufficient to need the employment of officials and councillors of some status. The most distinguished of these was Sir James Hobart, one of the king's leading councillors, who was chief steward of Surrey's lands in Suffolk as he had been for Surrey's father and still was for the dowager duchess. This sort of appointment did not, of course, necessarily imply subservience. Old acquaintance and Hobart's undoubted abilities probably counted less in this relationship than Surrey's desire to build links with the dominant figures on the Council. Among the earl's full-time household and estate officials, however, were Philip Tilney, Henry Chauncy, John Goldingham, John Mitchell and Benedict Brocas. Surrey also had connections among the higher gentry of the region, particularly his brothers-in-law, John Wyndham and John Tymperley, and possibly Sir John Heveningham who made Surrey overseer of his will in 1500. The marriage in about the same year of his daughter to Thomas, son and heir of Sir William Boleyn, provided a new and in the event fateful relationship.[59]

The effect of Surrey's growing wealth and status upon local government is difficult to assess. Perhaps the first sign of the revival of Howard influence was the addition of Tilney to the Suffolk peace commission in 1497 and his appointment as escheator in the same year. Surrey himself, though appointed

57. *RP*, vi, 479–80.   58. *CPR, 1494–1509*, p. 114.
59. Ibid., p. 114; *CCR, 1500–09*, 179, 361; PCC 9 Moone; Pembroke College Ms. B.4; Norfolk R.O., P.691/8. Wyndham's son, Thomas, was certainly a client of the Howards [PCC 3 Bodfelde].

treasurer in 1501, had to wait until 1504 for appointment to the commision of the peace in Norfolk and Suffolk. His eldest son, Lord Howard, joined him a little later but both had been preceded on the Suffolk bench by Surrey's younger son, Sir Edward, who married successively two East Anglian heiresses.[60] John Tymperley was added to the commission in Suffolk in 1503 and so were two members of a family long connected with the dukes of Norfolk, Sir Robert Southwell and his nephew of the same name.[61] Sir Robert, of course, was an important royal official with several East Anglian appointments, but the appointment of these men and the choice of Sir Edmund Jenney, also a former Mowbray servant, as sheriff in 1502, may reflect the increasing interest and influence of Surrey in local affairs.[62]

The earl of Oxford remained a real force in the region, in wealth and prestige superior to Surrey, but he was now ageing and childless, and men were bound to look to the future which, accidents apart, had to lie with the Howards. Until the death of Duchess Elizabeth, however, Surrey's landed wealth was not sufficient to give him his full power in the region. How far the duchess herself exerted any influence it is impossible to say, though she certainly tried to look after her servants' interests.[63] She seems to have been mainly resident in Essex or Derbyshire but she naturally employed a number of East Anglian gentlemen as estate officials and councillors. Sir James Hobart, steward of her Suffolk estates, and John Tymperley, overseer in Suffolk, appear to have been her closest councillors and were the main feoffees for her lands, but among her counsel were Edmund Jenney and Richard and Sir Robert Southwell, the last of whom was her steward in her later years and, with Jenney, was her chief executor. A number of influential gentlemen including Hobart, Sir Christopher Willoughby and Sir Thomas Montgomery, were in receipt of annuities from her estates but most of these were certainly not her servants or clients.[64]

60. *Complete Peerage*, ix, 220–1; Francis Blomefield, *Topographical History of (etc.) Norfolk* (1805–10), ix, 321.

61. W. C. Richardson, *Tudor Chamber Administration, 1485–1547* (Baton Rouge, 1962), pp. 458–62; *CPR, 1494–1509*, pp. 9, 355, 538.

62. Jenney appointed Surrey's servant, Philip Tilney, as overseer of his will in 1522 [Norfolk R.O., Norwich Consistory Court, 108 Brigges].

63. *Paston Letters*, vi, 155–56, 159.

64. PCC 25 Adeane; Phillipps Ms. 3840; Norfolk R.O., Rye Ms. 74 (a view of account of the lands of the duchess for 1505–6).

Some of these men were also connected with the Howards, and it is likely that in the duchess' last years her servants were preparing for the transfer of authority. Hobart, in particular, was much involved in the settlements that followed the death of the duchess in November 1506, by which in May 1507 Surrey and Lord Berkeley received licence to enter upon her lands and in the same month Surrey's feoffees settled the bulk of her East Anglian lands upon him in tail male.[65] Although her income seems to have dropped considerably after the early 1490s, most manors producing less cash, the duchess appears to have been receiving about £830 net from her estates in the last years of her life and Surrey inherited about three-quarters of this, thus for the first time having estates in East Anglia of the same order of magnitude as those of the earl of Oxford.[66] With the disappearance of the De la Pole and Radcliffe interest there was no serious rival. Relations between the two earls remained good and in 1511 Oxford married his young nephew and heir to Surrey's daughter.[67] On Oxford's death two years later Surrey was granted the wardship of the new earl.[68]

The reign of Henry VIII brought new favours to the Howards even before their triumph at Flodden in 1513. In 1510 the king granted to Surrey's heir, Lord Howard, and his wife extensive lands in lieu of the share of the earldom of March that she claimed as co-heir of Edward IV: they were granted only to Anne and the heirs of her body so Howard lost them on her death in 1511, but he retained two valuable manors that had been granted to him at the same time.[69] In 1513 Surrey's rights in some of the Arundel lands of the Mowbray inheritance were restored to him.[70] The earl's increasing influence may also be reflected in the appointment as sheriff or JP of a number of relatives and clients, among them Thomas Boleyn, Thomas Wyndham, Lionel Talmage and John Goldingham, or in the presents sent by the city of Norwich to Surrey and his son in 1513, apparently for the first time.[71]

65. PCC 25 Adeane; *CFR, 1485–1509*, 853; *CPR, 1494–1509*, pp. 541, 543–4; *CCR, 1500–09*, 766.
66. Norfolk R.O., Rye Ms. 74.
67. For some of the settlements involved, see C142/28/2 etc.
68. *LP*, i, 2694(80).
69. *Complete Peerage*, ix, 613–14; *Catalogue of Ancient Deeds*, v, 13566; *LP*, i, 1129.
70. *LJ*, i, vi; 4 Hen. VIII c. 13.
71. Norfolk R.O., Norwich Chamberlains' Accounts, 1512–13, 1514–15.

With the death of the earl of Oxford in 1513, the victory of Flodden and the restoration to the dukedom, the Howards' pre-eminence in the region might seem to have been limited only by their cautious subservience to the monarch.

In fact, however, new rivals were already gathering strength. The story of how Wolsey came to overshadow the old councillors need not be told here again. In East Anglian terms even more significant was the rise of the king's friend and brother-in-law, Charles Brandon, created duke of Suffolk in 1514 and later endowed with most of the forfeited De la Pole estates.[72] The Howards' endowment in reward for Flodden was, by contrast, in counties remote from East Anglia.[73] It is unlikely that this was deliberate policy by the king or Wolsey to prevent the total dominance of the region by the Howards, though not impossible. More probably it was a reflection of the king's own friendship with Brandon whose ancestry and natural interests lay in the region. Even after 1515 Brandon's landed wealth did not equal that of the new duke of Norfolk but his royal connections made him a potentially dangerous rival; he was, in fact, active in local affairs during the next two decades.[74] During the first years of Henry VIII's reign, Surrey had been powerfully represented at court by his second son, Sir Edward, one of the young king's closest companions. Brandon had also been a close friend of Edward Howard who had appointed him his executor and given him custody of one of his bastard sons (the other went to the king).[75] But after Edward's death at sea in 1513, relations between the two families were not without friction, though this seems to have been largely resolved by the late 1520s when the third duke and Suffolk were united in their hostility towards Wolsey.[76]

The old duke does not seem to have felt the same enmity towards Wolsey as his son was later to show. In his later years, as in those after Bosworth, he doubtless saw friendship with the dominant power at court as the essential foundation for the prosperity of his house. He is said by the Venetian ambassador, Giustinian, to have been intimate with Wolsey during the last

72. *LP*, i, 2684(5); ii, 94.
73. Ibid., i, 2684(1,2); 5 Hen. VIII cc. 9, 11; 6 Hen. VIII c. 19.
74. E.g. *LP*, ii, 2179; iv, 1260, 1318–19, 3883 etc. He was chief steward of Lynn by 1521 [BL, Egerton Roll 8796].
75. PCC 18 Fetiplace.
76. E.g. *LP*, i, 3355–6, 3376; A. F. Pollard, *Wolsey* (edn 1965), pp. 223ff.

years of his activity at court, from which he seems to have finally retired in 1522.[77] He continued to acquire lands, in particular benefiting from the fall of Buckingham by the grant of several Stafford manors in Norfolk, and he appears to have had ambitions to regain some of the Irish estates of the Mowbrays which had long since ceased to yield revenue.[78] But his last years were increasingly concerned with the disposal of his estates and his body. His will and earlier settlements make generous provision for his wife from his chattels but settle only about 500 marks of land on her—mostly in Sussex; nor were his younger children very generously endowed.[79] His achievement had been to rebuild the fortunes of his house and he would not see its essential landed basis dispersed.

The duke of Norfolk's estates were valued after his death at £2241 a year net.[80] This was probably a more accurate valuation than many, as his heir in order to obtain livery had to guarantee payment to the king of double the value of any land where an auditor appointed by the crown found under-valuation.[81] The lands in Norfolk and Suffolk were valued at just under £1300. The dower lands of his stepmother and certain other manors were not immediately inherited by the new duke but a receiver-general's account for 1525-6 shows him enjoying a total landed income of over £2800, with cash liveries of over £1900.[82] The increase over the valuation of 1524 can be largely explained by the inclusion of the lands previously held by the third duke as earl of Surrey. It is true that on the receivers' accounts most manors produced somewhat larger returns than in the valuation of 1524 but presumably the latter made allowance for repairs and fees which are separately listed on the accounts. Whatever the exact sum, the third duke had certainly succeeded to one of the two or three wealthiest peerages in England.

Norfolk's will is conventional enough save for the detailed provision for the completion of his great funeral monument at Thetford with its unique autobiographical inscription which

---

77. *LP*, iii, 402.   78. Ibid., iii, 2382; Pembroke College Ms. A. 9.

79. PCC 23 Bodfelde; Arundel Castle Ms. T.1. I am indebted to his Grace the Duke of Norfolk and his honorary archivist, Mr F. W. Steer, for permission to consult this and other manuscripts at Arundel Castle.

80. Arundel Castle Ms. G.1/4; Pembroke College Ms. B.5.

81. Pembroke College Ms. B.5.

82. Arundel Castle Ms. Q. 2/2.

emphasises above all his loyal service to the crown.[83] In spite of his wealth and power he still felt it necessary to sue to Wolsey 'in our most humble wise' to be 'good lord' to his executors. But there is no evidence that Norfolk had ever desired to be the first man in the kingdom. His success had been built upon patience, good service and a fair measure of humility. He left his house firmly established in the king's favour, with great possessions, an extensive network of relatives by blood and marriage among the greatest families of the kingdom and a prestige and magnificence that towered over the gentry of East Anglia, even if he never achieved the monopoly of regional authority possessed by his father or the earl of Oxford.

On this foundation his son built a political career in many ways very different from that of his father. By 1524 he was already a powerful figure at court and in the council and his authority was, of course, to increase after the fall of Wolsey in 1529. But although he was active in regional affairs during the 1520s, his great new estates do not seem to have brought him immediate supremacy in the region.[84] Even in 1525 the duke of Suffolk was equally active in East Anglia and there is little evidence of Norfolk's influence on local government appointments in the region before 1530. The knights of the shire and burgesses elected from Norfolk and Suffolk to the Reformation Parliament, for instance, show no obvious connection with him, though he had electoral influence elsewhere, and it was not until 1531 that several of his servants and councillors, among them Robert Holdich, Roger Wodehouse and Nicholas Hare, were added to an enlarged commission of the peace for Norfolk.[85] The fact that his servants were added to the Norfolk and not the Suffolk peace commission may have some significance. While earl of Surrey, the third duke had normally resided at the ancestral Howard home in Suffolk, Stoke-by-Nayland, but soon after 1525 he began to rebuild Kenninghall in Norfolk as his main residence. No doubt needs of convenience and prestige were mainly responsible for the building of a more modern, magnificent dwelling than Framlingham, the main seat of earls and dukes of Norfolk for more than three hundred years, but it also seems

83. William Dugdale, *The Baronage of England* (1675), ii, 269–70.
84. For Norfolk's activities in the region see *LP*, iv, 1235, 1261, 1319, 1231, 3664, 3703, etc.
85. These and others of the duke's entourage appear in Arundel Castle Ms. Q2/2; SC 6/Henry VIII, 6305 and elsewhere.

likely that the shift northwards represented, as it certainly encouraged, a real shift in Howard influence and interest. This was,
perhaps, in part due to the uncomfortable proximity of the
powerful Charles Brandon whose already great influence in
Suffolk was strengthened in 1534 by his marriage to the Willoughby heiress.[86]

Whatever the reason, it is clear that 'the county that bore his
name' took an increasing share of the attention of the third duke
at the expense of his Suffolk interests. The tendency was to continue under his grandson, the fourth duke. By the late 1520s, too,
it is possible to see an even more important territorial policy
developing. From that period Howard began to sell off much of
his outlying estates in the Midlands and elsewhere in order to
purchase a very large share of the East Anglian lands of monastic
houses dissolved by Wolsey in the 1520s and by Cromwell in the
following decade. It is unnecessary to list here his grants, purchases
and sales but by 1546 the consolidation of his estates had gone
very far.[87] Apart from his valuable lands in Sussex the duke's
territorial interests were overwhelmingly by this time in Norfolk
and Suffolk, and predominantly in the former county.

In a sense this consolidation of his estates conflicted with the
ambitions of the third duke, his son and grandson, to play a
major role in national politics. None of them, whatever the size of
their rent-roll, could rival the nation-wide landed interests of the
greatest fifteenth-century magnates. Nor was East Anglia the
reservoir of loyal, bellicose gentlemen and peasants such as could
be found in the North or West. The post-Reformation fortunes
of the house of Howard would probably have been happier if
their political ambitions had been more commensurate with the
nature of their landed estates. The crown still needed regional
lieutenants. As in 1485, so in 1546 and 1570, it was when Howard
ambitions moved outside the East Anglian context that they
ended in catastrophe.

86. *The Works of Henry Howard, Earl of Surrey and of Sir Thomas Wyatt the
Elder*, ed. G. F. Nott (1815), i, pp. v–xii and App. II.
87. For such a list see Grace, op. cit., app. II and III.

II

'Agaynst taking awaye of Women': the Inception and Operation of the Abduction Act of 1487

E. W. IVES

'Certainely his times for good *Common-wealths Lawes* did excell', wrote Francis Bacon of Henry VII, 'so as he may iustly be celebrated for the best *Law-giuer* to this Nation, after King EDWARD the first'.[1] The comparison apart, this high opinion of Henry VII's legislation has been generally echoed for the last three and a half centuries. Only recently has research shown that there is little evidence of any real attempt to enforce these vaunted laws, except where the king's own pocket was concerned, that a significant proportion of the two hundred acts he approved had been proposed to him, not by him, that, in the words of S. B. Chrimes: 'At best the government procured some measures which seemed to it sufficiently worthwhile to procure parliamentary sanction for them. But it is difficult to believe that the reign of Henry VII was particularly notable for its legislative activity.'[2] Yet to conclude that tradition has been wrong and that the first Tudor was no systematic legislator is to raise a new question. When the crown decided to proceed by statute, what lay behind that decision? Why was one problem singled out for parliament and not another, and why this remedy and not that? The less we see Henry VII as a law-giver, the more we need to ask why he gave the laws he did.

Some legislation was the product of committee work. The discussions among the crown lawyers in 1485–6 are well known,

1. Francis Bacon, *The Historie of the Raigne of King HENRY the Seuenth* (1622), p. 71.
2. S. B. Chrimes, *Henry VII* (1972), p. 136.

although these had most influence upon constitutional decisions and the one substantive proposal for legislation was ignored.[3] In 1494, however, a group of royal councillors did meet with the specific purpose of proposing reforms to the next parliament and the legislation of 1495 was in consequence substantial and comprehensive.[4] Where such specific evidence is absent, it is tempting to presume government interest from the legislation actually put through. This is especially true of law and order, which has always been associated with Henry Tudor. When in 1487 parliament passed the famous 'so-called star chamber act' plus statutes dealing with appeals of murder, bailing felons, royal officers and retaining, and discipline at court, when a bill of 1489 invited complaints against negligent justices of the peace, when in 1495 legislation covered vagabonds, corruption of juries, perjury and riot, the direction of interest may seem plain.

One of the least known of these 'law and order' statutes is the 'Acte agaynst taking awaye of Women agaynst theire Willes' passed in 1487, 3 Henry VII c. 2.[5] This made it a felony to abduct women, or rather what the act terms 'women having substances', an offence invited by the common law ruling that for the duration of a marriage the fortune of the wife was completely in the hands of her husband. He occupied any freehold she had or inherited, although he could not dispose of it beyond his own life time; as for his wife's chattels personal, here he was absolute owner; chattels real—leases, debts and the like—were from the early fifteenth century regarded as his also, although any outstanding at his death would revert to the widow.[6] In normal circumstances, these rights and the wife's reciprocal claims for dower would be modified by marriage settlements, but otherwise the law took full force and this put every unmarried woman of wealth at peril. To abduct her and compel her to marry, was immediately to secure all her wealth. And to compel the victim to marry was not impossible. Separated from friends, usually in a strange part of the country, surrounded by allies of the abductor, a woman had little

3. Ibid., pp. 160–1; it was suggested that parliament should deal with the falsification of *inquisitions post mortem*. *YB*, Mich. 1 Hen. VII, p. 3, f. 3.

4. C. G. Bayne, *Select Cases in the Council of Henry VII* (Selden Soc. 75, 1958), pp. 28–9.

5. The chapters of this parliament's statutes are variously numbered; this essay follows the *Chronological Table of the Statutes* (1971).

6. W. S. Holdsworth, *History of English Law* (1941), iii, 525–7.

alternative, and there was always the ultimate sanction of violation; equally, only an exceptional woman would complain afterwards.

English law did not distinguish initially between such abduction for gain and the offence of rape, sexual assault. Indeed, mere abduction was a trespass only and the requirement of physical violation always governed interpretation of this offence by the courts.[7] The required allegation was *'felonice rapuit'* which was taken to imply *'carnaliter cognovit contra voluntatem'*, though these words were often included as well.[8] By common law, rape was an offence to be prosecuted by its victim and only with Westminster I, c. 13 (1275) did it become a plea of the crown, punishable by two years in prison and a fine. Ten years later Westminster II, c. 34 advanced rape to the level of felony, whether or not the woman consented after the assault. It was not until 1347 that the property element in certain cases of rape attracted parliamentary attention, with the commons petitioning that this robust way to wealth was all too prevalent.[9] Nothing was done, for the obvious reason that Westminster II was adequate as law; the defect was in execution, since where a woman consented after rape, she was unlikely to continue to complain and so bring her husband under the statute. Abductions were, in any case, often collusive, with the woman's surrender to force a mere disguise.[10] Indeed, it was probably elopement which was being attacked when, after a century, Westminster II was strengthened. By 6 Richard II, st. 1 c. 6 (1382), where a woman consented to marriage after abduction, both husband and wife were disabled from all inheritance, dower and jointure, and the next of blood was 'incontinently' to have title to enter on any such property. What is more, prosecution of the ravisher was no longer to depend upon the woman. The nearest relative was given the right to sue for felony. This clearly provided those with an incentive with the means to sue, and the would-be abductor now knew that a determined family could deny him his profit. In 1453 the law was tightened again to defeat

7. *YB*, Mich. 11 Hen. IV, p. 30, f. 13: *'si il ravishoit & ne conustroit carnelment, ce n'est niy felonie, eins transgressione'*.

8. *YB*, Trin. 9 Edw. IV, p. 35, f. 26; Mich. 20 Hen. VII, p. 17, f. 7.

9. *RP*, ii. 172a; I. S. Leadam, *Select Cases before Star Chamber, 1477–1509* (Selden Soc. 16, 1903), pp. cx–cxii.

10. J. G. Bellamy, *Crime and Public Order in the later Middle Ages* (1973), pp. 58–59.

the *novelx invencions* of those who counted on abduction alone being no felony and compelled victims to enter into bonds signing away wealth or agreeing to marry which were perfectly good in law.[11] This was not made a crime, but a procedure was laid down for voiding such bonds.

Behind the act of 1487, therefore, lay two centuries of legislative concern and historians have been tempted to see Tudor decisiveness replacing inefficient tinkering. In fact, this legislation added up to a comprehensive code. For Henry VII to declare abduction a felony was in most respects to restate existing law. That of itself might have been useful, and the act does make clear that marriage under duress is covered where Westminster II speaks of consent following ravishment *a force*. Yet at only two points did the statute of 1487 add anything to current law. The first was the provision that accessories were henceforth to be principals, which meant that they could be tried for felony immediately, not deferred until the actual abductor had been dealt with. This may have been some additional deterrent, but the change was hardly substantial and was very undesirable in law.[12] The other extension promised more. The preamble refers to the problem of women of wealth 'oftentimes taken by mis-doers, contrary to their will, and after married to such misdoers, or to other by their assent, or defiled'; the enacting clause, however, penalises the taking of 'any woman so against her will', with no mention of forcible marriage or sexual assault. In other words, the statute could be held to extend felony to abduction *per se*. That it was initially read in this way is confirmed by a handful of indictments in which the words of felony are not 'feloniously raped and had carnal knowledge' but a formula previously invalid, '*felonice cepit et abduxit* (or *et accariavit*) *contra voluntatem*'. Four examples have been found for the decade 1488–97. In one, 3 Henry VII c. 2 is actually quoted and in two others it is referred to as 'the statute lately promulgated'.[13] Yet it would be wrong to follow Matthew Hale and talk of a new felony of forcible marriage.[14]

---

11. 31 Hen. VI c. 9.   12. Cf. Edward Coke, *Institutes* (1797), iii, 61.
13. KB9/391/40; 384/20 and 385/39; 409/17. The fourth case is KB9/402/52.
14. Matthew Hale, *Pleas of the Crown* (1736), i, 659. Commentators have had much difficulty with this act and the whole law of rape, ibid., i, 628–32, 637; Coke, op. cit, iii, 360, 434; William Blackstone, *Commentaries* (1794), iii, 208; William Hawkins, *Pleas of the Crown* (1795), iii, 307, 310. The earliest, William Staunford, *Les Plees del Coron* (1560) only refers to the point in the act re principals [f. 44v].

The abductor who raped his victim or compelled her to marry was already in danger of the law. What the act added, even when interpreted generously to include all female abduction, was one felony only, abduction without rape or forced marriage. In most cases this would be the taking of a minor. In two of the four known cases between 1488 and 1497 the victims are specifically described as children and it is noticeable that in three instances the abductors were labourers and the like, one group certainly from London's underworld.[15] Thus the practical significance of the act was for kidnapping. Even this did not last. To take the act in this way was to ignore the preamble and strain the phrase 'so against her will', and the preamble could not be distorted for ever. A judgement of 1556–7 ruled that the felony of abduction could only exist where there had been rape or its equivalent, forced marriage.[16] As a result, new legislation was necessary and 4 & 5 Philip and Mary c. 8 (1558) decreed a penalty of two years in gaol for kidnapping a female heiress. How far Henry VII had been discarded is shown by the penalty of five years where the offence had been aggravated by rape or marriage, unquestionably a felony under his statute. By contrast, Richard II's legislation was closely followed in dealing with heiresses who consented to their abductors.

The abduction act of 1487 is, therefore, a curiosity—in the main superfluous and for the rest impermanent. It is also doubtful if the abduction of wealthy women was as prevalent as the preamble claims. The king's bench indictment files for the ten years up to and including Michaelmas term 1487 contain, perhaps, fifty-three cases of rape.[17] Of these, one might have qualified under the preamble—the abduction in 1480 of Joan Fabyan from the home of Stephen Fabyan, the prominent London draper—though the identity of the abductors and the immediate raping of the girl suggest that another motive might have been revenge.[18] There are indictments for simple sexual assault, for example, the unnamed cleric who allegedly raped women in Dunwich and Beccles in 1482 and 1483 and who may well be the Robert

---

15. Children: KB9/384/20 and 385/39; 402/52. Labourers: KB9 391/40; 409/17; 384/20 and 385/39, with which last cf. KB27/915 Rex, m. 11.
16. William Dalison, *Les Reports des divers special Cases* (1689), f. 22.
17. KB9/346–8, 350–75, 949–53, 1000, 1001.
18. KB9/352/23: J. Wedgwood, *History of Parliament, Biographies* (1936), p. 311.

Burnet of Dunwich, clerk, accused of other similar offences in the area.[19] There are cases incidental to other crimes, abductions for immoral purposes and taking women away in the course of disputes about property and the like. But abduction for gain is almost unknown. This is highlighted by the one indictment in this decade which does attempt to use the Richard II statute. From Cornwall, it rehearses the act and then declares that since Matilda, widow of Richard Mourton of Launcells, gentleman, had been ravished against her will by William Smyth of Launcells, labourer *alias* yeoman, and had then consented to him, both were liable to the statute. Precisely why a jury should indict on a law whose enforcement belonged to the next of kin is made clear—and so too the unreality of the alleged rape—by an indictment of the couple by another jury for administering a fatal poison to the ailing Richard 'desiring to enjoy his goods, chattels, lands and tenements'. The accusations of abduction and poisoning were expressions of public condemnation of an unfaithful wife and her plebeian lover.[20]

It is true that a search of the king's bench rolls might reveal indictments to add to the two thousand or so in the files for these years. Equally, the files contain principally indictments called into king's bench on special grounds and more general sources, notably the assize files, are fragmentary. But the year books discuss no case after 1466 and nothing appears in the rolls of parliament. This contrasts with the situation earlier; a number of notorious abductions came under parliamentary scrutiny and three year book cases are known.[21] Unless, therefore, the sources mislead, abduction for profit had not been a significant problem for some years before 1487.

Henry VII's abduction act is far more probably a response to a particular incident than any concern for public policy. A king's bench indictment tells the story.[22] On Sunday, 9 September 1487, Robert Bellingham of Kenilworth, gentleman, with four named and a score of unnamed accomplices, and prompted by Thomas Wodeshawe, gentleman, of Berkswell, broke into the house of John Beaufitz (Bevis), esquire, at Temple Balsall near Solihull.

---

19. KB9/1001/41-3; 371/50.   20. KB9/358/2 and 3.
21. *RP*, iv, 498a; v, 14b, 70a; *YB*, Mich. 11 Hen. IV, p. 30, f. 13; Mich. 1 Hen. VI, p. 1, f. 1: Trin. 5 Edw. IV, p. 24, ff. 5-6; Edw. IV, Long Quint f. 58.
22. KB9/377/22, from which the following unless stated.

Beaufitz was assaulted and the household, which was at supper, was told to 'sitte still, for he that sterith shall die, whatsoeuer he be'. The target was Margery Ruyton, John's daughter and heir, whom the raiders carried off by force.

Nothing is recorded beyond the indictment but something can be reconstructed of the background to this episode. John Beaufitz was a leading Warwickshire gentleman. A justice of the peace, sheriff in 1476–7 and MP for Warwick in 1478, he was completing a second term as escheator.[23] He owned land in various places in the county, but he leased his principal seat, the preceptory at Balsall, from the Order of St John.[24] One of the busiest of local commissioners, Beaufitz was also receiver for the duchy at Kenilworth and for the crown at Feckenham in Worcestershire, and had been one of the new breed of officers accounting to Edward IV's chamber.[25] Public service and property in the town brought Beaufitz to Coventry and his daughter had married Thomas Ruyton, draper or mercer, eldest son of the wealthy ex-mayor, John Ruyton.[26] Margery received a life interest in an estate at Bubbenhall, near Coventry, to add to the three properties her father had given her 'to by hyr kerchurs' (kerchiefs), so that when her husband died she was already an obvious prize, and over and above was the expectation of the rest of the Beaufitz lands in due course.[27] Her abductor, Robert Bellingham, may not have been a Warwickshire man but he was indicted as 'late' of Kenilworth, Canley or 'of our [the king's] household in the county of Warwick, gentleman'.[28] What office he then held is unknown, but in 1494 he became bailiff of the royal estate at Sutton in Warwickshire and by 1496 was Henry VII's serjeant-

23. *CPR, 1467–77*, p. 634; *1476–85*, p. 576; *1485–94*, p. 503; *CFR, 1471–85*, 373. The official return for the 1478 parliament gives the name 'Thomas' [C219/17/3/3/136] but is almost certainly in error (although a Thomas Beaufitz, possibly John's son, was alive in 1484 [*CCR, 1476–85*, 1224]) and the references in Wedgwood, op. cit, p. 56 are to John; *CFR, 1437–45*, p. 285; *1485–1509*, p. 99.

24. *VCH Warws.*, v, 47, vi, 145, 235.

25. *CPR, CCR passim*; B. P. Wolffe, *The Crown Lands, 1461–1536* (1970), pp. 110–11; R. Somerville, *Duchy of Lancaster* (1953), i, 561–2; *CPR, 1461–67*, p. 189; pardoned 1484 as of Balsall and Kenilworth, gentleman or esquire, ex-sheriff and late receiver, C67/51 m. 19.

26. *Calendar of Ancient Deeds*, iv, 7514 [hereafter *CAD*]; PCC 12 Milles; *Coventry Leet Book*, ed. M. D. Harris (EETS 134, 135, 138, 146, 1907–13), *passim*; *Records of the Guild of Holy Trinity Coventry*, ed. G. Templeman (Dugdale Soc.19, 1944), ii, 58, 164.

27. *CAD*, iv, 7514; PCC 20 Milles.	28. Wedgwood, op. cit., p. 63.

porter.[29] Of the other major figure in the case, Thomas Wode-shawe, less is known, but he too belonged to this background of royal service and land management. Probably from Tamworth and described as a grazier, he occupied Berkswell as king's bailiff and in 1487 was appointed escheator of Staffordshire.[30]

With this cast, the scene at Balsall writes itself. The surprise is the violent reaction of the crown. Nine days after the abduction (and earlier action would have been impossible) the justices of the peace met at Warwick. They did so, most exceptionally, in the presence of William Hussey, chief justice of England, Edward Lord Hastings and Henry Lord Grey of Codnor, two leading magnates of the midlands, and the king's solicitor, Andrew Dymmock. None of these men belonged to Warwickshire or was JP for the county; each was a member of the king's council. The explanation must be a special instruction from Henry VII to attend and see that indictments were preferred against the abductors, while detaching the chief justice and the king's solicitor weeks only before a parliament assembled argues a determination to have the indictments good in law. Nor was the king's anger short-lived. On 2 March 1488 a commission was issued to deliver Warwick gaol of Bellingham and his four accomplices.[31] A month later the indictment was called into king's bench and the five principals surrendered to the Marshalsea.[32] Pressure was kept up and the trial held at the next Warwick assizes on 22 July 1488. There the prosecution collapsed. No evidence was forthcoming and the accused were found 'not guilty'.[33] Action against Wodeshawe as accessory thereby became impossible. In all probability, Bellingham had compounded with Beaufitz, so leaving the crown without a case. Robert certainly married his victim and when Beaufitz drew up his will in 1488, he left Bellingham his best silver cup—'it is bettyr than x *marcas*'— and instructed his executors to pay the £70 he owed him, possibly part of the marriage settlement.[34] When Beaufitz died the next year, Bellingham sued out probate on behalf of the

29. *CPR, 1494–1509*, p. 10; *VCH Warws.*, ii, 101.

30. *CPR, 1485–94*, pp. 4, 289; *CFR, 1485–1509*, 178. Wodeshawe and Beaufitz were both concerned with the 1477 Burdett treason. *CCR, 1476–85*, 122, 166, 346; *CPR, 1476–85*, pp. 50, 319.

31. *CPR, 1485–94*, p. 239.   32. KB9/377/21.

33. KB27/907 Rex, m. 7d.

34. *VCH Warws.*, v, 47; PCC 20 Milles.

widow, and when she died, 'Master Bellyngham' was overseer of her will.[35]

What is very much a puzzle is the reason for Henry VII's reaction. With Stoke only three months earlier, the king could be forgiven for being specially sensitive to disorder. Again, Beaufitz was an important man, perhaps with powerful patrons.[36] But hints in the indictment suggest that the principal concern was the flagrant challenge to Henry's authority by some of his own servants. Bellingham is specifically described as 'of the royal household', the attack on Beaufitz explicitly named as an assault on a justice of the peace, and the words used directly flouted his commission. If Henry could not rule his own men, there was no hope that he could rule the kingdom. At least two of the statutes in 1487 exhibit this same concern. 3 Henry VII c. 12 decreed loss of office for any royal servant who retained, was retained or tolerated retaining, except by the king, or who took part in any 'field, assembly or rout' without his orders. 3 Henry VII c. 14 created a special procedure to investigate suspected conspiracy in the king's entourage, whether against the king, his household officers or a nobleman, declared such plotting to be felony and set up a form of trial by a jury of the king's servants. In the end, as Edward Hall recalled, rigour became a set policy: 'there was no man with hym, beynge neuer so muche in his fauoure, or hauing neuer so muche aucthorite, that either durst or coulde do any thing as his awne phauntasye did serue him.'[37] It was not the abduction of Margery Ruyton which mattered but the identity of her abductors.

The connection between the assault at Balsall in September 1487 and the 'acte agaynst taking awaye of women' which was placed before parliament in November is circumstantial but it is strong. The abduction was the first of its kind since 1480 at least. The king's interest and anger are witnessed by the exceptional steps over the indictment. The act raised accessories to the status of principals and the one person difficult to reach immediately by existing law was the accessory, Thomas Wodeshawe. The act as first interpreted did not require evidence of rape or marriage

35. Ibid., 21 Horne.
36. Beaufitz had been a client of Ralph Boteler, Lord Sudeley (ob. 1473), e.g. *CAD*, ii, 2510; iii, B3927; PCC 20 Milles.
37. Edward Hall, *Chronicle* (1809), p. 504.

under duress and composition between Bellingham and Beaufitz would rob the crown precisely of that evidence. A year before, Henry VII had shown much impatience at delays in the Humphrey Stafford case.[38] If the king saw the Balsall offenders, and his own men at that, getting away scot free, he might well have demanded a change in the law. The function of the law, as Henry saw it, was to punish wrongdoers and to do so without obstruction. It was the same parliament of 1487 which passed the 'pro-camera-stellata' act to make easier the prosecution of the powerful.[39] Yet more striking was the statute to deal with murder suspects; all accused were to be kept in prison for a year and a day, even when acquitted after trial on indictment, in order to give more time for private appellants.[40]

If the abduction act of 1487 was an instantaneous reaction to a particular episode, it suggests that not all of Henry VII's law-making was marked by the rational thinking of 1495. Some was, frankly, what Bacon said it was not: 'made vpon the *Spurre* of a particular Occasion for the *Present*'.[41] In crude terms, the accident of a parliament allowed the king to legislate about his current pre-occupations. The act of 1487 on conspiracy in the royal household even admits that it was provoked by 'recent envy and malice' there.[42] We may wonder, indeed, if Henry began his reign with much conception of the distinctive nature of statute or of the potential long-term significance of legislating. And if law-making was random, we may have an explanation for feeble law-enforcement. Historians have been puzzled by the lack of vigour shown by the tribunal set up under 3 Henry VII c. 1, but if a special court to deal with the over-mighty subject was more a bright idea of the moment than a real need, its lethargy would be explained.[43] Where legislation was a reflection of a 'present' interest it mattered while that interest lasted, and except where money was concerned, that was not for long.

How far is this true of the abduction act and the king's indignation with ravishers for profit? To what extent were women now better protected and their assailants more surely disciplined? An answer must start from the evident truth that incidence of

38. Bayne, op. cit., p. 8; *YB*, Trin. 1 Hen. VII, p. 1, f. 26.
39. 3 Hen. VII c. 1.   40. 3 Hen. VII c. [2].
41. Bacon, op. cit., p. 71.   42. 3 Hen. VII c. 14.
43. Chrimes, op. cit., p. 156.

prosecution is no good measure of law enforcement. 'No prosecutions' may mean a one hundred per cent deterrent or, equally,
inaction; the explanation could also be an offence out of fashion,
misleading statistics or changes in enforcement. In the ten years
after 1488 indictments for rape do drop by approximately twenty
per cent but probably not thanks to the act.[44] The figure is not
really significant—it represents ten cases fewer in fifteen hundred.
Judicial decisions in 1482, 1491 and 1495 that indictments brought
at a court leet or a sheriff's tourn were no longer valid may have
discouraged complaints.[45] Above all, the catalogue of offences
does not change. Apart from the four cases where the statute is
cited, there is no evidence that the courts paid much attention,
still less of any campaign against abductors who had previously
escaped justice.

It is, nevertheless, possible for an act to prove its value in individual cases. The first of the four cases from the decade 1488–97,
the abduction of Agnes Levenger at Edgware in December 1489,
certainly produced some court activity. Yet only one abductor
and one receiver stood trial out of the nine people accused and the
ringleader chose to sue for a pardon instead.[46] The courts were
clearly unfamiliar with the act, for the receiver, who under it was
guilty of a felony, was charged not with receiving but with a
separate abduction dating from his taking over of the child. The
next indictment under the act was brought by the sheriff's tourn
of Kent, and hence was void.[47] In the third case, arising from the
abduction in 1493 of Margaret Harecourt, daughter and heir of
John Harecourt esquire, of Witney in Oxfordshire, two gentlemen
and two yeomen did surrender to the crown, but nothing more is
known.[48] In the final example, the abduction of Agnes Russell at
Watford in 1496, the accused seem never to have been arrested.[49]

For a substantially documented case which tested to the full
the act of 1487 and the whole law on rape for profit it is necessary

44. KB9/376–80, 382–9, 391–413, 934, 959.
45. *YB*, Mich. 22 Edw. IV, p. 2, ff. 22–3; Trin. 6 Hen. VII, p. 4, ff. 4–5; Pas. 11
Hen. VII, p. 11, f. 22.
46. KB9/384/20; 385/39, 40; 399/48 (i); KB27/915 Rex, mm. 11, 38d; 916 Rex,
mm. 14, 16; 917 Rex, mm. 9. 11d; 920 Rex, m. 23; *CPR, 1485–94*, p. 426.
47. KB9/391/40.
48. KB9/402/52—indicted 24 Feb. 1494, to king's bench Mich. 1494 but no
entries in Rex Roll for Mich. to Pas. 1494–95, KB27/933, 934, 935.
49. KB9/409/17—the names are not annotated 'mar[shalsea]'.

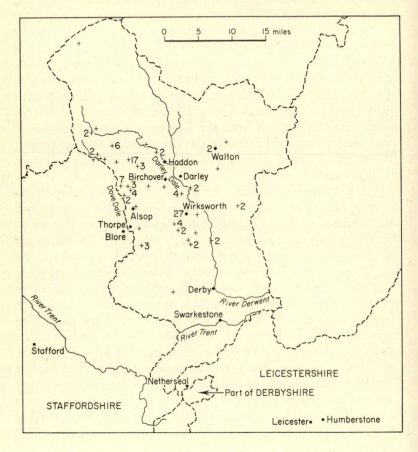

Map 1. The Abduction of Margaret Kebell

Parishes from which the abductors came are marked with a cross and where more than one person came the number is given

to go to the abduction of Margaret Kebell in 1502. Margaret was the widow of Thomas Kebell of Humberstone in Leicestershire, king's serjeant-at-law and justice at Chester, who died in 1500. She was wealthy on two counts. Her jointure was £40 a year for life and Kebell had bequeathed her one-third of his goods and chattels, worth £260.[50] Secondly, she was, as she said, 'enhabitable to landes and tenementes of gret yerly valew' as the female heir of the Bassett family of Blore in Staffordshire.[51] It was to Blore that she returned after Kebell's death, where her mother Eleanor kept house for her uncle, William Bassett the younger, esquire. Margaret could clearly not remain unmarried, she was only about twenty-five, and at the end of January 1502 a party assembled at Blore, probably to celebrate her betrothal or marriage to her mother's half-brother, Ralph Egerton of Wrinehill, a member of Prince Arthur's household.[52] But whatever was planned, it was interrupted.[53] At six in the morning of Tuesday, 1 February, the Bassett home was attacked by some 120 armed men, led by Roger Vernon of Wirksworth, the son and heir of Sir Henry Vernon of Haddon. Surprise was complete. Bassett put up a struggle but the raiders were too strong. Margaret Kebell's belongings were tossed into a wicker basket, the £100 she had with her confiscated and she was hustled out. Either she would, Margaret was bluntly told, come quietly and accept Roger as her husband, or she would be incarcerated in the wilds of the Peak until she saw reason. She was put on a horse and the raiders were away down the breakneck track which led to the River Dove and the crossing to Thorpe in Derbyshire.

The abduction had been well planned. The Vernon men came from the whole length of Darleydale and the Peak, one from as far away as Glossop. They were mainly yeomen with a sprinkling of labourers and small craftsmen; only four gentlemen rode with Roger Vernon, among them Thomas Folijambe of Walton near

50. C1/329/51; PCC 3 Moone; Wiltshire R.O., 88:5, 17a; C142/56/51.
51. E. W. Ives, 'Patronage at the court of Henry VIII: the case of Sir Ralph Egerton of Ridley', in *Bull. John Rylands Lib.*, lii (1970), 348.
52. Ibid., 346–9; Margaret's parents were married in 1474. HMC, *11 Report* (1888), vii, 136.
53. The following is based on KB9/425/28, 29, 34; 426/7, 11; 437/9, 10; KB27/966 Rex, mm. 6, 6d; 969 Rex, mm. 3, 3d; 973 Rex, m. 19; 990 Rex, m. 13; STAC1/19/17, 1–3 [printed in Leadam, op. cit., pp. 130–7]; STAC2/22/18; 23/4; 24/305; 25/68. The search for material relevant to this abduction has not been taken beyond the death of Henry VII.

Chesterfield and John Alsop of Alsop, only seven miles from Blore. It was probably at Alsop that the party had its rendezvous since the direct approach from Wirksworth ran through Bassett country. Precisely why the Vernons should go to such lengths is not clear. They knew the Bassetts well; Sir Henry, along with William Bassett senior, had been retained by William, Lord Hastings, and so too Thomas Kebell.[54] The estates and influence of the two families were contiguous; the Vernons ruled Darleydale, the headwaters of the Dove and the Peak, frequently serving as duchy steward or bailiff there; Bassett of Blore was 'of the country people called Kinge of the Morelande', the lower slopes of the Pennines, the southern reaches of the Dove and eastward towards Derby.[55] Was Roger a rejected suitor? Was it a case of *droit de seigneur* claiming a Vernon perquisite? Or had the Hastings retinue really been an expression of regional solidarity so that the Vernons would feel that Bassett and Kebell wealth should stay within the faction?

With the departure of the Vernons, Eleanor Bassett set about organising a rescue. Time was short. Blore is barely a mile from the Dove, and in Derbyshire the Bassetts would be the invaders. Two dozen managed to get to horse—Ralph Egerton and Thomas Haselrig, an old friend from Humberstone, were in the pack and so too four parsons—with Eleanor in the lead. They came up with the raiding party as it bunched at the river crossing, but Margaret was beyond rescue. Heavily outnumbered, the Bassetts sat helpless, noting those of the raiders they recognised. Margaret was taken to the house of Henry Columbell, gentleman, at Darley, to spend the night in the heart of the Vernon country. Next morning, needing now only an escort of sixteen, she was moved. Her treatment had convinced Margaret that the threats made at Blore had not been idle, so that when taken to a church in Derby, she consented to go through a form of marriage with Roger. But compliance did not deceive him; he was clearly in for a tempestuous few days and needed a refuge. His choice, or the prearranged next stop, was Netherseal where his uncle, William Vernon lived. Still at this date in Leicestershire, Netherseal was out of the

54. W. H. Dunham, *Lord Hastings' Indentured Retainers* (New Haven, 1955), p. 118; Huntington Library, Ms. history of the Hastings family by William Dugdale (1677), pp. 31-2.

55. Somerville, op. cit., i, 552-5; John Leland, *Itineraries*, ed. L. T. Smith (1906-8), ii, 171.

jurisdiction of both Staffordshire and Derbyshire, and since it lay
in a cul-de-sac with Derbyshire north and south and Staffordshire
to the west, retreat from the Leicester magistrates was guaranteed.
Despite the eighteen miles already travelled from Darley, Roger
pressed on twenty-two miles to Netherseal, crossing the Trent at
Swarkestone.

With the arrival at Netherseal late on Wednesday, 2 February,
Margaret Kebell takes up her own tale. William Vernon, she
remembered, came out to greet the party and she was taken
indoors, her arms held, one by the uncle, the other by the nephew.
While Roger explained to William, the latter's wife entered and,
somewhat surprised to see the bride so 'sad and hevy', asked
whether Roger had taken her against her will. The venom of
Margaret's reply disconcerted her, coupled as it was with the
threat to make Roger repent if ever she got free. Mrs Vernon then
made her opinion all too clear to her husband and nephew—'hyt
was pitee that Roger Vernon levyd by cause that [he] toke a wey
any good gentylwoman as the seyd Margaret ys, contrarie to her
mynd and wyll'. The dangers of female sympathy brought
Roger back at once to his reluctant wife: 'Alas Mastres, wyl hyt
be no bettur yit? I mervell gretly that ye wyll schew yowr mynd
to suche a strong strumpett & a hore as sche ys, for sche can kepe
no councell, & al that ye doo ys to vndoo me for euer.' To this
Margaret replied that 'sche wold do so, en eny place where so
euer sche came, & wold not let for no man'.

Roger's only course was to conceal Margaret and prepare his
friends in high places for trouble, a decision confirmed next
morning when Margaret made a scene at mass. John Alsop was
sent to London 'to dyuers of the fryndys' of Roger 'to labur for
hym'; William went to Haddon to tell Sir Henry. Roger took
Margaret, put her on horseback and the cavalcade set off. Their
destination was the Welsh border and an ally of the Vernons,
Sir Richard Delaber of Clehonger near Hereford. More than
eighty miles from Blore, Roger could hope to have shaken off
pursuit and with no prospect of escape in that alien spot, 'Mrs
Margaret Vernon' might be expected to face facts.

Out of sight was, however, not out of mind for the Bassetts.
Before the week was out, Eleanor had arrived at Darley with
men at her back, and finding Margaret gone, prepared to delate
Roger and his followers. Agitation in London brought a writ

dated 8 February to the earl of Shrewsbury and others, ordering an investigation and arrests in Staffordshire, although, as the earl was related to Henry Vernon, it was five weeks before the commission met.[56] The Bassetts also laid information at the Staffordshire quarter sessions on 21 February, and followed this at the March sessions at Chesterfield and Leicester. As late as the following October, the Leicestershire JPs were still receiving names of offenders.

Margaret, meanwhile, was looking to escape to London. Strictly, she should have gone to denounce her marriage before the bishop of Lichfield. But London was safer and promised access to the king. Soon after Easter she got away and, according to the version told in court, stopped some passers-by and persuaded them to provide a horse and take her to London. In fact, seven of the eight chivalrous travellers had been in the pursuit from Blore; it was a rescue party. This retreated via Pershore in Worcestershire, and there Roger Vernon caught up. Clearly feeling it unsafe to use force, he joined the party, bought Margaret a horse, sent ahead to arrange lodgings and played the attentive husband. And this paid dividends; his servants were later able to report a convincingly domestic journey during which Roger and Margaret lived as man and wife. Nevertheless, London spelled danger and Roger hurried off to sanctuary at Westminster. Margaret discovered that her lodgings at the *Saracen's Head* in Fleet Street were close to the *Bolt and Gun* where Sir Henry Vernon was putting up, and the father now became the suitor.

According to Vernon accounts, Sir Henry was bewildered by his son's runaway marriage. Immediately on her arrival, Margaret sent a Vernon servant, Edward Capull, to invite him to call. When he arrived, Sir Henry asked whether he should say, 'Welcome Doghter or Maistres'. Margaret replied, 'Doghter and it pleased [you], and so I trust ye will take me and be good fadur to your son and me'. Henry responded, 'So that ye be as ye say, the kyng pleased, I will be content'. He then asked about her treatment and was assured that she had not been misused or taken to any 'vile place'; she loved her husband and had consented to the whole escapade, indeed, her kinsman, Dr Standish, had celebrated the marriage. Next day there was, the Vernons recalled, a pleasing family episode. Roger, from the Westminster sanctuary,

56. Vernon was the earl's uncle by marriage. HMC, *Rutland* (1888–1905), iv, 190.

sent Margaret a pike and some herrings and she returned him a
dish of apples. The pike, when cooked, she sent to Sir Henry who
kept part for his dinner and returned the remainder for Margaret's
meal. This version was furiously denied by Margaret. Sir Henry's
visit, she said, was unsolicited, to persuade her 'for certain considerations' to accept the situation. She had been ill-treated, she
was not Roger's wife, she had never talked to Sir Henry except to
ferret out his complicity. As for the pike, this was a plot, and not
until the fish was on the table had she discovered Roger was the
sender; at once she had sent it, whole, to Sir Henry who kept a
portion and returned the rest, only to have Margaret send the
congealing mess back again. If Margaret was ever to have the
Derby marriage undone, such caution was warranted, but the
tone of her language leaves no doubt of her desire for revenge.
The Vernons were to pay.

On the face of it, everything was in Margaret Kebell's favour.
Although our information comes from indictments and other
allegations, the facts are not in doubt; there never was a clearer
case of abduction for profit. The law too was clear; everyone involved was guilty of felony and, by 3 Henry VII c. 2, accessories
like William Vernon, Richard Delaber, Henry Columbell and
Henry Vernon himself could be charged as principals. The crown
immediately called the indictments into king's bench but it was
not until 7 November that the first suspect surrendered to the
Marshalsea, Thomas Folijambe of Walton, a gentleman known
for riot.[57] He was bailed to appear at the Derby and Wolverhampton assizes and on 20 March 1503, the Derbyshire jurors, not
surprisingly given his Vernon friends, returned a verdict of not
guilty; the Wolverhampton jury seems not to have met. About
three dozen offenders in all surrendered to the Marshalsea, but
only four more were proceeded against, Richard Bargh of
Birchover and three other Derbyshire yeomen. Bailed to appear
at the assizes, they were acquitted at Stafford in July 1503 and at
Derby in March 1504.

Action or inaction by the king did not take away the right of a
victim to sue, and Margaret Kebell appealed her abductors of
felony in both Derbyshire and Staffordshire.[58] She also pursued

57. KB9/440/7.
58. KB27/979/mm. 44, 50; 980 mm. 65, 65d; 981 m. 109; 983 m. 29d; 984 m.
26; 987 m. 27d; 988 m. 20.

three civil actions in king's bench and another in common pleas,
and there may well be more undiscovered. Roger Vernon never
appeared to face her accusation of felony. Thomas Folijambe took
the lead yet again and he pleaded a technicality, error in the writ;
instead of 'Laurence Horsekeeper, *alias* Richardson, labourer',
Margaret had accused 'Laurence Hone, horsekeeper'.[59] Her
counsel, Serjeant Humphrey Coningsby, one of Thomas Kebell's
Inner Temple colleagues, argued that, if proved, this would
invalidate only process against Laurence, but the court disagreed.
Coningsby next tried to forestall trial of the fact at *nisi prius* at
Stafford, assuring the court that Hone was active in several lawsuits, but he was told to put this to the jury. Margaret successfully
challenged one panel for bias, but a second jury returned, in
August 1508, that Hone had not existed, and Folijambe was
discharged.[60] This defence was imitated by many of the thirty or
so others who appeared to answer Margaret. Process dragged on,
with frequent adjournments. Eventually all the defendants were
able to plead the Folijambe acquittal. [61]

The actions which Margaret Kebell brought in king's bench for
trespass and assault seem to have been even less effective, but she
faced considerable difficulty in civil litigation as is shown by the
professional interest taken in her common pleas action for trespass.[62] Vernon argued that Margaret was his wife and so, in law,
he was privileged against her. She replied by alleging that the
marriage had been procured '*per manasse & dures d'imprisonment*',
hence the privilege was barred. The court had to adjourn to consider this, but next day Thomas Frowyk, C. J., another of Thomas
Kebell's friends, announced that he had examined the authorities
and the plea was good. John Yaxley, the expensive serjeant-at-law
retained by Vernon, then claimed, first, that there had been no
threats, and second, that as the alleged threats had been in Staffordshire but the marriage at Derby, Margaret had not married under
duress.[63] This second point found no favour; this was not, Frowyk
ruled, a plea such as self-defence where threats had to continue

59. KB27/980 m. 65; *YB*, Mich. 21 Hen. VII, p. 13, f. 31; p. 35, f. 34.
60. KB27/980 m. 65.   61. KB27/981 m. 109.
62. KB27/983 m. 17; 987 mm. 40, 48; Robert Keilwey, *Reports d'Ascuns Cases*
(1688), f. 52v, 53. A search of the prothonotaries' entries for Trin. 1502 to Mich.
1504 has failed to discover this latter case [CP40/961 to 963, 965 to 969, 971].
63. For Yaxley's charges, see *Plumpton Correspondence*, ed. T. Stapleton (CS, iv,
1839), pp. 152-3.

from place to place; the marriage was '*per causse del primer manasse en l'auter countie*'. Frowyk also called on the Vernons to traverse the start of the threats, but Yaxley persuaded the court that this was unnecessary where counties joined. This was fortunate; otherwise the Vernons would have risked trial in Staffordshire on the issue, 'had Margaret been threatened at Blore?' But to deny generally that threats had been made was still dangerous and a stronger defence was soon produced. After threats and imprisonment at Blore (if any) Margaret had been set free; thus when she married she was a freely consenting party. In common sense as well as law, this had a certain plausibility; a woman might accompany an abductor under duress, but would she marry in a normal fashion in such a busy town as Derby under the stresss of her original terror? Frowyk accepted the plea, and the lead passed to Margaret. Did she manage a reply? The year books go no further. Yaxley had neatly exposed her weakness; until the church said otherwise, the law presumed she was Margaret Vernon.

Margaret was not allowed to test these various remedies at leisure. By Michaelmas 1504, Roger was already suing her rescuers for 'abducting' his wife, using the little known section of Westminster I c. 13, *de uxore abducta cum bonis viri*.[64] Coningsby, however, carried the court and despite some difficulty about Margaret not going to Lichfield or the archbishop, Fineux, C. J., delivered a substantial rebuff to the Vernons. Was a man who gave a woman a lift to market guilty of abduction? As for the wrong bishop, it was too much to expect the ordinary person to know the law on divorce. A second Vernon action was more threatening. Richard Bargh brought a writ of conspiracy against 'Margaret Vernon of Clehonger, gentlewoman', Eleanor Bassett, and others responsible for his 'malicious' prosecution at Derby in 1503.[65] In law, his acquittal had entitled Bargh to the writ and the £200 damages he claimed, and 'the case was divers times in argument and was perused by all the bench and also by all the bar'. Apart from the effrontery, there were the defences raised that Bargh had been seen with a party of rioters in warlike array, riding on the road the abductors had taken (did this deny

64. KB27/973, warrants; *YB*, Mich. 20 Hen. VII, p. 4, f. 2; Hil. 21 Hen. VII, p. 17, f. 13. Hale referred to the procedure as 'learning long antiquated', op. cit., i, 637.

65. KB27/973 m. 97d; 974 m. 70; 981 m. 100; 984 m. 30; *YB*, Mich. 20 Hen. VII, p. 21, ff. 11–12; Keilwey, op. cit., f. 81v.

the assize verdict?), and that 'common voice and fame' said that
Richard was at the abduction (was this ground for accusing him?).
Public interest argued that honest complaints should be protected,
but this raised the technical problem of avoiding jury trial at
Stafford on a plea of 'not guilty', which must have gone in favour
of Bargh. Fortunately for Margaret (and the law), the justices
declared the decision to lie in their hands and ruled on public
policy.

These Vernon lawsuits were only to harass, but even without
them Margaret Kebell had seen little from years of litigation.
That statutory felony was at issue is mentioned again and again,
the abduction act cited specifically. But crown prosecution fell to
Vernon influence, appeals of felony to the notorious technicalities
of the law, and civil remedies to uncertainties about Margaret's
status. This hardly demonstrated the protection afforded by the
law on abduction or the effectiveness of 3 Henry VII, c. 2 in bringing offenders to book. Thomas Haselrig might retaliate by bringing
an action for maintenance against Sir Henry Vernon, but this had
only nuisance value.[66]

For effective action we have to turn from the common law
machinery to the king. This was the hope behind Margaret's
journey to London, and she had a special interview with Henry at
Greenwich which seems to have produced prompt action by the
council.[67] Thomas Lovell and John Mordaunt, two of his closest
advisers, certainly examined William Vernon at an early stage.
However, they were convinced by his excuses, and when Margaret put in a formal bill (before June 1502), stressing that to har-
bour an abducted woman was felony by the 1487 statute, William
answered that he had already been cleared; action against him was
now restricted to common law.[68] Margaret's second bill in Trinity
1502 was against Sir Henry as the architect of the whole episode.
It is lost, but interrogatories make the accusations clear: Henry
'concellyd' Roger to abduct Margaret; he made his houses available and assisted with money; he advised Roger to 'convey the
company by the manour placez and liggynges off Sir Henry
Vernon and to the Marchez of Walez'; he sent letters of support to
Clehonger and, finally, put pressure on Margaret to drop her
complaint.[69] The replication and the rejoinder do survive, to-

66. KB27/983 m. 14; 987 m. 15.
68. Ibid., 19/17/1; STAC2/23/4.
67. STAC1/19/17/2.
69. STAC1/19/17/3.

gether with two depositions by Vernon servants, but deal only
with the journey from Herefordshire and the events in London.[70]
All this is *ex parte*, but the servants produced circumstantial
accounts of Margaret's conduct with Roger; either they were
lying—and some points are suspicious—or she had been guilty of
a certain duplicity, or both.

For manifest felony to be taken before the council is not as
strange under Henry VII as it would be when jurisdictions had
become more distinct. But there are two significant features of
Margaret Kebell v Henry Vernon in star chamber. One is speed.
The first rioter to surrender to indictment did not do so until
7 November 1502, but the next day the council received the completed pleadings and evidence of the case it was handling. The
second is the absence of any prosecution of Henry Vernon at
common law and any conciliar action against Roger. Part of the
explanation may have been the need for more investigation in the
case of Sir Henry (and William in so far as he was involved with
his brother); another aspect was political, the misuse of local
power and the misbehaviour of a great man who began his public
career in the Readeption crisis of 1470–1; there was, too, a
personal challenge to the king, as in the Beaufitz affair, for in
February 1502 Henry Vernon was controller to the prince of
Wales.[71] But a principal reason must be that in this case the crown
had no confidence in the common law courts. Roger and William
had been indicted in the immediate aftermath of the abduction,
and although not much could be expected of any trial, the threat
would serve to keep them under some pressure. But the head of
the Vernon clan was the key figure in the affair—without him,
Roger and William were men of straw—and the council knew
that it was pointless to threaten Sir Henry Vernon of Haddon
with a Derbyshire jury. In other words, the abduction act was
powerless against him. Abduction for profit was a crime of the
influential, but in restating common law in 1487 the crown had
remained dependent on machinery which was useless against the
influential.

What the crown wanted was a political settlement—surrender,
not conviction. The fact that all the crown prosecutions had

70. Ibid., 19/17/2; STAC2/22/18; 24/305; 25/68.
71. HMC, *Rutland*, i, 13–15. Roger was a duchy and possibly a royal servant.
Somerville, op. cit., i, 555.

failed was immaterial. The first step was calling in the final quarter sessions indictment in October 1503 and this was followed by a petition by Roger for a writ of *supersedeas*, freezing all process against himself and those indicted with him.[72] The text he submitted spoke of indictments procured 'by synyster meanes of their aduersaries', but also of 'dyuers and many singler consideracions' moving the king to exercise grace. The consideration was four hundred marks, a sum in which Roger had to be bound with three guarantors in November 1503, £100 to be paid in February and £100 in November 1504 and the rest 'within iij monethes after the determinacion or cohabiting had betwene Roger Vernon and Margaret Kebell'.[73] With the bond signed, a pardon was appropriate and this was issued on 9 December.[74] Neither *supersedeas* nor pardon should have impeded Margaret Kebell's appeal, but they certainly made it more difficult. She was able to insist that, before securing a final end of the indictments, Roger should offer the requisite surety to keep the peace towards her, £200 in his own name and two guarantors in two hundred marks each, one, ironically, Richard Delaber.[75] But he then seems to have used the *supersedeas* on royal actions to quash a stage in Margaret's appeal.[76] Of his men, few troubled to sue the pardon formally. But as late as 1509, perhaps because of continued harassment, a dozen did so.[77] As Sir Henry had never been indicted, this pardon did not cover him, and his return to favour took much longer. The council was certainly considering his position in November 1504, the cause papers are endorsed with that date, but he was not finally pardoned until the summer of 1507. His composition, too, was more severe, a total of £900, £100 down and £100 every half year until 1511.[78] This brought the total fine on the Vernons for the attempt to abduct Margaret Kebell to £1166.13.4., and it may also have cost Roger certain duchy offices.[79] They had certainly been made to pay, but by the prerogative, not the common law.

72. KB9/437/9; PSO2/3 [I owe the latter reference to the kindness of Miss M. M. Condon].

73. BL, Add., 21480 f. 99; E36/214 p. 440.

74. *CPR, 1494–1509*, pp. 336–7.

75. C244/153/117, 118 [I owe this reference to the kindness of Dr J. A. Guy].

76. *YB*, Mich. 21 Hen. VII, p. 22, f. 32.   77. KB27/990 Rex, m. 13.

78. BL, Lans., 127 f.45v; *CCR, 1500–09*, 749.

79. Somerville, op. cit., i, 555.

Margaret Kebell eventually secured the end of a marriage which she had resisted so long, either on Roger's death or by ecclesiastical litigation now lost. In June 1509, she and her patient suitor, Ralph Egerton, were dispensed for consanguinity and free to marry at last.[80] Not everyone found this a satisfactory ending; from his cell in the Tower, Edmund Dudley was writing at about the same time, 'Sir Henry Vernon was to sore delt withall'.[81] This one can well believe. It is improbable that he had set out to offer naked defiance to the king. Vernon sources hint that Margaret's adamant hostility was unexpected; her marrying at Derby, the servants' accounts of her subsequent behaviour and her own admitted playing of Sir Henry to see 'yff he wold haue discoueryd any thyng off hys demenur tovchyng ye riotus & felonys ayenst her' show that she could certainly mislead them. Perhaps Roger set out on what was intended to be little more than an encouraged elopement and his mistake was to persist when he found he was unwelcome. Margaret's resistance had also owed much to the perseverance of the Bassetts and here, too, Henry Vernon must have been surprised. Unless he was indifferent to a feud with his neighbours and unless he was pursuing an existing quarrel, Vernon must have expected the Bassetts to accept the situation without too much fuss. Perhaps he had not reckoned with Ralph Egerton being the half-brother to Margaret's formidable mother. Whatever the truth, Margaret outlived the other actors in the drama, drawing until 1534 her Kebell jointure and impoverishing that family in the process.[82] Her second husband had more bastard children than he could remember, but his rise in Henry VIII's service made her Lady Egerton and mistress of the fine mansion of Ridley in Cheshire.[83] Her grandson Thomas Egerton was the famous Lord Chancellor Ellesmere.

The great loser from the Kebell abduction was the law itself. Statute and common law process were shown to be helpless. Legislation, both recent and long established, might as well not have existed. The legal machine had laboured, and brought forth perjured juries, legal ingenuity and a blanket of frustration. Whatever was to come, in the England of Henry VII there was

80. HMC, *11 Report*, vii, 135.
81. C. J. Harrison, 'The petition of Edmund Dudley', *EHR*, 87 (1972), 88.
82. C142/56/51.
83. Ives, *Bull. John Rylands Lib.*, lii, 365, 369–70.

simply no alternative to personal rule. Then, as now, Englishmen were proud of the superiority of the common law to foreign systems. But the law on abduction demonstrates that, at any rate under Henry Tudor, executive justice was infinitely superior to the due process of the common law.

III

Cardinal Wolsey and the Common Weal

J. J. SCARISBRICK

Kinder things can be said about Thomas Wolsey than most historians have conceded. We have lived too long under the influence of A. F. Pollard's hostile biography and given too much credence to John Skelton and Polydore Vergil, the spokesmen—most of the time—of political enemies, whom the cardinal had in plenty. One cannot deny his greed, vanity and worldliness (to name but a few of his shortcomings); they were well-developed. But there were other things as well, without which a portrait will become a caricature.

In his foreign policy Wolsey sought international peace as well as international prestige. He presided over the burning of heretical books but never over the burning of any heretic. He tried to promote overseas exploration (but was repulsed by a London too content with the Antwerp market to be eager for heroics). He was a patron of the arts (especially music) and a builder on the grand scale. Thanks to his grammar school at Ipswich and his most ambitious college in Oxford, he deserves a distinguished place in the history of English education. He failed, of course, to use his enormous powers to carry out the root-and-branch renewal of the late-medieval church in England which it desperately needed (and himself embodied several of its worst abuses). But he did try with the Black Monks and some friars; and the new dioceses set up a decade after his fall originated in a scheme which he presented to Rome in 1528.[1]

He combined, therefore, some of the interests of Erasmus with the urbanity of Leo X, and was more interesting and open than has sometimes been supposed. It will be argued here that there is

---

1. For some of this, see my *Henry VIII* (1968), pp. 41–96, 123–5, and J. Summerson, *Architecture in Britain, 1530–1830* (1958), pp. 1–7. On the new dioceses, see *LP*, iv, 4896, 4900, 5607–8, 5638–9, etc.

another side to him which is more interesting still, namely, his involvement in the agrarian problems of his day.

This is not the place to embark upon a discussion of the facts of the early Tudor agrarian scene, not least because economic historians have in recent years proved that the terrain is so dangerous that a non-specialist is almost certain to come to grief if he dares to trespass; and the subject has enough scalps to its credit as it is. Suffice it to say, at least for the moment, that the problem as it presented itself to Wolsey following an enquiry initiated by him (as distinct from what we today may think it was or are convinced it must have been) was of apparently large-scale conversion of land during the late-fifteenth and early-sixteenth centuries from tillage to pasture—usually sheep pasture—often accompanied by forcible rural depopulation and unemployment as a result of a change to an economy which employed only a shepherd or two where previously perhaps dozens had tilled the soil and left only a couple of cottages where previously a whole village had stood. In this view of things, therefore, the reversion of arable land to pasture, frequently accomplished by enclosing with hedges and ditches, meant ploughs left to rust and families often driven off the land into either neighbouring villages or towns or vagrancy, which in turn caused human suffering, dearer bread, a decline in taxable rural wealth, loss of manpower to serve in the king's wars, and so on.

The story of how this became a major preoccupation of Wolsey's chancellorship was first told at the turn of this century by I. S. Leadam and E. F. Gay. In his *The Lost Villages of England*, M. W. Beresford did much to unravel the complexities and, of course, placed the whole history of enclosing in a new light. Since then there has been much work by agrarian historians and further reappraisals of the subject.[2] On the whole, however, the debate has turned on such questions as the timing, extent, character and effects of reversion to grassland and enclosing, and has been more interested in those responsible for these things (or in those who spoke out against them) than in those who acted against them. No one has asked how sincerely and effectively Wolsey was

2. In particular, see J. Thirsk, *Tudor Enclosures* (Hist. Ass. pamphlet, 1959); *Agrarian History of England*, iv, ed. J. Thirsk (1967), chap. iv; I. Blanchard, 'Population Change, Enclosure and the Early Tudor Economy', *EcHR*, Ser. 2, 23 (1970), esp. 436–43.

involved. Indeed, it has rarely been allowed that Wolsey could have been concerned for anyone but himself.[3]

The story can be begun in 1489 with a statute against the throwing down and decay of rural houses and depopulation. Though there was reference to conversion of land from tillage to pasture, there was no explicit concern here with enclosure. In 1514 and 1515 two new statutes, for which Wolsey may well have had some responsibility and in which he again showed a readiness to resume an initiative from the previous reign, were passed, largely reaffirming the principles of the first act and repeating the previous penalty, namely, forfeiture of half of the annual value of the houses in decay or destroyed and of the land converted.[4] Moreover, someone (maybe Wolsey himself) had apparently perceived the truth that there could be no effective enforcement of the law until it was known how many houses had been affected, and how much land converted, by whom, when and where. The result was the decision to institute an almost nationwide enquiry by royal commissioners touring the counties and collecting information from panels of local men. The commissioners carried out the first phase of the work in late summer and early autumn 1517, acting usually in groups of three or four; they resumed operations in August 1518.

In 1897 I. S. Leadam, who had already unearthed and published extensive material relating to the commissioners' work, produced a large corpus of additional records of this 'inquisition', as contemporaries called it, in his *The Domesday of Enclosures*. Yet further (and abundant) material has since come to light, some of

3. In *Tudor England* (1950) pp. 75–6, S. T. Bindoff had some appreciative things to say about the cardinal's concern for the poor. E. F. Gay also allowed that Wolsey's campaign against enclosure could have been sincere. See his 'The inquisitions of depopulation in 1517', *TRHS*, n.s., 14 (1900), 236. Pollard virtually ignored the whole affair in his *Wolsey*; and the cardinal receives only one (rather dismissive) mention in vol. iv of *Agrarian History of England*. R. W. Heinze, *The Proclamations of the Tudor Kings* (Cambridge, 1976), pp. 94–8 takes Wolsey seriously, however. Wolsey's reputation as an enlightened judge has been much enhanced by Dr J. A. Guy's recent study, *The Cardinal's Court* (Hassocks, 1977).

4. 6 Hen. VIII c. 5 and 7 Hen. VIII c. 1. The first was to remain in force until the following Christmas only; the second, almost identical otherwise, was perpetual. That two statutes should have been necessary suggests bargaining and manoeuvring. (Cf. *LP*, i, 3600—a draft bill and proclamation in the event replaced by the statutes just noted.) *LJ*, i, 26a, 29b, 30a, b, 31a, 32a, 33a, 34a, 35b, 41b is eloquent testimony to the opposition: the first bill was read five times and committed twice in the Lords before being sent to the commons. Cf. the excellent account in Heinze, op. cit., pp. 94–6.

which has been edited by Leadam himself.[5] Even so, it is clear from the subsequent legal proceedings that the records of the commissioners' work are now seriously defective—even, as Leadam noted, for some of those Midland counties where the evidence is most plentiful. Thus, for example, the large-scale enclosing of Richard Knightley of Fawsley in Northamptonshire, involving the destruction of seventeen houses and the removal of 400 acres from tillage, is not to be found in the two stout volumes of Leadam's *Domesday*.[6] Nor is the case of the prior of Daventry, who converted 60 acres in a nearby village, or that of Magdalen College Oxford, which involved three houses and 200 acres in Golder in Oxfordshire.[7]

Though the total acreage affected thus in early Tudor England was, as we have often been reminded, a very small fraction of the total area of the kingdom, it was a considerably larger fraction of the total *arable*. It would have quickly been obvious that it was not only concentrated in the Midlands but often concentrated within individual Midland counties. Wolsey was presented with a record of hundreds of homes deliberately destroyed or allowed to fall into decay (the commissioners made this distinction; and the majority of cases were of allegedly direct and deliberate destruction), of hundreds of folk being driven out of their homes, as well as of hundreds of presumably already empty houses, i.e., potential homes, being lost, of hundreds of ploughs lying idle and tens of thousands of acres converted from arable to tillage. He would have known as well as we do that allowance has to be made for malice and honest error. Accounts of families departing from their homes and being driven out of their villages '*lacrimose et dolorose*', etc., would have been seen for what they often were, namely, attempts to make the worst of bad stories. They would have included witting and unwitting embellishment, particularly if they told of events which had taken place decades before and had since become part of local folklore. All the same, after full allowance had been made for all this, Wolsey would have received a catalogue of rural violence which had left whole villages stricken

5. Leadam had already published some returns (from the BL) in *TRHS*, n. s. 6, 7, and 8 (1892–4). He published the returns for Nottinghamshire in Thoroton Society, record series, ii (1904).

6. E159/298, Mich. 11 Hen. VIII, m. xiv. All references to these rolls will be to the *communia* section therof.

7. Ibid., mm. xv and xil.

or at least semi-derelict; and since neighbouring villages had often
been similarly affected the victims could not be quickly or easily
absorbed, but would have to travel far to find a new life. When
William Willington of Barcheston, for instance, allegedly enclosed 530 acres, threw down four houses and left twenty-four
homeless, he added yet another enclosure to the already lengthy
list for his part of Warwickshire.[8] Not far away one Henry Smith
had enclosed 640 acres in one village, destroyed sixteen houses and
driven out eighty inhabitants to face misery and unemployment.
The church was in decay; animals wandered over the graveyard.[9]
The village was evidently in ruins. And so were several others in
south-east Warwickshire.

The abbot of Abingdon and his farmers bore major responsibility
for a swathe of destruction which had cut through villages of
Berkshire between Wantage and Reading. Another ran from
Bedford to Banbury; a third from Northampton to Peterborough.
There was heavy conversion and enclosing around Bedford and
the south-west and south-east of Leicester, and in pockets of
north Oxfordshire in particular. In some places, therefore, it would
have seemed that sheep were indeed 'eating up men' and that the
toll of destruction and human suffering, though localised, was
high.

If we turn from what a lord chancellor was told had happened
to what modern historians assure us actually took place, we meet
a different picture. Enclosure was slow, erratic and piecemeal, and
as much the work of peasants as of big men. It had begun generations before. In the main, villages had dwindled, houses had
tumbled and land been given over to grass not so much because of
aggressive landlordism but because landlords had been unable to
find tenants and been forced to accept an often less profitable use
of their acres by turning them over to pasture.[10] The conversion to
arable was often a consequence of the voluntary abandonment of
dwellings rather than the other way round. When enclosure had
taken place, therefore, it would have harmed only the lingering
remnant of inhabitants of a village already almost emptied by
plague and migration. The arithmetic of the jurors of 1517–18 is
suspect: their acreages are guesses expressed in convenient round
figures; a standard multiplier is used to reckon the number of

8. Leadam, *Domesday of Enclosures* (1897), ii, 416f.
9. Ibid., pp. 431ff.   10. Blanchard, op. cit., pp. 436–8.

'homeless' and of rusting ploughs. Since we know that a number of the accused were acquitted, we have another reason why we cannot use the returns of the inquisition as evidence of the extent either of depopulation or enclosure: a charge is not the same as a verdict.[11]

On the other hand, if there was no particular new problem to be dealt with, it is difficult to explain why the statutes of 1489 and 1514–15 (let alone the enquiry of 1517–18) came about. If it is true, as has recently been suggested, that the population of England did not begin to pick up until the 1520s—and that we have therefore antedated the demographic recovery hitherto[12]— our statutes are doubly difficult to explain, particularly as their preambles suggest that the destruction of houses and forcible eviction of villagers and conversion of land from tillage had recently become serious. Legislators are commonly wrong about the facts, of course; but in this case it would presumably have been in the interests of a parliament composed of landlords to suggest that evils against which they were legislating were not the work of landlords but of Nature. The jurors in the enquiry may have been spinning yarns or innocently telescoping events and re-writing them in the process. But they were giving testimony to local men and their returns were destined for scrutiny by a hard-headed chancellor. Most important of all, if they were wrong in suggesting that there had been much decay and destruction of houses in the previous two or three decades and a great deal of conversion of land to pasture, and if they had mistaken a long-term process for a recent one, most of those accused of offences against the statutes would have been acquitted. A number were—on the ground that their offences had taken place before the beginning of Henry VII's reign, the limiting date of the statutes. But, as we shall see, a large number either pleaded guilty or were not dismissed until they had allegedly rebuilt the houses or restored the lands concerned; that is, their cases implicitly or explicitly confirm the returns of the commissioners. In other words, it is difficult not to suspect that there had been an upsurge in the amount of eviction and conversion in those decades, that the problems had acquired a new urgency.

11. This point has been made vigorously by E. Kerridge in his article 'The Returns of the Inquisitions of Depopulation', *EHR*, 70 (1955), 212–8.
12. Cf. Blanchard in his article cited above, n. 2.

This, however, is not central to our purpose. Let us return to the enquiry itself. We know very little, alas, about how it was conducted, that is, about how the jurors who presented information to the commissioners were selected and how they went about their work. All we have is the results—a major bureaucratic achievement. Its chief executant, John Veysey, dean of the chapels royal and later rewarded with the see of Exeter, merits a place in the Valhalla of state servants. His and his colleagues' work deserves to stand alongside that other famous Tudor compilation, *Valor Ecclesiasticus*, and could even bear comparison with Domesday Book itself. Moreover, unlike either the *Valor* or Domesday, or the *Quo Warranto* enquiries of the three Edwards (another rival to fame) it was designed for the benefit of the king's subjects rather than for the enhancement of either royal finances or royal authority.

The commissioners made their returns to chancery. There, in the autumn of 1518 and using criteria which cannot now be wholly recovered, it was decided whom to proceed against. The first writs of summons (*scire facias*) to the sheriffs concerned were sent out as early as June 1518. There was only a trickle of them then. By December dozens of landlords were being cited to appear in chancery in the following months.

The records of the common law side of chancery, which was involved here, are so patchy that we have only a haphazard picture of what happened next. However, because the crown had a financial interest in them—that moiety of the annual value of lands illegally enclosed or houses destroyed—the cases moved on from chancery to the exchequer, whose records are happily intact. The defendants came into exchequer along two paths: one, for those who (for reasons we will discuss shortly) had won a writ of *supersedeas* from chancery discharging them, permanently or temporarily, of financial liability to the crown and who found their way on to the memoranda rolls of the king's remembrancer; the other for those who had not succeeded in placating the lord chancellor and whose cases were entered on the rolls of the other remembrancer, the lord treasurer's.[13]

Using these two sets of rolls as well as records of king's bench

13. The best discussion of the procedure is in Kerridge, art. cit., pp. 215ff.

(but eliminating names which 'repeat') and then adding a handful of names of persons for whom writs of *scire facias* or other chancery documents survive or who appointed attorneys in exchequer—i.e., who were certainly proceeded against—but whose cases have inexplicably been omitted from the rolls, I have arrived at the following conclusion: between 1518 and Wolsey's fall in late 1529 legal action was taken against 264 persons alleged in the enquiry of 1517–18 to have offended against the statutes.[14] This figure is, of course, considerably lower than the total number of offences which were involved, because some of the defendants faced two, three or even more charges of illegal destruction of houses or conversion to grassland. Furthermore, except when the tenant became directly involved, they include only the landlords—for it was they, not the farmers (who were usually the people who had done the damage), who had to answer for the offences.

Of these 264, seventy-four pleaded guilty and entered into recognisances to rebuild the houses and restore to arable the lands concerned by a certain date.[15] The recognisances or bonds varied from £20 to over £200. The highest was £240—which was for the abbot of Reading. Some defendants acquired several—Lord Mountjoy, for instance, entered into three to a total of £208; the abbot of Tewkesbury the same number to a total of £200. The terms of the bonds were usually that the restoration should be completed within a year, but in complicated cases or where large numbers of houses were involved, the work was to be done in two stages—half the houses rebuilt or half the land returned to the plough by, for example, the following Michaelmas, the remainder by twelve months later. Our picture of procedure is far from perfect. But we have enough evidence to see that defendants often appeared in chancery before Wolsey in person and that, after the defendant had placed himself on the king's mercy, a decree in chancery named the date by which the rebuilding, etc., was to be done: and we have examples of defendants subsequently

14. The sources used are: E159/298–308; E368/293–303; C43/2 and 28; KB27/1035–50.

15. My figure, slightly lower than that of E. F. Gay in 'The inquisitions of depopulation in 1517', p. 288, is from king's remembrancer rolls (E159) which mention bonds entered into in chancery and from memoranda of recognisances which survive among chancery pleadings (C43/28/1–8), checked against and augmented by two lists of recognisances on the close rolls of 1520 and 1526 (C54/388 and 395).

returning to chancery, under a *subpoena*, to swear that this has been done.

Many defendants, of course, pleaded not guilty. There were all manner of pleas. Some claimed that the land had been enclosed before Henry VII and hence was outside the scope of the statute. We hear of a house abandoned, not because of enclosure, as the commissioners alleged, but because the nearby river flooded it or because it was very isolated and on poor soil or because it had been accidentally burnt down. Some defendants simply denied outright what the commissioners had found; others admitted enclosure, but claimed that it had been done with local consent and with no harm to local folk, or that they had since made amends.[16]

Some of these pleas were immediately successful. Hence fifteen defendants, together with forty-one of those who had pleaded guilty and entered into recognisances, normally had all further action against them in the exchequer halted by writs of *supersedeas omnino*. That accounts, therefore, for fifty-six of the 264.

Forty were not immediately successful with their pleas. Their cases were adjourned and writs of *supersedeas usque* (or *pendente*), that is, a stay of execution until a subsequent term, were sent from chancery to the barons. Many of these cases dragged on for years.

Seven defendants died before their cases had come to judgement. Occasionally proceedings were halted by the crown '*ob insufficientiam materie*' or for other reasons, or they crossed over to the other set of remembrancer's memoranda rolls (the lord treasurer's) and were concluded there. Those who traversed the commissioners' presentments, that is, denied the facts of the accusations, in turn passed to king's bench and to trial at the assizes. Twenty-eight verdicts from the assizes have been found—invariably dismissing the defendants *sine die*.[17]

Putting together all the known verdicts from the records of

---

16. A very incomplete set of pleadings for eight counties (C43/28/1-8), which also contains writs of *scire facias* and *non omittet*, can be amplified by reference to proceedings in the exchequer—E159/298-308.

17. Assize verdicts are recorded in exchequer proceedings (when a full record of process is given), chancery pleadings (C43/2) and on *coram rege* rolls (KB27). That assize juries contradicted what the juries of the recent enquiry of 1517–18 had said raises a problem: which jury was telling the truth? Since the motive to defeat a genuine charge is likely to be greater than that to invent a phoney one, we should put more trust in the original findings

chancery, exchequer and king's bench, we have verdicts for 188 of the 264 defendants—a figure which includes the seventy-four who entered into recognisances, the twenty-eight dismissed at the assizes and others dismissed *sine die* on the lord treasurer's remembrancer's rolls. We can add a further thirty-four whose cases were terminated by death or for some other reason are marked as discontinued—which commonly indicates that the crown recognised that the case was to be dropped and is therefore the equivalent of dismissal *sine die*. The total of cases which came to some declared decision is, therefore, 222—though the number of certain verdicts is 188.

Using these 188 cases we can tackle the obvious question: was Wolsey—indeed, was this whole operation—serious?

A priori, it is difficult to believe that so laborious a business as the huge and tedious enquiry or the scores of later legal proceedings were intended to be merely a charade. It is no less difficult to believe that Wolsey did not hope and intend that they should serve some useful purpose and equally difficult to believe that an experienced man of affairs like him would have entertained groundless expectations in the matter. Then, when we come to look at the details of the story, that is, the details of those 188 cases which came to a known verdict, we have to pause for thought increasingly often.

For instance, when one Robert Lee appeared in chancery under a *subpoena* on 19 December 1519 and swore an oath that he had cast down enclosures in Fleet Marston in Buckinghamshire and 'a C acres or theruppon did sowe with beans', as well as rebuilding a barn, we cannot assume that he was lying.[18] When the abbot of Reading, 'in the full court and before my lord cardinall chancellor of England and other lordes of the kyngis most honourable counsell', acknowledged himself guilty of destroying eight houses and two cottages and enclosing 210 acres in Buckinghamshire and Leicestershire, and then entered into a recognisance of £240 to restore all to former use, was he intending no such thing and were chancellor and chancery merely going through the motions of law enforcement?[19] And when exchequer, having accepted that he had indeed rebuilt the houses and restored the land to arable cultivation by 12 June 1522, dismissed him *sine die*,

18. C43/28/3, no. 5.
19. C43/28/5, unnumbered; E159/298, Mich. 11 Hen. VIII, m. xxvid.

it is difficult to believe that all the parties were engaged in an elaborate piece of self-deception.[20]

Recognisances were not infallible instruments and we cannot know how intently the crown checked the stories about re-building, etc. But when Sir Nicholas Vaux appeared in person in chancery on 8 November 1518 and was bound by Wolsey in £100 to cast down hedges which illegally enclosed 200 acres and to rebuild four houses in Stantonbury in Buckinghamshire, there was presumably some intention that the bond should bind him—as also the other seventy-odd defendants in similar case.[21] That, for example, the abbot of Rewley forfeited his recognisance of £100 suggests that some vigilance was exercised and that bonds were not cancelled on the nod.

There are other considerations. First, legal proceedings were set in train very swiftly after the commissioners' enquiry was completed. As has been noted, by December 1518 writs of *scire facias* were going out by the fistful. By Hilary term, i.e., February 1519, dozens of doubtless angry landowners were either making their own way southwards to Westminster or having to instruct attorneys to act for them. All this betokens a determination on someone's part to roll up his own and others' sleeves. Secondly, every student of legal history is familiar with the phenomenon of cases fizzling out—disappearing into the sands—inexplicably and exasperatingly. But here some 83 per cent of the cases came to a known verdict or some explicit conclusion (owing to death, etc.), which is a very high proportion and again argues that there was official determination to get on with the business. Thirdly, we can catch glimpses of landlords being sufficiently alarmed by the mere preliminaries to make amends before any chancery process began. There are two possible examples of enclosures being removed simply in the wake of the act of 1515—or, more probably, when the offenders first got wind of the enquiry.[22] Then there is the case of the abbot of Stoneleigh who was reported by the commissioners

20. E368/296, Hil. 14 Hen. VIII, m. xiii.
21. E159/298, Hil. 11 Hen. VIII, m. xxiii. Cf. C43/28/6 no. 2. Vaux was a vigorous encloser: eight cases were brought against him in chancery.
22. Sir Richard Eliot said he had rebuilt six houses in June 1517, four months before the commissioners came to his part of the world (the houses were in Chaddleworth, Berks). See E368/293, Mich. 11 Hen. VIII, m. iii. The prioress of Goring claimed that her farmer, William Young, had rebuilt one house and restored forty acres to the plough in Gatehampton (Oxon) by 5 April 1517. So E368/296, Trin. 14 Hen. VIII, m. vii.

in 1517 as having enclosed 300 acres and destroyed one house, contrary to the act; but in the following year, when the commissioners
returned to Kenilworth to continue their work, they were told
that the house was in good repair and that the lands had been
enclosed 'ex antiquo', that is, before the fourth year of Henry VII,
the limiting date.[23] Perhaps the jurors had been wrong on that
first occasion in 1517. Perhaps the abbot had done some successful
bullying since. Whichever it was, he was evidently sufficiently
worried to want to get the record put straight. At least three more
landlords claimed to have seen the warning light immediately
after the enquiry in 1518 and to have acted before chancery
could get at them. Thus one John Percival swore in chancery that
he had rebuilt a house in Higham Ferrers—in obedience to the act
—'immediately after the enquiry but before the scire facias was
returned to chancery'.[24] He had taken fright.

We have grounds for thinking that the operation was, at least
to some extent, seriously meant and was seen to be by some of
the victims, therefore. But was it successful? How far did Wolsey
succeed in forcing offenders to act against their economic interests?
How many houses were rebuilt, how many acres put back under
the plough?

There can be no exact answer to these crucial questions. But
we can offer an imprecise and tentative conclusion, after giving
due warning of the hazards involved.

We cannot accept every recognisance at face value—that is, as
proof that amends were made; and when a defendant secured a
supersedeas omnino on the ground that he had undone an enclosure
and rebuilt a house, we cannot be sure that he was telling the truth.
On the other hand, we cannot dismiss either the recognisance or
the writ as worthless. Next, we are faced with just over 100 cases
on the second set of memoranda rolls in which the defendant was
eventually dismissed because he (or she) also pleaded that houses
had been rebuilt and lands returned to tillage since the commissioners had reported in 1517–18. In every case the defendant
named the date by which the restoration had been completed and

23. E159/300, Hil. 13 Hen. VIII, m. xvi.
24. C43/28/6, no. 5. The other cases are: the prior of Axholme (E368/296, Eas.
14 Hen. VIII, m. xli) and the abbot of Garendon (ibid., Mich. 14 Hen. VIII, m. ix).
They claimed to have rebuilt, etc., by September 1518 and February 1519 respectively.

the king's attorney accepted the plea: whereupon the barons gave their verdict.[25]

But what did it mean to say that a house had been rebuilt '*bene et sufficienter*' to support agriculture? There may have been merely a temporary or token patching-up of one or two dwellings rather than genuine reconstruction of all or most. How complete and, more important, how permanent was the alleged conversion of the land to arable? Latimer told us of the landlord who escaped the law merely by cutting a single furrow through the grassland. Sometimes the defendant said that the land had been restored for 'agriculture and the sowing of seed'; sometimes that it was being put to the 'customary use' of that part of the country—which could have been an honest acknowledgement that not all land was suitable for ploughing or could have covered a multitude of evasions.[26]

In many cases there may have been no rebuilding and no conversion of any kind, but merely lies. In the lord treasurer's remembrancer's rolls the tales of virtuous obedience are so continuous that we must be sceptical. But we cannot always assume that the crown and the barons, consciously or otherwise, were having wool pulled over their eyes. The crown never accepted the defence until there had been further enquiry. Sometimes, as we have seen, this involved handing the case over to the assizes— where the defendants invariably won, and where juries, local men, may have been suborned (but we cannot prove this). Exchequer dismissed the defendants forthwith. In many other cases local enquiry was carried out by *ad hoc* commissioners. Their testimony may have been equally unreliable, and the king's attorney may have been equally misguided in a story at which he had previously demurred. But we cannot dismiss as untrue every story of rebuilding and every claim to have taken away land from the sheep. Sometimes one of the original commissioners, Roger Wigston—a leading colleague of John Veysey in 1517–18 and subsequently conspicuous in Wolsey's household (which was, in a sense, the true centre of the government of England for a decade

25. The defendant was dismissed *sine die*, saving any claim which the crown had to the moiety of the annual value between the time of the enclosure, etc., and the restoration, if this were carried out after 1515–16. The pardons of 1523 and 1529 restricted royal claims yet further.

26. Cf. Beresford, *The Lost Villages of England* (1954), pp. 122ff.; L. A. Parker, 'Enclosure in Leicestershire, 1485–1607' (London Univ. Ph.D. thesis, 1948), p. 47.

and a half)—was among those commissioned to investigate claims about rebuilding, etc. Occasionally he acted alone. It is not credible that he was always mistaken or bribed and hence always reported untruths to Wolsey and the exchequer. When the crown accepted the truth of the defence 'ex relatione Rogeri Wigston' (with or without others) it was on fairly firm ground: and so are we.

A few examples may show the strength of the claims that sometimes face us. An Oxfordshire farmer of the abbot of Kenilworth, for example, was accused of having converted forty acres to grass and of destroying one house. The abbot, who was legally responsible, was bound in £20 to make amends by the following Christmas. In the Michaelmas term of 1523 he claimed that he had indeed done so by 20 December 1520. As often happened, the crown then sought repeated adjournments and it was not until Easter 1529 that a verdict was given—when Richard Lister, acting for the crown, accepted the abbot's story 'ex relatione Rogeri Wigston' and others, and the abbot was dismissed sine die.[27] The recognisance, the abbot's plea and the testimony of Wigston come together in a coherent sequence. Then we may take the case of Thomas Lovett, a gentleman of Northamptonshire, who entered into a recognisance to restore six houses and 300 acres in Wappenham in two stages by Michaelmas 1521, and was likewise dismissed sine die (eventually) after the same Richard Lister on the testimony of the same Wigston (this time acting alone) reported that Lovett's claim to have observed the terms of the bond were true.[28] The abbot of Leicester told the court in Easter 1523 that three houses and 180 acres in Kirkby Mallory had been restored and all the enclosures had been removed which, in 1517, had been described as causing four ploughs to be 'put down' and eighteen villagers to quit their homes 'dolorose'. By Hilary term 1525 Wigston and others had verified the story, and the abbot was acquitted.[29] His verdict came quickly. Sir John Longvile, who had been bound in £100 to restore nine houses and 252 acres in Wolverton (he had figured conspicuously in the returns of 1517), claimed to have done so by 28 August 1520 when his case began in exchequer in Easter 1527; but it was not

27. E368/297, Mich. 15 Hen. VIII, m. lxxviii; C54/388.
28. E368/298, Mich. 16 Hen. VIII, m. lxvi; C54/388.
29. E368/297, Eas. 15 Hen. VIII, m. xxxvii; Leadam, Domesday, i, 236-7.

until Easter 1535 that the crown, again on the assurance of Wigston, accepted the story.[30] On the other hand, in many cases the king's attorney accepted the defendant's story about rebuilding, etc., at once, and the case was dismissed in the term in which it first occurs on the exchequer roll—and we are left to speculate about what has really happened.

Defendants usually took care to give precise dates by which rebuilding, restoration of land '*pro usu iconomie et seminatione granorum*', and the destruction of enclosing hedges and ditches had been completed. And we have several interesting examples of the crown, for its part, showing care and thoroughness. The abbot of Malvern, for instance, was pursued for years in respect of the crown's moiety of the annual value of eight dwellings and 140 acres in Shuttington in Warwickshire. Eventually the sheriff distrained some of his property, including two cows, and the abbot appeared in court (in Trinity term 1527). He claimed that he had rebuilt the houses and restored the lands and was therefore cleared of all liabilities by virtue of the act of pardon of 1523, which, as we shall see, was to play an important part in this whole story. By Easter 1533, after continual crown adjournments, he won his case.[31]

Anthony Catesby was probably telling the truth when he told chancery that the house in Irchester in Northamptonshire which he had been accused of destroying had been accidentally burnt down and that the twenty-four acres associated with it had not been under grass, as alleged. He was scarcely liable to the act, therefore. Nonetheless chancery pursued him and on 14 November 1519 he swore an oath that the house had been rebuilt '*de novo*'. Again, he seems to have been telling the truth.[32] On 11 July 1519 one William Fermour took an oath before Wolsey that the house in Hardwick in Oxfordshire which his farmer had allowed to decay had been rebuilt and that husbandry was kept there. But he was not dismissed *sine die* until Hilary 1525, by which time the king's attorney could report that the truth of his plea had been verified by local enquiry.[33] One John Bassett was not picked up by the commissioners of 1517 at all: an escheator's inquisition held

30. E159/301, Trin. 14 Hen. VIII, m. ii; E368/301, Trin. 19 Hen. VIII, m. iv.
31. E368/295, Trin. 13 Hen. VIII, m. xxvii.
32. C43/28/6, nos 26 and 27; E159/298, Mich. 11 Hen. VIII, m. xxxiiid.
33. E159/300, Eas. 13 Hen. VIII, m. xid; E368/298, Hil. 16 Hen. VIII, m. v. There are three Hardwicks in Oxfordshire: this one carries the addition of 'Audley'.

at Dartford in July 1518 discovered that he had destroyed a house and converted 26 acres in Foots Cray, and as a result of this official vigilance Kent is unexpectedly represented among Wolsey's victims.[34] Bassett pleaded that he had made amends by 21 May 1522. If this is true, he had obviously thought discretion the better part of valour.

Care had been taken with the original enquiry: when the commissioners came round again in 1518 they corrected many of the presentments of the previous year. Then, as chancery sifted the cases, many were dropped because of omission or error or because the defence would be very strong. A case in Chesham in Buckinghamshire was discontinued when further enquiry revealed that most of the land, which was poor, was nonetheless being ploughed.[35] The prior of St John of Jerusalem won his case when he argued that some land in Melchbourne in Bedfordshire was in some years in tillage and in others in pasture. In other words, the court was sensitive to the agricultural facts of the situation and could appreciate a need for convertible husbandry. But he was bound in £100 to rebuild devastated homes.[36] The case of John Spencer of Wormleighton in Warwickshire shows clearly both the complexity of the situation and the genuine dilemma which faced contemporaries. Spencer argued that the enclosing of land for grazing (in fact it had been done by the previous owner) had brought prosperity to the village: he had built some new houses, the hedges themselves and woods yielded useful firewood for the poor, the local church had been generously endowed by him. Were he forced to put the land back to tillage, fine cattle and sheep would have to be slaughtered, and the land, which was not good arable anyway, put to less valuable use. Wolsey apparently would not relent. Spencer was bound by a recognisance in 200 marks to rebuild the houses and throw down his precious hedges. He pleaded afresh with Wolsey, begging not to be forced to sell cattle 'now in the ded tyme of wyntyr' and to be allowed longer time to pull down his hedges.[37] Alas, we cannot be sure about

---

34. E368/302, Mich. 20 Hen. VIII, m. xx.
35. E159/299, Mich. 12 Hen. VIII, m. ix.
36. E159/298, Mich. 11 Hen. VIII. m. xl; cf. Kerridge, art. cit., p. 216.
37. Leadam, *Domesday*, ii, 485–9. Spencer's plea has rightly received a good deal of attention and been printed several times in later collections of documents. It is the most persuasive and elaborate defence of all those presented by the enquiry of 1517–18.

what happened next. All that we can say is that Spencer was clearly convinced that Wolsey was in earnest.

Ironically, one of the defendants in this story was Sir Thomas More. He had been granted lands belonging to the former Sir Thomas Lovell, which included thirty acres in Fringford reported in 1518 as illegally enclosed. In Hilary term 1527 More in person swore before the barons that the lands had been returned to arable and a house rebuilt.[38] He pleaded as many other defendants pleaded, and his case was dismissed. It is unlikely that More would have lied. If he was telling the truth, may not some of the others have been doing the same?

Then there is the case of Thomas Haselrig of Noseley in Leicestershire, whom the enquiry of 1517-18 found guilty of destroying five houses, reducing six others to cottages and enclosing 480 acres. He came to the exchequer in Easter term 1523 and claimed that the eleven dwellings had been rebuilt by December 1518. The crown denied the story, as it often did. Usually the crown subsequently retracted. But on 20 November 1526, after a familiar run of adjournments, Haselrig confessed that he had lied and was committed to the Fleet. He came before the barons again on 28 November, was examined '*diligenter*' and released on bail. On 3 November 1529 he was back in the Fleet for contumacious non-appearance.[39]

The outcome of this story can wait for a moment. The important thing now is that Haselrig's defence was not accepted automatically by the crown and that he was committed to prison for perjury. Alas, this is the only example of such vigilance. But one example is enough to show that there was some control, some attempt to winnow the pleas, and that the *sine die* was not granted as a matter of course after perhaps merely formal recourse to a local enquiry.

If we accept at face value all the defendants' claims to have mended their ways—which we cannot—we have a total of hundreds of houses rebuilt and many thousands of acres restored to tillage. If we are more circumspect and accept only those stories in which we are explicitly told that the defendant swore

38. E368/301, Hil. 19 Hen. VIII, m. xxxix.
39. E368/297, Eas. 15 Hen. VIII, m. xxiv. His plea had been that the enclosures (which he admitted) had brought prosperity to his village and a hundred folk (thirty-six resident in his own new mansion) were employed thereby. His defence was almost on a par with Spencer's. See C43/28/5.

before Wolsey that he had rebuilt (normally after previously being bound by recognisance to do so), or in which there is such precise evidence that we can be reasonably confident, or in which the crown immediately accepted the defence after having made further enquiry in which Roger Wigston himself was involved, we are left with forty-three cases in which Wolsey's efforts seem to have met success (i.e., just over one-sixth of the total), involving the rebuilding of ninety-seven houses and two barns and the return to arable of 3260 acres.

These figures are fraught with uncertainty, for reasons already explained, and may be a serious underestimate. But they are enough to suggest that the operation had some success and did, on occasion, bring the king's subjects to heel.

Wolsey was hamstrung by the notorious inefficiency of the common law. He was restricted, too, by the fact that the statutes limited his action to conversion of land, etc., since the beginning of Henry VII's reign; and we now know that a considerable amount of enclosing had taken place before then. It was not his fault that he was prevented from reaching the whole of the problem—nor that it was an easy escape for defendants to plead that their alleged offences pre-dated the act of 1489.

Enclosures were but one issue among many crowding in upon the cardinal and demanding his attention, and there were times when they must have been at the wrong end of a long agenda. He was constantly distracted by diplomacy; he had to find time and energy for desperate money-raising, for frequent bullying of Rome for his own advantage and the king's, for keeping Henry content, for the incessant business of star chamber and suitors seeking his favour. Had he been able to give more time to enclosures, the story could have been different.[40]

As it was, the numbers whom he brought to book were probably small, the total acreage restored to arable but a tiny fraction of the whole, the total number of homes and ploughs brought back to life insignificant. But perhaps statistics are not the most important thing.

40. There are three main periods of activity concerning enclosures: 1518–20, following the enquiry; 1525–6, when there is a surge of new cases, based on that enquiry, coming into exchequer and the three proclamations (see below, p. 65); and 1528–9, when many cases which had been pending are brought to a conclusion and two more proclamations emerge. To some extent these fluctuations coincide with Wolsey's involvement in other business, especially foreign affairs.

We should be surprised that Wolsey ever tried, not that he met only modest success. The enquiry of 1517–18 was itself remarkable, because so ambitious and disinterested. So were the subsequent legal proceedings. Wolsey's victims included nine peers, three bishops, thirty-two knights and fifty-one heads of religious houses, plus well over a hundred other gentlemen and five Oxford colleges (together with Eton). The list reads like a roll-call of the possessing classes of the Midlands, with such names as Spencer, Brudenell, Barentine, Vaux, Sacheverell, Dudley, Knightley, Lucy and Verney to the fore. The peers include the dukes of Norfolk and Suffolk, and the religious the abbots of Reading, Crowland, Peterborough and the like, not to mention the prior of St John of Jerusalem, Thomas Docwra. In attempting to enforce anti-enclosure legislation against such as these, he was challenging some of the sturdiest members of the 'political nation', and challenging them in their 'countries', that is, precisely where the natural leaders of society would most resent any attempt to trespass. This was intervention of a kind to which Englishmen would not become accustomed for centuries. The writs of *scire facias, subpoena* and *non omittet* brought over 250 members of the possessing classes into chancery and thence exchequer, not a few of them perhaps having to endure the humiliation of taking down hedges and fences or filling ditches and restoring houses before the gaze of tenants and those of 'the rude and common sort'; it brought to all the expense of either employing attorneys or coming to Westminster in person to plead their causes. Wolsey's sins may have been scarlet, but his writs were read. And that made the affront a biting one.

His motive cannot have been merely financial, for no more cumbersome or less successful way of raising cash could have been devised. In 1515, when the act of 1489 was renewed, parliament had apparently insisted that new legislation should include a pardon for all who had complied with the law by rebuilding, etc., by 13 November 1515. The crown's financial benefit was therefore waived in order to resuscitate the campaign against enclosure; and defendants regularly pleaded the act thereafter to escape payment of the crown's moiety. There was probably a furore over enclosing in that most interesting (but mysterious) of Tudor parliaments in 1523 and the pardon act which it produced was perhaps part of a larger 'package' negotiated between a fractious commons and a chancellor desperate for the cash originally expected from a swingeing new subsidy. The act gave special attention to the story which we have been tracing and granted pardon for destruction of houses or enclosure done before 8 August 1515, provided that the enclosures were down by Easter 1524 and the houses rebuilt by Michaelmas 1524. It further provided that 'almaner processes', as well as fines, amercements and the like, arising from any inquisition concerning decayed houses and converted lands should be put 'in suspence and respite'.[41] A doubtless angry parliament had therefore felled a large tree across Wolsey's path. Thereafter, though actions did continue in exchequer, defendants were able to escape any financial penalty if they could convince the barons that they had met the deadlines of the act of 1523 (and many claimed to have done so well before). So, if money was the object, the exercise failed, and was allowed to fail, easily.

Wolsey would have been hard-headed enough to know that enclosure and depopulation bred grievances among the dispossessed and hungry which could easily lead to insurrection. He knew of the Peasants' Revolt of 1381, of Sir John Oldcastle, and of how popular insurrection had afflicted fifteenth-century Bohemia.[42] But whether he wanted simply to de-fuse a potentially dangerous situation by forcing landlords to stir themselves betimes and thus avert punishment for their own landlordism is another matter. He would not have known (presumably) the full size of the problem, and hence of the threat, until after he had taken the most costly step in the whole enterprise—the first one, the enquiry of 1517–18 itself. There had been little popular protest hitherto to alert anyone to the dangers of the situation. And would a sixteenth-century Englishman have thought in such narrow terms anyway? Would not his motives have been both moral and pragmatic? The throwing down of houses, the rapid conversion of land, the victory of sheep over plough and the eviction, unemployment and vagrancy, the rise in food prices and the hunger which resulted caused both dangerous discontent and pitiable

41. *SR*, iii, 242ff. The pardon (14 & 15 Hen. VIII c. 17) is a very interesting document.

42. See his long harangue of Sir William Kingston, after his arrest in November 1530, reported in Cavendish, *The Life and Death of Cardinal Wolsey*, (ed. R. S. Sylvester, EETS, 243 [1959]), p. 180.

human suffering. In short, they were bad for the common weal.[43]

The chancellor counter-attacked with statute and commissioners and the weaponry of the common law courts. In the last three years he added proclamations: one in July 1526 (apparently to be enforced by new commissioners) requiring all illegal enclosures to be undone forthwith; two more in the following November requiring all offenders to appear under writs of *subpoena* in chancery and enter into recognisances to reform under pain of 500 marks; the fourth in May 1528 promising secrecy to anyone who informed against an encloser—so that he should not incur 'any indignation or displeasure of any man for his said disclosing'; and the fifth in February 1529, which threatened that sheriffs and other royal agents would destroy the hedges and ditches if the guilty persons did not do so themselves—an astonishingly bold measure which apparently encouraged some sheriffs to act.[44]

A few months later Wolsey himself had been laid low. The immediate reason for his fall was that the king had abandoned him. But his power and wealth, his greed and highhandedness, not to mention the mere fact that he was a prince of the church (and an arrogant one), ensured that he would be quickly dragged down once royal favour faded.

There were, indisputably, various reasons for seeking his downfall. But perhaps we have been considering here one of the more important. Wolsey had finally committed political suicide by recklessly intruding into what his victims would have regarded as their private affairs and by his readiness to galvanise the engine of the law—without regard for 'any indignation or displeasure of any man'—on behalf of underdogs against their social betters. His action was bound to provoke an angry response.

43. As Bishop Longland put it in a letter to Wolsey, 'your heart would mourn to see the towns, villages, hamlets, manor places, in ruin and decay, the people gone, the ploughs laid down, the living of many honest husbandmen in one man's hand, the breed of mannery by this means suppressed, few people there stirring, the commons taken away from the poor people, whereby they are compelled to forsake their houses'. *LP*, iv, 4796. Longland's views did not accord with the modern version of what had happened.

44. *Tudor Procs.*, 110, 113, 114, 119, 123. The reference to new commissioners comes from the two of November 1528. C47/7/2–3, f. 7 is a schedule of names of Northamptonshire folk, drawn up by such commissioners, involved in crown actions concerning illegal enclosure. Bishop Longland refers to these commissioners in the letter quoted in the previous note, which should perhaps be re-dated to 1526 (instead of 1528, as in *LP*). Cf. Heinze, op. cit., p. 98.

Plenty of Wolsey's victims were in the parliament which met in November 1529: in the upper house, bishops, abbots, the prior of St John of Jerusalem and lay peers; in the lower, knights of shires and burgesses with such names as Barentine, Sacheverell, Harrington, Parr, Knightley and Haslewood. They were men with scores to settle. 'We have begun to execute the statute of enclosings', said one of Palsgrave's articles against Wolsey.[45] Indeed he had.

Parliament soon passed another act of pardon, which again covered enclosures and hence again wiped the slate clean. Of the eleven peers who signed the articles for the proposed attainder against Wolsey, six had been involved in litigation concerning enclosures.[46] Most interesting of all, perhaps, that Thomas Haselrig, the encloser who lied to the barons of the exchequer and was put in the Fleet twice for his misdeeds, on 13 December 1529 received a royal pardon.[47] It was only a few weeks since Wolsey's fall. Perhaps Haselrig's release was a symbol of victory won, and revenge taken. Cases continued to come into exchequer after Wolsey's fall—still arising from the enquiry which Veysey had led over a decade before—but the most vigorous times were over.

If this assessment of an important and neglected strand in Wolsey's career is correct, we can understand better the remarks of Wolsey's gentleman usher and biographer, George Cavendish, who recalled that in November 1530 the poor commons turned out to watch the ex-chancellor on his journey from Yorkshire to London to meet the king (his last journey, and one ended prematurely at Leicester) and fêted him and wept as he went by. Perhaps we must allow for conventional literary embellishment here. Perhaps the poor commons wept easily, especially at the sight of so great a fall. But perhaps they knew what they were doing. 'They lovyd hyme so well', we are told, 'for suerly they had a great losse of hyme bothe the poore and the Riche, ffor the poore had of hyme great releafe'.[48]

It is notoriously easy both to overstate the originality of one's subject and to push backwards in time—ad absurdum—the search for origins and foreshadowings. Wolsey, of course, did not invent concern for the king's poor subjects. The demands of

45. *LP*, iv, 5750.   46. *LP*, iv, 6075.   47. *LP*, iv, 6135 (22).
48. Cavendish, op. cit., p. 163.

social justice were the stock-in-trade of many medieval preachers and of most chancellors in their orations at the opening of parliament; and the Piers Plowman tradition ran deeply through and beyond late medieval England. The act of 1489 was a notable precedent and was itself the product of an upsurge in the early years of Henry VII's reign of official interest in social problems which has several pre-echoes of later times. All the same, Wolsey's arrival on the scene transformed the anti-enclosure movement— lifted it on to a new plane. Nothing so ambitious had been attempted before. What came later, in the time of Thomas Cromwell or under Edward VI, was probably neither as determined nor as successful. 'Reform and renewal' had deep roots in Wolsey's gifted household, which, of course, nurtured Thomas Cromwell himself; and it may be permissible to describe Thomas Wolsey as a begetter, but not the only begetter, of the 'Commonwealth men'. As Bishop Longland of Lincoln said to him, 'there was never thing done in England more for the commonweal than to redress these enormous decays of towns and making enclosures'.[49]

49. *LP*, iv, 4796.

IV

The Sessional Printing of Statutes, 1484-1547

G. R. ELTON

Once statute became accepted as the supreme form of law-making, those living under the law needed to know what parliament had done, and lawyers in particular required copies of new statutes as quickly as possible. Such copies probably circulated even before the invention of printing, but there cannot have been many of them. The printers discovered the profitable market almost at once, and their activities came effectively to alter the very nature of parliamentary law itself: once sessional printing became the norm the product superseded the older records—the Rolls of Parliament and even the Original Acts—as the commonly used authoritative version of parliament's output.

The first set of printed statutes ever produced was for Richard III's only parliament (1484); neither of the two printers to whom the work has been ascribed could really have started earlier. William Caxton returned to England about 1476, while William de Machlinia is not found active till the later 1470s;[1] at most they missed the parliament of 1478. This branch of printing developed rapidly. Particular acts were put out as well as the statutes of particular parliaments and, by stages, collections of acts both ancient and recent; reprinting was frequent, dating was unknown before 1539 and far from conscientious thereafter, type was sometimes set up afresh and sometimes kept standing with new headlines supplied for successive printings. The highly successful collection of Henry VIII's statutes published by Thomas Berthelet in 1542 was reprinted in 1562, after his death, with his name still in the colophon.[2] In the course of time, such collections were often

1. E. G. Duff, *A Century of the English Book Trade* (1948) pp. 24, 97. The elegance of the 1484 production suggests to me that the longer-standing ascription to Caxton is correct.

2. Berthelet died in 1555 (*The Diary of Henry Machyn*, ed. J. G. Nichols, CS, (1848), p. 95).

broken up and sometimes rebound in a muddle of different printings, and many libraries have holdings of seemingly well-ordered volumes that are in fact a bibliographer's nightmare. A historian who is not a bibliographer must be rash indeed to embark upon materials that can be dated only from a study of typefaces, borders and ornaments.

Though a full-scale attack on the problem ought perhaps to have involved the comparing of all extant material side by side, this was both physically impossible and quite beyond my skill. Happily, I had earlier labours to assist me. The famous introduction to *The Statutes of the Realm* provides some useful clues but also contains some confident assertions for which no grounds are given; it is a mixture of learning and imagination which is very unsafe to use and has been trusted too readily. In 1900, Robert Procter attempted to track the work of Berthelet, the most prolific pioneer of this kind of printing, in an article which relied only on the holdings of the British Museum and in fact missed some of the Berthelet statutes available there.[3] Insufficient as his effort was, it did provide the first usable chronological framework. The listings in the British Library Catalogue and the *Short-Title Catalogue of English Books 1475–1640* are of some help, though the former does not attempt to distinguish between sessional printing, parts of collections and later reprints, while the second gives only a small selection from the extant mass. Much the most important analysis is found in J. H. Beale's great bibliography, which tried to base itself on a really comprehensive survey: Beale searched twenty-four libraries in England and America. He modestly disclaimed any pretensions to completeness or total accuracy and has indeed been found wanting here and there, but his work must nevertheless form the starting-point of any enquiry.[4] With the help of these guides I have worked through a selection of the extant printed acts from Richard III's only parliament to Henry VIII's last, and I have satisfied at least myself that I have seen all but two of the sessional prints that were produced and survive. The two absentees are listed by Beale and

3. R. Procter, 'A short view of Berthelet's editions of the statutes of Henry VIII', *Trans. of the Bibliographical Soc.*, 5 (1901), 255ff.

4. J. H. Beale, *A Bibliography of Early English Lawbooks* (Cambridge, Mass., 1926); see also the pamphlet of supplementary material by R. B. Anderson (ibid., 1943). I shall cite these works by authors' names only and printed statutes sometimes by the numbers attached in their lists.

Anderson as found at Harvard only. If my identification of a particular statute as sessionally printed should on occasion be suspect, the error would matter the less because from a certain date the fact of sessional printing can be proved obliquely and because the reprints were scrupulous: from the first, texts were regarded as sacrosanct, and compositors seem to have exercised a care quite unusual among sixteenth-century printers, practices upon which the legal authority of those productions naturally depended.

When did the king's printer start to produce sessional acts for the public use? The first positive evidence is also utterly un-ambiguous. On 3 May 1510, a warrant was issued to Lord Chancellor Warham, instructing him to deliver to Richard Pynson, king's printer, a true copy of the statutes passed in the last parliament, so that he might put them into print.[5] The first parliament of the reign had been dissolved on 23 February, so that it was only two and a half months after it went home that Pynson got the opportunity to set about his task. He produced the desired set, a somewhat primitive affair without any title, the first act opening on page 1. The print concludes with a table of the fifteen acts printed (out of the twenty passed); the colophon explained that these were 'the Statutis holden at Westmynster [*sic*] the. xxi . daye of January in the firste yere of ye most noble reygne of Kynge Henry the . viii', and claimed a two years' sales monopoly for Pynson by royal privilege.[6] We may note, for later reference, that Pynson had printed the tonnage and poundage act separately and that it was not included in the sessional set.[7]

This fine start was not immediately followed up. The next parliament sat for three separate sessions, and the novelty of a parliament so prorogued seems to have bewildered both printer and clerk. No copy of any statute has been found for the session of 5 Henry VIII, but those extant for the first two sessions of this parliament (3 and 4 Henry VIII) were printed together, being signed through and having a colophon only at the end of the double set.[8] There must be some doubt whether 5 Henry VIII ever produced a sessional printing, though the acts for that year are in the reprint collections of 1542 and 1562, and the disap-pearance of one sessional set among so many is much less sur-prising than the survival of all the rest. At any rate, while the

5. *LP*, i, 485 (4).   6. BL, C. 38. c. 2.   7. Beale, S110a.
8. BL, C. 122, f, 10 (2, 3).

routine of sessional printing was clearly not yet established for Henry's second parliament, it had arrived by the time the next one met; for each of its two sessions (6 and 7 Henry VIII) a separate and sessional statute can, with some difficulty, be ident- ified.[9] Thereafter we find sessional acts right through the reign, and from the session of 31 Henry VIII (1539) the sets carry the year date of printing.[10] From 1531 the work was done by Pynson's successor, Thomas Berthelet, who remained king's printer to the end of the reign and evidently put the whole business on a firm and regular basis. His carefulness appears, for instance, in the fact that the 'cum privilegio' in his colophon was promptly altered in 1539 to 'cum privilegio ad imprimendum solum', to accord with the order proclaimed on 16 November 1538, the full formula thereafter remaining in use:[11] this detail can help in dating stray copies. Berthelet got so efficient that he could publish (if his colophons are to be trusted which in 1543 and 1544 give the day of publication) within three to four weeks of the end of the session, an efficiency which did not endure; in 1555 the statutes did not become available until three months after parlia- ment had risen.[12]

Before Henry VIII, the situation is markedly less clear. Printed

---

9. 6 Hen. VIII: Beale S117, alleged to be found at Harvard and Cambridge, has not been tracked at the former by Anderson; the CUL copy (Syn. 4.83.9) is badly mutilated and lacks everything after sig. A iv. Beale S117a seems to be a mistake, since his table gives that number to the statute for 7 Hen. VIII which his list calls S117b. Anderson S116a is probably a reprint—7 Hen. VIII: Anderson S117c, which from its collation appears to be a separate piece of printing.

10. 14 & 15 Hen. VIII: Anderson S122a (Harvard). 21 Hen. VIII: BL, 506.d.31 (1) [Pynson's last]. 22 Hen. VIII: BL, 505.g.13(2) [rather than 506.d.31(2) which adds chapter numbers]. 23 Hen. VIII: BL, 506.d.31(3). 24 Hen. VIII: ibid. (4). 25 Hen. VIII: BL, C.64.e.10(1) [rather than 506.d.31(5) and 506.d.33 which look to be rushed reprints]. 26 Hen. VIII: BL, 506.d.34 [once owned by Sir Roger Cholmeley, then recorder of London, who when chief baron of the Exchequer gave it to his nephew Ralph]. 27 Hen. VIII: BL, 506.d.31(7). 28 Hen. VIII: ibid. (8). 31 Hen. VIII: CUL, Bb*.8.31.7 [the first printing, but BL, 505.f.5(11) probably also belongs to 1539]. 32 Hen. VIII: BL, C.64.e.10(4) [subsidy and pardon, separately printed, exceptionally bound in and added to table, without chapter numbers]. 33 Hen. VIII: BL, 505.f.5(13). 34 & 35 Hen. VIII: C.64.e.10(5). 35 Hen. VIII: BL, 506.d.8 (19). 37 Hen. VIII: ibid. (20).

11. *Tudor Procs*, i, 186.

12. The parliament ended on January 16, but it was only on April 24 that John Parkyn, who had been anxiously looking for the printed set, could despatch one to a friend in Yorkshire: A. G. Dickens, 'John Parkyn, Fellow of Trinity College, Cambridge', *Procs. of the Cambridge Antiquarian Soc.*, 43 (1950), esp. pp. 23–4

statutes exist for all but one of Henry VII's parliaments, but the copies now found come in the main from the collection for the reign which Pynson published, probably early in the next.[13] However, he utilised earlier printings, and some of these may well have been sessional. This seems most certain for the acts of Henry VII's last parliament (1504), printed by William Facques, the first man known to have held the title of king's printer, though the set is not dated and the elaborate production contrasts with Pynson's later rushed jobs.[14] Nothing survives for 12 Henry VII (1497); since Pynson's collection also omits this year we may suppose that no one printed anything for this parliament. 11 Henry VII yielded an elegant, even extravagant, set from Wynkyn de Worde; the only extant example of it is hand-coloured and hardly looks like print.[15] It may not have been sessional, but it was used in Pynson's collection, which follows its lay-out. Pynson's version for 7 Henry VII (no separate printing found) has no table and is altogether more primitive. The uncertainties posed by these sessions are overshadowed by the problems which the first three parliaments of the reign raise: for these we have a single printing covering all three (probably Caxton's work),[16] and Pynson's volume (by running through all three sessions before supplying tables for them which are not in Caxton's print) confirms that this collective set was all that ever appeared.

In fact, the set for the first three Tudor parliaments must be considered together with that for Richard III's—the first for which a printed statute exists. This has always been treated as contemporary (that is, sessional), though the grounds for that conviction are not clear. The editors of *Statutes of the Realm* simply stated it as a fact that the extant print[17] appeared soon after the end of the session, and they seem to have relied on the sort of enquiries summarised in one of the Record Commission's *Reports* (1806) which claims to have found copies, said to be sessional, in the Inner Temple Library and the King's Library at the British Museum.[18] But we are there given no grounds for these

13. BL, C.71.ff.6, a continuous set brought out by Pynson as king's printer, an office to which he did not succeed until after May 1508 (Duff, op. cit., pp. 126–7).
14. BL, C.122.f.9.   15. BL, IB. 55195.   16. BL, G. 6002.
17. BL, C.10.b.20.
18. *SR*, ii, 477 note; *Report of Searches for Originals, Records and Manuscript Copies etc.*, 1806 (ordered to be printed by the House of Lords, 30 June 1807), App. 19, pp. 49–51.

confident assertions which may be nothing more than the often unreliable fruits of Charles Abbot's love affair with muniments;[19] this very note calls up serious doubts when it locates copies of 31 and 37 Henry VIII at Winchester, despite the fact that, according to the same Report, 'no Originals, Records or Manuscripts were found at Winchester'. In short, the established conviction that Caxton (or Machlinia) printed the acts of Richard III immediately after the session has rested on no discoverable evidence. Nevertheless, of course, it may be correct.

Let us then look at the two productions for 1484-9 which, though they raise some tricky problems, also help to solve some of the mysteries of early statute-printing. Both look alike and differ from later prints. They are not in black-letter but in a rare cursive intended to look like handwriting; they run the acts recited into one block; and they open with a space left for an illuminated initial which in the surviving examples has not been filled in. The editors of *Statutes of the Realm* drew attention to the likeness of this format to that of the medieval Statute Roll and concluded that the Roll, now extant only to 1468, must have been continued and must have formed the original from which the printing was 'manifestly copied'.[20] This is not so. The Statute Roll has neither chapter numbers nor titles of acts: 1 Richard III has the first, and 1-4 Henry VII the second. The Statute Roll is in French, as is 1 Richard III; 1-4 Henry VII is in English. The transformation of the Roll of Parliament from its medieval into its modern form (from a record of proceedings to an enrolment of acts passed) was initiated in 1484: and it was this that made the Statute Roll superfluous. Even if any such Roll ever existed after 1468, it is much more likely that it ceased after the last parliament of Edward IV and was never written up for 1484. Every single Statute Roll covered long periods, and even if a new one was started in 1472 it would only have had material from two parliaments to enroll before the reformed Parliament Roll made the labour supererogatory: at that point the barely-started Roll would likely be discarded. For practical purposes, the Statute Roll always in effect terminated at 1468.

However, this does not necessarily mean that manuscript

---

19. Abbot was the moving spirit behind the Record Commission and also chairman of the editorial committee for *SR*.

20. *SR*, i, p. xxxv.

collections of sessional statutes also ceased. The Roll consisted of transcripts—from what? The form in which the acts appear there reflects no known original. The public acts of the session could not be got from the Parliament Roll, where they appeared in the form of petitions with the king's response: the whole purpose of the Statute Roll was to enregister the positive ordinances made on this basis, and this involved turning petition into act. Moreover, since the bills and petitions in parliament were by this time invariably in English (the Parliament Roll faithfully following suit), the acts had to be specially translated into the French of the Statute Roll. Thus the parliamentary bureaucracy had to prepare a document which could be enrolled in chancery. We may therefore, with some confidence, posit the existence, before 1484, of sessional manuscripts of statutes put together for this purpose; and it would have really been surprising if copies of these had not become available for sale to interested parties.

The conjecture seems probable, and it can be supported by something like firm evidence. Where else but from such copies could the scribe have got his text who composed the splendid volume of statutes kept in the king's remembrancer's office in the exchequer?[21] It is not credible that it could have been copied from the Statute Roll, kept in chancery. *Statutes of the Realm* noted that the text of the volume 'agreed in general with those of the Printed Copies', which is the less surprising because the volume was, once printing started, quite manifestly copied from the print; before that, therefore, it would have used something like our conjectured manuscripts. Another manuscript collection favoured by *Statutes of the Realm* looks also to have been copied from such sessional productions. This is Ms. Petyt 511/6 at the Inner Temple, a volume in which the acts down to the last parliament of Edward IV were transcribed about the end of the reign, those for Richard III and 1

---

21. E 164/11—very handsome and with lots of illuminated initials and borders. A note inserted by Hilary Jenkinson shows that originally one volume covered the parliaments from Edward IV to 11 Hen. VII, all written in one hand. From 1 Ric. III the book manifestly relies on the known printed statutes, reproducing some of their oddities and faithfully following their order of the acts. Like the prints, it has nothing for 12 Hen. VII. The correction of a repeated phrase in 1 Ric. III shows the copyist at work. The exception is 7 Hen. VII which, adding the royal assent and using phrases found only on the Roll, evidently derived from thence. A new copyist picked up in 19 Hen. VII, and yet another added 1–7 Hen. VIII, again using the printed statutes.

and 3 Henry VII being added thereafter.[22] This manuscript uses French throughout and in both the sessions of Henry VII omits the last act included in the print, while in 1 Henry VII it added the act for the king's title which was not printed. Thus, unlike the exchequer volume, it derived its entries for the last three parliaments it transcribed from a source other than the prints: it offers further circumstantial evidence for the existence of our conjectured manuscripts, while its omissions indicate the advantages which were to be gained from the security of printing.

I therefore suggest that before printing began some copies at least of the sessional statutes were circulating in manuscript, that these were copies of the material prepared for the Statute Roll, and that that material continued to be put together even after copying on the Roll was abandoned. Thus when Caxton decided that there was money in the printing of statutes, he first quite simply (in the manner familiar from other areas of early printing) put an existing manuscript style into print and made the product look as like the familiar predecessor as possible. The Petyt Ms. indicates that a French text was still available for 1 and 3 Henry VII, but not thereafter. Consequently, when Caxton next came to produce printed statutes (for Henry VII's first three parliaments) he no longer had the old French manuscript to work from and obtained copies of the acts in English, possibly from the Parliament Roll (with which his text agrees), though he added titles. Since, therefore, the second statute he printed differed from the first in the most important detail of all, the source of the copy used, it is indeed likely that the statute of 1484 was in effect sessionally printed—more or less at once. However, Caxton did not immediately continue to print every session; his successors played around with various formats; and before 1504 the whole business remained very haphazard.

Thus the earliest printing was not really innovatory; rather the story again demonstrates that printing did not so much produce new reading matter as give greater cheapness, celerity, distribution and reliability to already existing publications. Nor was this enterprise in any real sense official, though it is clear that once the conjectured 'Statute Roll manuscripts' ceased to be prepared the printers could not have produced sessional statutes

22. Cf. *Catalogue of Manuscripts in the Library of the Honourable Society of the Inner Temple*, ed. J. C. Davies (Oxford, 1972), i, 217–18.

without the aid of the clerks of the parliaments who controlled the records on which the prints depended. However, it was only in 1504, when Facques claimed the work for himself as king's printer, that the obvious association of official printer with officers of the parliament was made patent. In 1510, the coincidence of a new printer and a new clerk, which has provided us with the first evidence of official support for the printing of statutes, opened the real history of the regular sessional practice. It is worth remembering that the clerk, John Taylor, also did much to reform the keeping of a Journal:[23] very likely the regularising of sessional printing owed something to his tidy and organising mind. Though the full routine of the business enterprise awaited the coming of Thomas Berthelet in 1531, it is apparent that sessional printing is yet another aspect of parliamentary record production which, on the basis of somewhat halfhearted earlier efforts, became regular from the beginning of Henry VIII's reign. What had started as the application of the new technology to the serving of a much older lawyers' market for acts of parliament came to be a part of the government's running of parliamentary affairs.

The printers did not confine themselves to producing collections of acts either sessional or later. Some acts were printed separately. Thus supply acts, including that granting tonnage and poundage for life, were treated so from the first[24] and were not reprinted for sessional statutes, though sometimes copies of the separates were added to those publications.[25] These financial acts, which had to be distributed to all the commissioners for assessment and collection, called for immediate and numerous copies; separate printing was obviously convenient. For similar reasons, acts of general pardon received the same treatment and also do not appear in sessional sets. The 1543 statute for Wales (34 & 35 Henry VIII c. 26), not included in the sessional statute, was printed separately and is sometimes found in surviving sets where it has been bound in at the end of the year's acts.[26] Its length and

23. Cf. G. R. Elton, 'The early Journals of the House of Lords', *EHR*, 89 (1974), 481ff.

24. Above, p. 70.

25. Some sets include subsidy acts and pardons in the table (printed when the set was made up) but without chapter numbers; tables were printed last.

26. E.g. CUL, Rel.b.55.3, a collection made up from later reprints which at the end of the 1543 session inserts the original printing of c. 26. A more complete collection (Sel.3.207) achieves the same effect by using a 1547 reprint of the statute.

the lack of general interest in it may well have counselled against putting it into the sessional print, but, as Berthelet's accounts show, forty copies were wanted for proclamation in Wales, so that separate printing became necessary.[27] To these practical and accidental reasons, politics from 1533 added more pressing ones.[28] The first act which is known to have been specially printed by order of the government was that in restraint of appeals to Rome which it was decided in December 1533 to publish in the form of a proclamation.[29] This must have involved a fresh setting up since the multi-page format of the sessional statute was not suitable for posting. Very soon after we come across the extraordinary possibility that acts may have been available in separate copies even before the end of a session. On 28 March 1534, two days before the prorogation, a correspondent informed Lord Lisle in Calais that he was sending him the acts passed to that day, a purpose for which he could have had nothing available except printed versions.[30] It is thus possible that Berthelet set up the acts as they passed both houses, presumably in readiness for the sessional set, but that he was also willing to sell copies at once, before the assent was given.[31] In 1539, a well-informed observer reported the passing of the act of six articles on 13 June, a fortnight before the end of the session, and confidently expected it to be shortly published in the form of a proclamation, which would have meant 'premature' printing and publication; on the other hand, the French ambassador, markedly less well-informed, expected that printing would be done only after parliament had risen.[32] Over a fortnight after the end of the 1545 session, the imperial ambassador reported that its acts were being kept secret;[33] while this was probably no more than an ignorant complaint that the sessional print had not yet appeared (three days after Twelfthnight) it does show that no acts had become available

---

27. For Berthelet's accounts see below, n. 35.
28. Sometimes with disconcerting results: for what happened to the acts posted at Coventry see G. R. Elton, *Policy and Police* (Cambridge, 1972), pp. 134–5.
29. *LP*, vi, 1487 (1).   30. *LP*, vii, 384.
31. In this period, the indispensability of the royal assent may in practice have been something of a myth, a subject too large for proper discussion here. The Original Acts of the sessions of 27 and 28 Hen. VIII have no formulae of assent inscribed on them; and the 1539 act for the seating order in the lords (31 Hen. VIII c. 10) was carried into effect when it had passed that house, before the commons had seen it and months before it was assented to.
32. *LP*, xiv (1), 1108, 1207.   33. *LP*, xxi (1), 37.

earlier, as had happened in 1534. All very confusing and in-conclusive, but it cannot be helped that the evidence maliciously raises questions which it is then insufficient to answer.

However, it looks as though normally separate printing, except of subsidies and pardons, was confined to the production of acts in the form of proclamations, intended for publicity throughout the realm.[34] This appears from the king's printer's accounts for work supplied to king and council which happen to survive for 1541–3; they also show that by then such proclaiming had become commonplace and was no longer confined to matters of high political interest.[35] On 8 April 1543, in the middle of the session, Berthelet supplied 'iij little bookes of the Statutes' to the privy council, but this is most likely a reference to his 1542 collection of the acts of the reign. Separates he produced after the end of the session, though so promptly that printing had evidently been going on before the assent. On 20 April 1542, less than three weeks after the prorogation, he sent five hundred copies each of the first nineteen chapters of the sessional set, presumably in proclamation form; on 21 May 1543, just nine days after the prorogation, he sent five hundred copies of the first eleven acts, fifty each of two more,[36] and forty of the act for Wales, which last did not reappear in the sessional set—and this time he ex-plicitly stated that these copies were 'made out in Proclamacions'. Further small quantities of some of them were required by 12 June. In 1542, forty-six acts passed of which thirty-nine were printed and nineteen proclaimed; in 1543 the figures were forty-eight, twenty-five and twelve (plus three separates: the act for Wales, the subsidy and the general pardon). At first sight the distinction between acts printed in the sessional sets and those printed for proclamation might appear to lie in their general significance, but though those not proclaimed included a number

34. The suggestion in *LP*, xviii (I), 67 (2, 4) that two private acts of the session were printed and then certified by the clerk of the lords is misleading. Those documents are printed copies of certified manuscript transcripts, even the certi-fication and the clerk's name being in print. They were most probably prepared round about 1666, as evidence in a bastardy case (HMC, *8 Report*, 102).

35. W. H. Black and F. H. Davies, 'Thomas Berthelet's bill, as King's printer, for books sold and bound, and for statutes and proclamations furnished to the government in 1541–43', *Journal of the British Archaeological Assoc.*, vii (1853), 44–52. Cf. *LP*, xviii (II), 211.

36. cc. 12. and 13 for paving streets in London, and for knights and burgesses for Chester, both of local interest only.

of distinctly local or private acts the principle does not work out consistently. Why, for instance, should the lord chancellor in 1542 have wanted five hundred copies of the act freeing Manchester from the burden of being a sanctuary town, but none of those which barred justices of assize from sitting in their county of origin or provided for the naturalisation of certain kinds of children born abroad? In 1543 the crown paid for five hundred proclamations touching the manufacture of coverlets at York, but did not require any copies of the important acts amending the statutes of proclamations and fines. Perhaps temporal sequence accounted for the distinction: did the printer supply what had been got through in time? Against this is the fact that in 1542 he did not print proclamations of two acts later included in the sessional set, the attainder of Catherine Howard and that touching treason committed by lunatics, which specially received the royal assent by commission on 11 February, two months before the end of the session.[37] At any rate, the delivery dates confirm that in those years printing must have been well under way before parliament rose.

How, then, were acts chosen for printing? Who did this, and who supplied the printer with his copy? In the absence of direct evidence something may be inferred from the printed sets themselves. The warrant of 1510, which directed the lord chancellor to supply the necessary material, might suggest a reliance on the Roll, but, if this was so, practice manifestly soon changed. The notion, recently advanced, that the Roll was not made up between 1529 and 1555 is mistaken;[38] but it does look as though none was deposited in the chancery during those years, so that the clerk of the crown could not have supplied copies. More conclusively, from the time (1540) that the officers ceased to enroll every act passed, it is plain that certain acts could have been printed only from the original parchment bill: thus 33 Henry

37. *LJ*, i, 176b.
38. C. G. Ericson, 'Parliament as a legislative institution in the reigns of Edward VI and Mary' (London Univ. Ph.D. thesis, 1973), pp. 154–8, misinterprets a council order of 1556, which concerns certification into chancery, to mean that no rolls were written. For a variety of reasons it is out of the question that the rolls for the twenty-four sessions involved (all of which now exist in contemporary hands) should have been put together after 1556; but it is quite likely that the clerks of the parliaments tried to retain the rolls so as to keep complete control of copying and copying money. Another topic worthy of examination which awaits a study of the rolls.

VIII cc. 2, 8, 14, 15 and 21, though not on the Roll, appear in the sessional print. If the Roll was used, copies had to be made for the printer, as the warrant of 1510 envisaged; while this was supposed to be the practice also in using Original Acts, it seems only too likely that from an early date the clerk saved himself this unpaid labour by lending out the Original Acts themselves. Such improper evasion of duty perhaps accounts for the disappearance of the Original Acts of 1523 and 1529, Sir Brian Tuke's first two parliaments. On the other hand, the original of the act of 1532 for the conditional restraint of annates (23 Henry VIII c. 20) should still have been available when Berthelet printed the sessional statute. It is now missing and has been so since at least Henry Elsyng's day in the 1630s: his calendar of acts at the parliament office, based on 'the old calendar', fails to list it and numbers through as though no such act had ever existed.[39] We know in fact what happened: on 31 August 1533, Lord Chancellor Audley (in no great hurry to execute a warrant received on 9 July) sent for the annates act in order to have it transcribed into the letters patent which were to put it into effect. Evidently it never got back into the archive.[40] But clearly it was there before this, and yet Berthelet did not include it in his sessional statute. We may suspect that someone, most probably the clerk, exercised discretion in not sending to the printer a 'public' act of general interest which was awaiting confirmation by letters patent.

In all probability, therefore, the later standard practice was followed from the first: it fell to the clerks of the parliaments to provide the king's printer with what he was to print, and for this purpose they used the Original Acts in their keeping—either the documents themselves or copies made from them. The series of Original Acts now starts in 1497, that parliament of Henry VII which does not seem to have resulted in sessional printing. It is not impossible that Facques's demand for copy in 1504 induced the clerk to become more careful about preserving the acts of the session even after their enrolment on the Parliament Roll had rendered them superfluous under the traditional system; master record or not, the Roll was no longer sufficient once printing

39. Nat. Lib. of Wales, MS 17016D (cf. 'Calendar of Carew MSS', HMC, *Fourth Report*, App. 369a). The acts for 1523 and 1529 had also disappeared before that date.

40. *LP*, vi, 1049; the patent (whose date, of course, is that on which the warrant was delivered into chancery) is printed from the Parliament Roll in *SR*, iii, 387 n.

became regular. What are in effect Original Acts are found scattered among the Ancient Petitions at the Public Record Office; but in view of the strong probability that no proper sets were kept before 1497 it seems unlikely that the 'unofficial' printing of those early years had such first-hand copy to rely on. I have already suggested that Caxton used a 'Statute Roll manuscript' in 1484 and switched in 1489 to a copy of entries on the Parliament Roll, presumably bought from the clerks; much the same thing may have happened in 1491 and 1495. However, it may be said with reasonable confidence that from 1504 the Original Acts always formed the foundation of sessional printing and that the printer depended on the clerk of the lords for what he got into print. Whether the clerk was also responsible for the order in which acts were printed, or whether this was left to the accidents of the printing-house, cannot be determined. The point is not without interest, for the chapter numbers supplied in the print became the standard manner of legal reference to acts of parliament, though it is very noticeable that parliamentary drafting itself (for instance in acts confirming or repealing earlier acts) studiously avoided chapter numbers and preferred the dubious precision of *ad hoc* titles. Until 1536 the numbering of the printed statute nearly always differs greatly from that on the Roll, which (except for 1529) started with private acts that were not printed; at all times even the Roll's order of acts that did get into print practically never agrees with that adopted in the sessional set. Since, in their antiquarian fashion, the clerks continued to ascribe ultimate authority to the Roll, this fact may well explain why they would not use the printer's chapter numbers. But it also makes it more likely that those numbers came to be imposed as part of the printing process.

The clerk, of course, never sent all the acts to be printed; he (or whoever instructed him) made a selection. The principle of that selection is indicated by a phrase which recurs with little alteration in most of the titles of the sessional sets where it is stated that these are the acts of a given parliament for the honour of God and Holy Church and the profit of the common weal—in other words, the acts regarded as 'public'. Whatever precise meaning this term may have had before (and the Roll for the first time, and for one time only, recognised it in 1539), it became effectively fixed once printing started: it was not so much that the printer published the public acts, but that such acts as he printed were regarded as public, especially in the important sense that they could be alleged in court without special pleading (which involved the production of a certified true copy).[41] It was print that made the acts public or private, generally knowable or knowable only upon the inspection of the unprinted original. However, though print ossified the distinction, the principle of selection preceded it: someone had always had to select the acts that were enrolled on the Statute Roll and that were grouped on the Parliament Roll as the *communes peticiones* without being transcribed. After 1484, 'public' acts, too, were enrolled in full on the Parliament Roll, at first in what was effectively a separate section of it; but before long enrolment took the acts as they came, mixing those later made public with those left private. At this point, the clerk's selection of what to send to the printer finally settled the difference between the two kinds.

Of course, according to the textbook theory the clerk had no choice: he ought to have separated out those acts that bore the royal assent in the form 'le roi le veult' and sent them for printing. But that rule looks better in the books than in reality, even supposing that we can rely on the assent as recorded on the Parliament Roll, a dubious supposition.[42] In 1 Richard III the Roll included among the common petitions assented to by the public formula an act touching wardship of lands held of the duchy of Lancaster; this was not printed. The important act of Henry VII's first parliament which confirmed his title to the crown was not printed, perhaps because it was taken to be more a declaration in, than an act of, parliament; yet in form it was a commons' petition to which the king gave his consent in a barely modified version of the public formula. 1 Henry VII c. 10, the repeal of an earlier act hostile to Italian merchants, was the product of a petition from the interests affected, received the assent *soit fait*, and appears on the Roll among the private acts, forty-six items before the first properly public act; yet it was printed, being for the purpose turned 'public' by various rephrasings which made the king ordain it, having considered the petition (recited) and been ad-

41. The principle that public acts did not need to be specially pleaded was well established by the late fifteenth century (W. S. Holdsworth, *History of English Law*, xi, 290).

42. Even in the later part of Henry VIII's reign, Roll and Original Act do not always agree.

vised by both Houses. Two acts of 3 Henry VII (attainting certain rioters, and proclaiming certain acts of murder) have the public assent on the Roll but were not printed, which suggests that an arbitrary decision was made to the effect that their contents did not merit publicity or that they were really particular (in which case the assent was wrong). 4 Henry VII c. 5 was enrolled with a number of provisos; these did not make it into print, perhaps for no better reason than that they had become detached from the Original Act.

In the next reign, however, selection for printing does seem in general to agree with selection by assenting formula on the Roll— provided it is remembered that there is evidence (which it still needs a full study of the Roll to evaluate) that the clerk was capable of amending formulae on the Roll so as to reduce things to what he had come to regard as the proper order. The Roll, of course, was by this time written at a date later than the sending of the acts to the printer; it cannot have helped to control printing but is more likely to have been adjusted to what had been settled when the printer got his copy, and it may even (conceivably) have been copied from the print. Sometimes, however, formulae of assent were heeded with disconcerting results. It was presumably for this reason alone that the act of 1536 for the dissolution of the lesser monasteries, as palpably public and general an act as one could wish to find, which nevertheless was assented to *soit fait* (according to the Roll: none of the Original Acts of that session bears the formula of assent), was not printed in the sessional statute. According to Robert Aske, this helped to unleash the Pilgrimage of Grace. Aske told his interrogators that opposition to the Dissolution was enhanced by the discovery that the only printed act to refer to it (namely that which set up the court of augmentations) appeared to be so poorly phrased—it did not even define the dominions within which the houses were to be suppressed—that he and his fellows thought it void. He admitted that he had always supposed that another act, not printed, had actually authorised the confiscation.[43] In this he was right; but the argument shows the weight that a lawyer as early as this could place on the printed statutes with their general publicity.

By Henry VIII's time, therefore, the distinction between public and private acts had nothing to do with their import or the

43. *LP*, xii (I) p. 411.

initiative behind them, nor necessarily with the formula of assent, which could be overridden or at other times adjusted to the real distinction: whether an act had been chosen for printing or not. And since the choice was made from among the parchment bills accumulating during the session in the house of lords, the responsibility fell upon the clerk, who no doubt had his guide-lines but on occasion acted independently. Once he ceased to enroll all acts, he omitted not only any private acts whose beneficiaries neglected to pay the fees, but even some acts he sent for printing and thereby defined as public. It will need a study of the Rolls and the Original Acts to discover what he was up to—if indeed he was up to anything and this can be discovered. Why, for instance, did he not enroll Catherine Howard's attainder and yet allow it to appear in print?

It should be added that at this early date no sessional statute supplied the list of acts passed but not printed which was always (or nearly always) included in the sessional statutes from 1571 onwards.[44] In a way this gave the print even more exclusive authority because it left the generality without guidance as to what other legislation might have passed and aware only of the matter in print. We have seen how this fact troubled Aske.

One last point about these early printed sessional statutes deserves a little attention because it throws an unexpected light on constitutional developments. The title-pages always carried some formal introductory description, and changes in this are not without significance. Pynson originally settled for a title which announced that the king at his parliament held at a stated time and place, with the assent of the lords and commons, 'hath do to be ordained, made and enacted certain statutes and ordinances', and this was used down to 1523. In 1529, the title, for no obvious reason, switched to Latin and brevity, announcing simply that these were '*statuta ad rem publicam spectantia, edita in prima sessione parliamenti*', etc. In the next session, Berthelet's first effort in effect adopted the same formula: '*statuta bonum publicum concernentia edita in parliamento*', etc. Next year (having perhaps looked over Pynson's earlier work) he reverted to a cleaned up version of the original phrasing according to which the king had 'ordetaned [*sic*] established and enacted certayne good statutes lawes and ordinances'; but on this occasion it was not only said that the acts

44. Holdsworth, op. cit., xi, 292.

had been made with the assent of parliament but also 'by auctoritie of the same'—the full enacting clause which was coming to be customary for every individual act. From 1533 to 1536 (six sessions) the print baldly announced that these were 'Actes made in the parliament' etc., and this was also in effect the description employed in 1543 and 1546. In between, more solemn and lengthy phrases took over, according to which the king (full title) had held a session of parliament 'wherein were established these actes folowyng' (1539, 1542, 1544, varied in 1540 by saying that the acts following were among many other acts). Thus, while originally the legislative authority was placed solely in the monarch, from 1529 onwards, with the single exception of 1533, the statutes were declared to have been made in the parliament, there being no mention of the king ordaining them. One does not wish to place too heavy a burden on such formulations, but these title pages at first followed custom so regularly that innovations cannot be regarded as entirely meaningless. The meaning would seem to be that by the early 1530s the legislative authority had come to be seen as resting with the king, lords and commons as a body, a change of view which coincides notably with the clear signs that about that time the concept of parliament (which now included the king) as a sovereign lawmaker replaced the concept of the king's high court of parliament giving authority by its consent to the laws made by the king.[45]

In this transformation of the institution the sessional printing of statutes played its part by providing a public and authoritative version of the acts produced in these sovereign parliaments, available very soon after the end of each session. It may well be the case that so far as the courts are concerned even today 'in no case is the official print made conclusive evidence of the text of a statute'.[46] There may still be occasions when the courts might wish to ascertain the correct text of an act by looking at 'the original', but for the reigns of the first two Tudors they might

45. Cf. G. R. Elton, *Studies in Tudor and Stuart Politics and Government* (Cambridge, 1974), ii, 32–6.
46. P. H. Winfield, *The Chief Sources of English Legal History* (Cambridge, Mass., 1925), p. 94. There is a hint that Thomas Cromwell, that conservative radical, shared these doubts about printed copies. In 1535 he paid the clerk for certified copies of three acts (*LP*, xi, 135), two of them private and not printed, but the third the statute of uses. Surely he had a copy of the sessional print which contained it?

have some difficulty in doing so. No Original Acts before 1497 or for 1523 and 1529, some acts printed that are not on the Roll, clear signs that allegedly independent and semi-official collections like that of the exchequer volume were in fact copied from the print, the question marks that hang over the Rolls (especially those not signed by the clerk by way of certification into chancery): in that state of affairs, the printed acts not only will but must become the normal evidence for the wording of an act—the version that people in general and the courts in particular will rely on. Printing made the acts rapidly known all over the realm, whether they were formally proclaimed by order of the crown or privately sent out to the likes of Lord Lisle, Robert Aske and many others; and thus it gave equitable sense to the old principle that laws made for the commonwealth must be obeyed by all the commonwealth. For practical purposes, and virtually for all occasions of the law, printing settled the effect as well as the text of parliamentary law; it is no wonder that developments in judicial interpretation which restricted the freedom of the judges and elevated the authority of statute did not come until after the acts were regularly in print.[47] In the circumstances it was just as well that, despite his haste, his often muddled foliation, and his frequent and bewildering reprints, the king's printer took good care to print sound texts.

47. Cf. the discussion in S. E. Thorne's introduction to his edition of *Discourse upon the Exposicion & Understandinge of Statutes* (San Marino, Calif., 1942).

V

Henry VIII's Unwritten Will: Grants of Lands and Honours in 1547

HELEN MILLER

'Remembre what youe promysed me in the galerye at West-mynster, before the breathe was owt of the body of the king that dead ys. Remember what youe promysed immediately after, devising with me concerning the place which youe now occupie... And that was to folowe myne advise in all your procedings more then any other man's.'[1] Sir William Paget's letter to Protector Somerset has long been appreciated for the shaft of light it throws on the shadowy events surrounding the death of Henry VIII. Relatively little attention has been paid to the parallel negotiations conducted by Paget which ended in the promotion within the peerage of three noblemen besides Edward Seymour, earl of Hertford, the creation of four new barons and the distribution of crown lands valued at over £3200 per annum. Yet this episode also illuminates a dark corner of the Tudor scene.

Again the informant is Paget. At the request of the protector and council, he and the two chief gentlemen of Henry VIII's privy chamber, Sir Anthony Denny and Sir William Herbert, reported certain conversations they had had with the late king. Their signed statement was copied (omitting the signatures) and inserted into the council's register between the entries for 6 and 7 February 1547.[2] Paget recorded his testimony first, taking as his starting-point the arrest of Henry Howard, earl of Surrey, and his father, the duke of Norfolk, in mid-December 1546. When these two were 'in the daunger of the lawes for high treason', the king, Paget declared, 'devised' with him for the

---

1. SP10/8/4; printed from BL, Cott., Titus F III, in John Strype, *Ecclesiastical Memorials* (1822), ii(2), appendix HH.
2. PC2/2, ff. 12–16 [*APC, 1547–1550*, pp. 15–22].

disposal of their lands, 'thinking it expedient that the same shuld
be liberally dispersed and geven to divers noblemen and others his
majestes good servauntes'. Moreover, the nobility as a whole
being to the king's mind 'greatly decayed', the discussion also
covered 'th'advauncement of divers to higher places of honour'.
Paget suggested some names and the king asked him to prepare a
'booke' of those selected. This he did. Paget included the names
in his statement to the council: Edward Seymour, earl of Hertford,
to be a duke, William Parr, earl of Essex, to be a marquess, John
Dudley, Viscount Lisle, William Paulet, Lord St John, John, Lord
Russell and Thomas, Lord Wriothesley to be earls, and ten
knights, headed by Sir Thomas Seymour, to be barons. When
the list had been read over to the king, Paget urged him to turn
his attention to the land grants he might make, 'seing he had
advaunced these men to honour and was mynded to distribute by
wey of gift' the estates of the fallen Howards. Consulting the
valuations of the Howard lands brought him by John Gates,
Henry ordered Paget to 'tot' upon the heads of six men the gifts
he would assign them: lands worth yearly 1000 marks for Hertford,
£200 each for Lisle, St John and Russell, £100 for Wriothesley
and £300 for Sir Thomas Seymour. 'All which', Paget reported,
'I sayde was to litle, and stode moch with him therin.' A final
decision was therefore deferred until the men concerned had been
consulted. Paget next put in a plea for Denny to have the priory of
Bungay, 'which I had herd he moche desired'. The king said that
Denny should have lands worth £200, and Herbert lands worth
400 marks a year, 'which he sayd he had promised him to help
him out of debt', and two more of the privy chamber, Sir
Thomas Cawarden and John Gates, lands worth 100 marks each.[3]
The total value of the lands to be distributed was thus £2266.13.4.
per annum.

However, when Paget sounded out those on the king's honours
list who were at court, he found that they were 'not well satisfied,
some laboureng to remayne in their olde degrees, and th'others
thinkeng the lande to litle for their mayntenaunce which was
appoynted to them'. Reporting this, Paget pressed for the grants
to be increased. Henry then told him that he had been informed
that Norfolk, acknowledging his guilt, had requested that his
lands should be given to Prince Edward; and that he had decided

3. Cawarden's gift misprinted as 200 marks.

to keep the duke's lands, 'except a certein in Sussex and Kent'. Nevertheless, the king agreed to a revised list of promotions (reduced to four by the omission of St John and Russell) and creations (reduced to six), accompanied by additional land grants to the value of £700 per annum. The question of where the lands were to come from was shelved, at Paget's instigation. A further grant to Hertford of six of the best prebends of any English cathedral, already authorised, was then amended, at Paget's suit, to include a deanery and a treasurership, previously disallowed, instead of two of the prebends. The final list, which included the redistributed Howard offices, Paget then read to the king. Henry put it in his pocket and agreed that Paget should tell everyone what they were to receive. This time 'all were pleased'. But before the grants could be put into effect, Henry VIII died. 'Heruppon was it', Paget concluded, 'that being remembred in his deathe bed that he had promised grete thinges to divers men, he willed in his testament that whatsoever shuld in any wise appere to his counsell to have ben promised by him, the same shuld be parfourmed.' Denny and Herbert joined Paget in deposing that the conversations reported were 'true in effect, and for the substaunce of them'. They added that they had pointed out to Henry that one man had been omitted: Paget himself. The king responded by ordering a grant to him of lands to the same value as Herbert's, bringing the total value of the crown lands to be given away to £3233.6.8. a year. After considering the statement, the privy council resolved to respect the king's last wishes and to go ahead with the distribution of the lands.

On this occasion Paget's evidence must obviously be treated with great caution. Yet some parts of his report can be corroborated. The process whereby the first list of beneficiaries was transformed into the second list may be reconstructed from a document in the state papers, amended by Paget.[4] From this it appears that the decision was quickly taken to reduce the number of new barons, for the state paper made no mention of Sir Thomas Cheyne nor of two men whose Christian names failed to surface in Paget's mind as he composed his statement for the council, Sir . . . Wymbish and Sir . . . Vernon of the Peak. Neither was in fact a knight until George Vernon was created K.B. at the coronation of Edward VI on 20 February 1547. Thomas Wymbish

4. SP10/1/11.

received no honour although it seems unlikely that he would have refused a barony, even without a gift of land, since he had a few years earlier applied to be summoned to parliament in right of his wife, heiress to the Tailboys barony, and had his petition rejected. But some curtailment of the new creations was not unreasonable. However 'decayed' the nobility in quality, in numbers it was not reduced and even the removal of Thomas Howard, duke of Norfolk, hardly called for recompense on such a scale. Another potential nobleman disappeared when 'Sir Thomas Arundell to be a baron' was deleted by Paget as he amended the state paper. The names of the two barons rejected for promotion were also scored through. After these alterations the state paper honours list was identical with the second list of Paget's statement.

His report that 'all were pleased' with the revised arrangements appears equally dubious when the land grants are examined. The total amount of land to be disbursed was indeed substantially increased, but the value of the grant to both St John and Russell was reduced—cut from £200 to £100 per annum with the loss of their earldoms. Lisle, on the other hand, had his £200 raised to £300 and Essex, originally the only peer to be promoted without a grant, was put down for lands worth £200 a year on the state paper, although this was reduced to £100 in Paget's amendments. Sir Richard Rich joined Sir Thomas Seymour in receiving a land grant as well as a barony, although in his case the lands were worth only 100 marks per annum. The master of the horse, Sir Anthony Browne, was added to the beneficiaries with a grant of lands worth £100 per annum. These decisions were, according to Paget, all accepted by Henry, together with three significant changes recorded nowhere else. The annual value of Sir Thomas Seymour's land grant, originally £300, was increased to £400 by an addition on the state paper; in Paget's account of the late king's dying intention it had grown to £500. Hertford's grant was increased on the state paper to £800 a year and amended to give him as well £200 'of the next bishopes landes'; in Paget's statement to the council the addition had become £300 of the next bishop's lands to fall vacant. The grant to Wriothesley, at first to be lands to the yearly value of £100, was entered on the state paper as £200 and raised again, to £300, in Paget's statement. The two Seymours and the lord chancellor were intimately involved in the realisation of Paget's plans. The final decision on their land grants was probably taken only shortly before Henry VIII died, perhaps about 23 January when Sir Thomas Seymour—on Paget's declaration that this was the king's desire—was sworn a member of the privy council.[5]

The state paper itself was almost certainly drawn up in the second half of December and amended early in January. All the projected grants of office which it recorded were dependent, directly or indirectly, on the fall of the Howards. Norfolk had been appointed lord treasurer for life and earl marshal in tail male; both offices were to go to Hertford. Lisle was to become great chamberlain (in succession to Hertford), Sir Thomas Seymour lord admiral (in succession to Lisle) and Sir Philip Hoby master of the ordnance (in succession to Seymour). Other men were chosen to be stewards of Howard lands and to take over stewardships and fees held by Norfolk and Surrey. The information needed for the local appointments was soon in the king's hands, impounded by commissioners sent to Kenninghall on 12 December, the day of the duke's arrest.[6] One of the commissioners was John Gates, who produced the books (so Paget testified) when Henry began to consider what to do about the estates. The early discussion of this question is credible; even perhaps the king's readiness to dispose of the lands. But what of his change of mind, the decision to keep most of them for his son, prompted by a request from Norfolk as he acknowledged his guilt? Immediately after his arrest Norfolk had offered the king his lands and goods for a return to favour, although protesting his innocence; it was not until 12 January that he confessed to high treason.[7] By then, however, the idea of endowing the prince with Norfolk's lands had become decidedly opportune. William Lord Grey in Boulogne had just heard that 'the creation of the prince's grace' was shortly to be solemnised.[8] Edward himself later recorded that preparations for his creation as prince of Wales had been interrupted by his father's death.[9] Indeed, lord chancellor Wriothesley informed parliament on 27 January that he and his fellow

5. *APC*, 1542–47, p. 566. 6. *LP*, xxi(2), 548.

7. Edward, Lord Herbert of Cherbury, *The Life and Reign of King Henry the Eighth* (1672), pp. 629–33 [*LP*, xxi(2), 540, 696].

8. *LP*, xxi(2), 694.

9. *Literary Remains of Edward VI*, ed. J. G. Nichols (Roxburghe Club, 1857), ii, 210.

commissioners had been empowered by Henry VIII—too ill to attend in person—to give the royal assent to the attainder of the Howards specifically in order that certain of the duke's offices might be conferred on others, to be exercised at the imminent 'coronation' of Prince Edward.[10] The slip betrays the reality: the cermony to be expected now was the coronation of a king rather than the creation of a prince. But either event would require the services of the earl marshal. Only within hours of Henry VIII's death was this office legally vacant; but before he died the king granted it and the lord treasurership to Hertford—or so the councillors of Edward VI alleged.[11]

If true, the appointment must have been by the king's word or sign. What else did Henry VIII authorise in this way, leaving no record? The destruction of the Howards was needed not only to make sure of Norfolk's offices but to ease the passage to power of Hertford and his friends. The royal assent to the bill of attainder was given by a commission appointed on the day itself by letters patent signed by the dry stamp.[12] Did Henry order the stamp to be applied? Under regulations issued in August 1546 authority to affix the stamp was given to Sir Anthony Denny, John Gates and William Clerk, a clerk of the privy seal, with the proviso that a list of the documents stamped should be entered in a book or in schedules to be signed each month by the king's own hand.[13] In practice, Henry VIII occasionally signed the paper schedules, but not often; he never signed the parchment fair copies.[14] Yet even if he had been meticulous in this, the use made of the stamp in the last hours of his life could never be checked. By 27 January it was clear that the king was dying. Would not men with so much at stake feel justified in taking action on the slightest indication of the king's wishes? Even perhaps on a gesture construed as assent to a question put to him by one of his attendants? The frail basis of such a warrant need not become public knowledge. Parliament was not told at the time that this commission was signed by stamp: only that it bore the sign manual and the great seal.[15] In the autumn of 1553, when Norfolk was at last free to challenge the validity of the attainder, the justices at Serjeants' Inn in-

10. House of Lords R.O., LJ, i, 688 [LJ, i, 289].
11. APC, 1547–50, p. 10.
12. Annexed to original act, House of Lords R.O.
13. LP, xxi(1), 1537 (34).   14. All in SP4/1.   15. LJ, i, 289.

spected the act and the commission annexed to it but concluded only that the signature on the latter was probably not the king's own since it appeared beneath the *Teste*, not at the head, where Henry VIII used to sign, and the writing was too good to be that of a man on the verge of death; and also because, 'some farther said', it was a stamp.[16] The question of fact was settled in parliament. When the house of commons considered the duke of Norfolk's private bill to annul the act of attainder, Paget attended and deposed that the commission to give the royal assent had not been signed by Henry VIII personally but stamped by William Clerk.[17] All the same, until the opinion of the judges was sought by Norfolk, there had been no suggestion that a signature by stamp was of less authority than one in the king's own hand. The declared intention of Henry VIII had been to authorise his three named servants to sign on his behalf, and the validity of most documents so stamped was never contested. Norfolk's bill itself implicitly recognised this by taking ground on technicalities. The commission was defective because it contained no statement that the king 'did himself give his royall assent' to the attainder, besides being signed with the stamp, put at the end of the commission and not at the head 'as his highnes was accustomed to doo'. Moreover, it was possible to claim that this was a special case. Norfolk petitioned for a declaration that 'the lawe of this realme is and allwaies hath byn' that the royal assent to bills ought to be given by the king personally or 'by his lettres patentes under his great seale assigned with his hande', as prescribed in a statute of 1542—the act of attainder passed against Catherine Howard which authorised for immediate and future use the alternative procedure under letters patent 'to be signed with your most gracyous hande and to be putt undre your greate seall of England'.[18] Norfolk's bill became law, but only after he had promised to accept arbitration over the recompense to be made to the present owners of the lands sold or given away by Edward VI, whose rights were expressly (if illogically) safeguarded in the act.[19]

On this argument, Henry VIII's will was also a special case, since he had been empowered by statute to settle the succession either

16. James Dyer, *Reports of Cases in the Reigns of Henry VIII* (etc.), ed. J. Vaillant (1794), i, 93.

17. Ibid., i, 93n., corroborated below.   18. 33 Hen. VIII, c. 21.

19. 1 Mary sess. 2, c. 27 (original act). References to concessions over lands in *CJ*, i, 32, in Norfolk's will (PCC 14 More), and below.

by letters patent or by his will signed with his 'gracious hande'.[20]
The debate on Norfolk's attainder evidently raised a query about
the will and Paget testified to the facts in this case too. He declared
that William Clerk had signed the will by stamp: Edmund
Plowden in his treatise on the succession recorded that he had
heard Paget make the declaration in the house of commons.
Plowden saw no reason to doubt Paget's word. He had affirmed
on his honour that he was 'privey to the beginning, proceding
and ending of the said laste will' and, Plowden added, 'if I be not
mervelously forgetfull, he tolde me he wrote the will itselfe or the
first draughte therof with his owne hande'. (The extant will is in
the hand of William Honnings, one of the clerks of the council.)[21]
Furthermore, Paget's evidence had been given when there were
many still alive who had been present 'at the publishing of the
said will, and putting to the stampe, yeven as he was, and called
therto as witnesses', one of whom—Sir Henry Neville—had assured
Plowden that Paget's account was trustworthy. Admittedly
the final words of the will declared that it had been signed with
the king's own hand, but Plowden pointed out that this could not
have been true at the time the words were written: they prove
only that it was intended that the king should sign it.[22]

The will was undoubtedly stamped by William Clerk, who
included it in his list of documents signed by stamp in January
1547, entering it as the penultimate item, followed by the commission to give the royal assent to the Howards' attainder.[23] The
fact did not, however, become generally known. Only as the
proponents of the Stuart claim to the throne, ignored by Henry
VIII, began to dispute the will in Elizabeth's reign, was the attempt
made by Plowden and others to prove that it had never been
signed by the king. Maitland of Lethington had heard of Paget's
evidence and cited it in a letter to Sir William Cecil in 1567.[24]
He called for depositions to be taken from, among others, Sir
Anthony Denny, 'if he be lyving', and three surviving witnesses
to the will, Dr Huick, Sir Henry Neville and Edmund Harman.
Further, Maitland was prepared to assert that Cecil, too, knew
the inside story: how, the king's 'death approching, some, as well

20. 28 Hen. VIII, c. 7; 35 Hen. VIII, c. 1.   21. E23/4.
22. BL, Harl., 849, ff. 32, 34v–35.
23. SP4/1/19 [LP, xxi (2), 770; StP, i, 892–8].
24. The Egerton Papers, ed. J. P. Collier (CS, 12, 1840), pp. 41–9.

knowne to yowe as to me, caused William Clerk, sometyme servaunt to Thomas Henneage, to signe the supposed will with a stamp, for otherwise signed it was never. And yet notwith-standing, ... procured diverse honest gentlemen, attending in sondrie romes about the kinges person, to testifie with their hand-writinges the contentes of the sayde pretended will, surmised to be signed with the sayde kinges owin hand'.

Indeed, Cecil should have been well informed on this matter since his father had been yeoman of the robes at the time of Henry VIII's death. In the last weeks of his life Henry had been cut off from the outside world, seen only by privy councillors and gentlemen of the privy chamber.[25] Access to the king was controlled by Sir Anthony Denny, head of the privy chamber since the dismissal of Sir Thomas Henneage in October 1546; Denny also controlled the dry stamp, which was kept by his brother-in-law, John Gates, William Clerk being no more than Denny's assistant.[26] The will was witnessed by Gates and five other gentlemen of the privy chamber, four of the king's medical attendants, and William Clerk.[27] It was not the role of witnesses to testify to the contents of a will, as Maitland supposed, but to an act: to the signing or the sealing of a document. William Clerk, when he recorded the king's will in his final list of documents signed by stamp, described both the will and the ceremony at which the king formally acknowledged it. This probably took place only shortly before the king died, when he was—as Paget described him in his statement to the council—on his deathbed. The will, however, was dated 30 December 1546, as Clerk was careful to note when he entered it on his list: 'Your maiesties last will and testament bearing date at Westminster the thirtie daie of December last past written in a booke of paper signed above in the beginning and beneth in th' ende and sealed with the signet, in the presence of th'erle of Hertford, Mr Secretarie Pagett, Mr Denny and Mr Harbart, and also in the presence of certain other persons whose names ar subscribed with their own handes, as witnesses to the same, whiche testament your maiestie delyvered then in our sightes with your own hande to the saide erle of

25. *LP*, xxi (2), 605, 675, 684.
26. D. R. Starkey, 'The will of Henry VIII: a question of interpretation'. I am grateful to Dr Starkey for sight of this unpublished seminar paper.
27. E23/4 [*LP*, xxi (2), 634; T. Rymer, *Foedera* (1739–45), vi (2), 142–5].

Hertforde as your own dede, last will and testament, revoking and adnulling all other your hieghnes former willes and testamentes'.[28] The councillors present were the four men whose influence most completely encompassed the dying king. The will itself, written under Paget's direction, provided the essential basis for the new regime. Once the document had Henry's signature upon it, had been sealed and witnessed and placed in safe custody, the future was secured. Henry VIII's will empowered the sixteen men named as councillors and executors, or a majority of them, to do anything they thought necessary for the welfare of Edward or the realm, which enabled Hertford to be appointed protector by his fellow councillors 'by vertue of th'authorite gevin unto us by the saide wille'.[29] It required the executors, for discharge of the king's conscience, to make good all his grants and promises left unfulfilled, which safeguarded in principle the distribution of lands and honours after his death. The quality of Henry's assent to these provisions of his will must remain a matter of conjecture. There was—and is—no way of breaking into the closed circle that served and perhaps betrayed him at the last.

The council, when the time came, showed no compunction in altering the late king's plans for the nobility. The honours agreed upon by Henry VIII, according to Paget's testimony, were revised after his death. Of the six barons named, only four were created; neither Sir John St Leger nor Sir Christopher Danby was among the men ennobled by letters patent a few days before the coronation of Edward VI. Changes were also made in the names to be assumed by those raised in the peerage. Lord St John's proposed title had been earl of Winchester. When his promotion was rescinded the title was transferred to Thomas, Lord Wriothesley, initially down to become earl of Chichester; yet Wriothesley was in the event created earl of Southampton. Russell would have been earl of Northampton if he had received an earldom at this time; William Parr, earl of Essex, was named marquess of Essex in Paget's statement but became marquess of Northampton. The title for John Dudley, Viscount Lisle appeared as earl of Leicester, amended to Coventry on the state paper and as earl of Coventry in Paget's statement. But he put in a successful claim to do service at the coronation as the heir (through his mother) of Richard Beauchamp, earl of Warwick, and it was

28. SP4/1/19 (original punctuation).   29. *APC, 1547–50*, p. 5.

no doubt at his request that the earldom of Warwick was given to him.[30] In the case of Hertford, alone, was Henry VIII's decision upheld. The state paper had only grudgingly met the earl's preference. It carried Paget's interlining, as italicised: Hertford was to be 'duke of *Somerset, Exeter or* Hertforde and his sonne erle of Wilteshire *if he* [*be*] *duke of Hertford*'. Reluctance to allow either of the added alternatives, with their royal connotations, had not, it seems, died with the king. The inducement of an earl-dom for his son failed to persuade Hertford to renounce the name borne by the Beauforts in the mid-fifteenth century, then in turn by Henry VII's third son and Henry VIII's bastard, Henry FitzRoy; but his son as a consequence enjoyed only a courtesy title.

The councillors of Edward VI evidently felt more vulnerable to criticism over the dispersal of crown lands and in this took care to adhere to the letter of Paget's declaration of Henry's wishes. Yet their acquisitive spirit could hardly be disguised. Three months before the king's death Richard Cox had written to Paget to castigate the greediness of 'the woulves of the worlde' who were preying upon the church. Even Paget, he had heard, had obtained something.[31] Paget had in fact just acquired large estates from two bishoprics. In September 1546 he had put forward for stamping with the king's signature a warrant to the chancellor of augmen-tations to 'practise' with the bishop of Chester and the bishop of Coventry and Lichfield for the surrender of these lands, together with letters to the bishops and their deans and chapters demanding their acquiescence.[32] On 29 September the formal surrenders were signed and in October Paget was granted the estates for £5700.[33] When parliament met in January 1547 Paget had prepared a bill, already signed by the king's stamp, to confirm his right to the lands.[34] (It was read in the lords for the first time on 29 January, the house still ignorant of the king's death early the previous day.)[35] The gift to Paget under Henry VIII's unwritten will was largely made up of further lands taken from the church. His grant—the first to be completed, late in May 1547—contained the lordship of Harmondsworth, Middlesex, and associated manors valued at

30. SP10/1/7.   31. SP1/225, ff. 202–3 [*LP*, xxi (2), 282].
32. *LP*, xxi (2), 199 (133–7).
33. Ibid., xxi (2), 182–3, 331 (54), 332 (76).
34. Ibid., xxi (2), 770 (80).   35. *LJ*, i, 290.

£95.8.7. per annum, surrendered by the college of St Mary near Winchester, and the lordship of Iver, Buckinghamshire, valued at £98.13.2½ a year, which had belonged to St George's, Windsor. The rest of the grant comprised less valuable items, including two priories in Lancashire.[36] On the patent roll the total grant appears to add up to slightly over the £266.13.4. per annum allotted to him, but the particulars show that the valuation of the property by the court of augmentations came to the exact amount, tenths and an annual rent to the king deducted.[37] Since the court's auditors were only concerned to establish the current value of the property to the crown, free of charges upon it, the real worth of any grant to a new owner might vary considerably. Paget's gift, for example, included the abbey of Notley, Buckinghamshire, valued at £11.3.0. a year. This estate was charged with an annual fee of £6.1.8. to Sir John Williams as keeper of the site, which had been reserved for the king's use. Paget was able to sell Notley to Williams for £450, forty years' purchase on the valuation at which he had received it—double the normal rate.[38]

Sir William Herbert did even better with his grant in July 1547. Woods and advowsons were generally included without being counted in the valuation, and Herbert received as extras the woods and advowsons of six rectories in the diocese of Llandaff. He also obtained, besides lands mainly in Wales and south-west England, the lordship of Hackney, which had been sold to Henry VIII by Thomas Percy, earl of Northumberland. The mansion house was included without being priced, although when it had been surveyed in 1536 it had been described as 'a fayre house all of bricke', and money had been spent on it in the mid-1540s before Henry lent it to Wriothesley for his London residence.[39] Herbert did not want the house for himself and immediately sold it for £1000.[40] The ultimate value of his grant was further enhanced by the inclusion of a number of reversions, valued at half rate. The gift to Herbert was therefore worth, on paper, exactly the £266.13.4. a year assigned to him, but substantially more in reality. Sir Anthony Denny was somewhat less fortunate. He

36. C66/800, mm. 43–46 [CPR, 1547–48, pp. 45–7, valuation of Harmondsworth recte of Iver, Harmondsworth omitted]; DL42/23, ff. 10v–12.

37. E318/1834.   38. C54/454, no. 67.

39. CPR, 1547–48, pp. 193–8; E318/1685; LP, xix (1), 368; ibid., xx (1), 557; ibid., xx (2), 268, 280.

40. C54/451, no. 1.

never received Bungay, which he had apparently wanted, but Warwick wrote to Paget on his behalf for the site and demesnes of Waltham Holy Cross, which Denny already leased, and these he was granted, with other lands, in June 1547.[41] As he paid no rent for the site of the abbey, it was given a nil valuation in the grant. Waltham Park was also entered as producing no income because it was reserved for deer, although the auditor noted that if ever it were disparked it would be worth over £40 per annum. Denny was keeper of the abbey's mansion, Waltham Grange, as well as keeper of the park and steward of the monastic lands, and his fees totalling £27.13.4. a year were deducted from the value of the estates, bringing his grant down to the required £200 per annum.[42] After Waltham the most valuable property in Denny's allocation was the abbey of Sibton, Suffolk, which had belonged to the duke of Norfolk. No notice was taken of Henry VIII's intention to keep the duke's lands 'except a certein in Sussex and Kent': Howard estates wherever they lay were freely dispersed. Edward VI's councillors had at the start been worried about some aspect of the Howards' attainder and called for legal opinion upon it; the master of the rolls returned the documents on 5 July 1547.[43] If their concern was over the safe title to the lands, the report must have been reassuring. Many who received these lands retained them; those who preferred to sell apparently had no difficulty in finding purchasers. In the event, though, Denny's decision to keep Sibton proved a mistake. In 1555 his heir joined in a petition to parliament to save the rights of the patentees of Howard lands.[44] Mary's first parliament, 'shewinge itself of moost soveraign iustice and dexteritie', had inserted a proviso on their behalf into the duke of Norfolk's bill and only with this, 'and uppon the offer of the said duke in open parliament to take a honorable and reasonable ende' with the patentees, had the act been passed annulling his attainder. But it had also included a section invalidating all exemplifications of the act of attainder which failed to include the commission for the royal assent, and that, together with an arbitration award allegedly made without consulting the petitioners, had led to the eviction of some of them without recompense. They argued bitterly that parliament should not 'make suche lawes as shall in one same acte bothe give

41. SP10/1/30; *CPR, 1547–48*, pp. 243–5.   42. E318/1572.
43. *APC, 1547–50*, p. 106.   44. SP46/8, ff. 59–62.

and take awaye', but their bill, passed by 152 votes to 125 in the commons, was rejected on the third reading by the house of lords.[45]

Sir Anthony Denny's brother-in-law, John Gates, received lands worth only 100 marks a year under Henry VIII's unwritten will; the largest item in the grant was the manor of Cheshunt, Hertfordshire, of which Denny was steward.[46] But Gates had in December 1546 been given the lands of Pleshey college, Essex, recently surrendered to the crown.[47] In December, too, Sir Thomas Cawarden had been granted all the possessions of Lingfield college, Surrey, and the reversion to the manor of Bletchingley, with the house there in which he was living.[48] This property he evidently prized more than the three manors he was given under the will, valued at 100 marks per annum, since before the end of 1547 he obtained licence to sell two of them.[49] Grants authorised as free gifts in December 1546 probably affected the land allocations under Henry VIII's will, not only to these two gentlemen of the privy chamber, but also to the master of the horse and the queen's brother. Grants stamped then and delivered into chancery early in January 1547, gave to Sir Anthony Browne church lands in Sussex, Kent and Essex and to William Parr, earl of Essex the reversion (falling due in 1553) to estates in the north leased to his father in 1513 at an annual rent of £340.[50] In these circumstances it is the less surprising that neither Browne nor Essex appeared among the first beneficiaries suggested by Paget to the king, and that the grants eventually allotted to them were kept relatively low at £100 per annum. The gift to Browne included manors in Sussex and Surrey and a house in London.[51] William Parr, by then marquess of Northampton, was granted Pipewell abbey in Northamptonshire and two manors in Essex, with a number of reversions, some to lands which he already leased, and the duke of Norfolk's Lambeth house, unvalued in the grant since the marquess claimed to be already the custodian of it by gift of Henry VIII.[52]

45. *CJ*, i, 43–45; *LJ*, i, 505–6.
46. *CPR, 1547–48*, pp. 22–3; E318/1628.
47. *LP*, xxi (2), 647 (33), 648 (61).
48. *Ibid.*, xxi (2), 647 (27), 648 (50).
49. *CPR, 1547–48*, pp. 17–18, 53; E318/1474.
50. *LP*, xxi (2), 647 (49, 60), 771 (3, 12).
51. *CPR, 1547–48*, pp. 240–1.   52. *Ibid.*, 168–70; E318/1816.

No grant was made to Sir Richard Rich beyond the lands worth annually 100 marks allocated to him by an addition to the state paper, which brought him two manors and two hundreds in Essex.[53] (However, Sir William Willoughby and Sir Edmund Sheffield were made barons with no land grants at all.) No gifts of land before the death of Henry VIII came the way of St John or Russell either, although each suffered a cut of £100 in their grants in Paget's amendments. But St John's grant, in August 1547, seems to have been worth nearly £10 a year more than the £100 allotted to him, and in September he was given another grant of lands, worth nearly £60 per annum, which the patent declared it had been the late king's wish that he should have.[54] Russell also received a second grant—at the same time as the first, in July 1547 —but this was by way of exchange and payment, not as a gift. His grant under the will brought him the reversion to Woburn abbey, with £100 a year from the current rents until the leases expired, mostly in the mid-1560s.[55] The significance of Woburn for the Russells lay hidden in the future; at the time the grant must have seemed a meagre reward for the lord privy seal in comparison with the gifts enjoyed by members of Henry VIII's household on the one hand and on the other by the four men who (with Paget) dominated the political scene at the beginning of 1547, Lisle, Wriothesley and the two Seymours.

Lisle, after his creation as earl of Warwick, turned his attention to the land grants. He wrote to Paget asking for Waltham for Denny, an estate in Sussex which had belonged to Lord De la Warr for Sir Anthony Browne—which he did not get—and, for himself, the lordship of Warwick.[56] He was afraid that some might argue against this because Warwick was 'a great royalte', although actually much decayed. He was already constable of the castle and high steward of the town and was anxious to be given the whole property 'becaus of the name' and because he 'came of oon of the doughters and heyres of the right and nat defyled lyne'. He asked Paget 'to move the reste of my lordes to this affect', offering to 'rebat my fees in my portion' if it went through; or, second thoughts breeding caution, 'parte of my fees'. Alternatively,

53. CPR, 1547-48, pp. 109-11; E318/1906.
54. CPR, 1547-48, pp. 42-3, 66-8.   55. Ibid., pp. 6-8; E318/1920.
56. SP10/1/30 [P. F. Tytler, England under the reigns of Edward VI and Mary (1839), i, 28-9].

he would settle for Tonbridge and Penshurst, which had been the duke of Buckingham's, and Halden, Kent. In either case he wanted Canonbury in Middlesex as well. The grant when it was made in June 1547 included the lordship, manor, town and castle of Warwick, other manors in the county which had belonged to the Beauchamps in the fifteenth century, and the lordship of Canonbury, which had been Thomas Cromwell's. Further lands, some in reversion, brought the grant up to the stipulated £300 per annum.[57] Six months later Halden was included in a grant to Warwick of lands worth £100 a year for his services in the Scottish war.[58] Estates to the annual value of £300 were granted to Thomas Wriothesley, earl of Southampton in July 1547: they included former monastic lands in the south-west and the manor of Dogmersfield, Hampshire, with its house and park, which had been bought by Henry VIII from the bishop of Bath and Wells. Although the earl had been dismissed as lord chancellor in March, there was no attempt to interfere with his grant; indeed, when it was later found that it had been wrongly valued by £6.13.4. a year, an additional grant was authorised to make up the difference.[59]

Admiral Seymour, however, received lands worth much more than his allocation. His grant in August 1547 listed the properties given him in fulfilment of Henry VIII's intention to give him lands worth £500 per annum without recording their individual valuations. The particulars survive but the document is in parts illegible and now lacks the final summary.[60] But the figures which can still be read add up to nearly £500 clear of all charges; the lands whose valuations are now lost to view include the barony, castle and borough of Bramber, the manors and boroughs of Horsham and New Shoreham, the manors of King's Barns, West Grinstead and Knepp, with the parks of Knepp, Bewbush and Shelley, Sussex, all former possessions of the duke of Norfolk. They had constituted the greater part of the lands assigned to the duke after the attainder of his stepmother, for which he had had to pay the crown over £200 a year during her life.[61] They must have represented a large, concealed extension of Seymour's grant, the preamble to the patent masking the truth. The individual

57. CPR, 1547–48, pp. 252–7; E318/2042.
58. CPR, 1547–48, pp. 170–1; E318/2044.
59. CPR, 1547–48, pp. 23–24; ibid., 1548–49, p. 131; E318/2107.
60. C66/800, mm. 11–22 [CPR, 1547–48, pp. 25–33]; E318/1933.
61. SC6/Hen. VIII/3496.

valuations of the lands given to Protector Somerset were not entered on the letters patent to him either and the particulars of his grant are not extant; there is no way of knowing whether these lands were valued at the £800 per annum they were alleged to be worth.[62] However, the other promise of Paget's statement—lands worth £300 a year from the next bishopric to fall vacant—was generously fulfilled at the expense of the see of Lincoln. The old bishop died on 7 May 1547, and his successor received the temporalities on 16 August, the day after a licence had been signed giving him permission to grant to the protector the castle, borough, hundred and manor of Banbury and ten other manors.[63] No value was put upon these estates but Banbury and eight of the manors had been entered in the *Valor Ecclesiasticus* as worth, together, nearly £400 a year before payment of tenths. The indenture between the bishop and Somerset, dated 21 August 1547, mentioned 'certeyne grete sommes of money' paid by the duke and 'other causes and consideracions' about which the bishop was equally reticent.[64] The deanery, treasurership and four prebends agreed upon in principle by Henry VIII were also granted to Somerset with advantages, in this case four extra prebends and the archdeaconry of Wells; the grant was made on 9 July 1547, in exchange for tithes in Ramsbury, Wiltshire.[65] But an indenture between Edward VI and Protector Somerset later in July declared that Henry had seen this grant as preliminary to a larger exchange with the crown, now to be implemented. Somerset sold to Edward VI most of the properties he had just been granted, with other prebends, rectories and tithes and a house in London, valued at £1684.3.1¾ a year, and received in return 17 manors in Somerset, a priory and nine manors in Dorset, and other properties including Thame abbey, surrendered by the bishop of Oxford, valued together at £1679.15.3. per annum, and the remission of an annual rent of nearly £45 due on an earlier grant. Somerset paid £806.12.1. to balance the exchange.[66] It was perhaps disappointing that the first bishopric to

62. C66/802, mm. 42–50 [*CPR, 1547–48*, pp. 124–33].

63. *CPR, 1547–48*, p. 184.

64. C54/454, no. 21; printed from bishop's copy in *Chapter Acts of the Cathedral Church of St. Mary of Lincoln, 1536–47*, ed. R. E. G. Cole (Lincoln Rec. Soc., 13, 1917), pp. 150–2.

65. C66/805, mm. 7–9 [*CPR, 1547–48*, pp. 190–1, treasurership omitted].

66. C54/450, no. 1; *CPR, 1547–48*, pp. 118–24.

fall vacant should have been Lincoln, its estates lying outside the protector's area of land concentration in the west country, but chance soon offered a fresh opportunity. The bishop of Bath and Wells died in late September 1547, less than three weeks after Somerset's victory over the Scots at Pinkie. Early in October, at the request of the council, Edward VI expressed his gratitude to the protector by writing—with his own hand, it was said—the warrant for a gift to him of lands worth annually £500. In view of the king's great expenses, the warrant claimed, Somerset had asked instead for a licence for the bishop of Bath and Wells to sell him certain lands. In July 1548 the new bishop was licensed to alienate to him seven manors in Somerset, including Wells, and Edward VI made up the full amount of his reward by giving him lands valued at £106.14.9. per annum.[67] The protector's son, years afterward, was prepared to admit that his father had been 'his owne carver' after the death of Henry VIII, taking what lands he liked.[68] Admiral Seymour, resentful of his brother's gains, was alert to forestall criticism of his own, his wife making it known that he intended to return Sudeley castle to Edward VI when he came of age.[69] As for those who plundered the church, Seymour exclaimed: 'I wolde not be in soome of theyre cotes for fyve markes when he shall here of these matiers.'[70]

The possible reaction of Edward VI was in fact in the mind of his council from the beginning. The king, waiting in the Tower for his coronation, understood that the councillors were discussing his father's will, but took note only of the decisions they reached on creations and promotions in the peerage.[71] When the names were announced in council on 16 February it was implied that the new titles had been chosen by Henry VIII; no reference was made to the reduction in the number of baronies.[72] Paget had probably already composed his statement to the council with its different version of Henry's intentions but it was not

67. CPR, 1547–48, p. 275; ibid., 1548–49, pp. 27–9 (reference to 1547 warrant in preamble). For the effect on the bishopric see P. M. Hembry, The Bishops of Bath and Wells, 1540–1640 (1967), pp. 105–15.

68. HMC, Bath, iv: Seymour Papers, 1532–1686, ed. Marjorie Blatcher (1968), pp. 179, 180.

69. S. Haynes, A Collection of State Papers (etc.) left by William Cecil (etc.), (1740), p, 104.

70. SP10/7/8 [Tytler, op. cit., i, 168–73].

71. Roxburghe Club, op. cit., ii, 210.

72. APC, 1547–50, pp. 34–5 (misprinted 15 February).

considered until after the honours had been awarded—and Paget nominated K.G.—on 17 February.[73] Action was taken upon it by the protector and 'others of the privy council', unnamed; the record of their deliberations, neither dated nor signed, incorporating Paget's statement, was bound into the register after the entry for 6 February, which finished at the bottom of a page. A copy of the whole text was kept by Paget and included in his letter book.[74] Designed to justify the council's resolve to make free gifts of crown lands, it might also serve to protect him individually against any charge of having abused his trust.

Yet Paget's statement—even if accepted as true 'in effect'—revealed more, perhaps, than he intended. It showed the workings of faction in the last weeks of Henry VIII's reign, the pressure on the dying king to destroy the Howard inheritance and to create for his son a group of advisers bound to him by self-interest. It exposed Paget's unblushing pride in his pursuit of lands for his colleagues. It explained the inclusion of the unfulfilled gifts clause in Henry VIII's will, an unprecedented extension of the normal request to executors to pay the testator's debts. Read with hindsight, it demonstrated how little respect the councillors had for Henry's wishes. Nevertheless, a scrupulous regard for the late king's will was the compelling reason they put forward for distributing the lands: 'we think we cannot otherwise discharge ourselfes towardes God and the worlde'. Only if the performance of the will were actually prejudicial to 'the honour and suretie' of Edward VI would the council be justified in taking no action. The condition did not apply since 'suche londe as now is disposed by his majestie, or herafter shalbe upon greter occasion disposed, shalbe redye, with all the rest that every honest true subiect hath, to serve his majestie'. (The process, evidently, was to continue.) It was in the young king's best interest for the lands to be given away as then his councillors would be 'of abilitie and power to serve hym'. All in all, they professed themselves confident that Edward would approve their decision when he reached 'th'age of knowledge and judgment of the worlde'. The story of Henry VIII's unwritten will could in itself have provided his son with an education in Tudor politics.

73. References to Paget as 'knight of th'order' in the introduction and to 'degrees of honour' already assumed in the closing section.

74. Northants R.O., Fitzwilliam (Milton) Corr., 21, ff. 23–6. Obvious slips, most but not all corrected, rule out any possibility of this being an original draft.

VI

Francis I, 'Defender of the Faith'?

R. J. KNECHT

Francis I was not in the same class as Henry VIII where paradox was concerned; he never executed three Protestants and three Catholics on the same day.[1] Yet his religious policy does not strike one as a model of consistency. Until the autumn of 1534 he seems to have been on the whole well-disposed towards reformers, protecting them from persecution by the Sorbonne and the parlement. Then, after the Affair of the Placards, in which a Protestant broadsheet was allegedly fixed to the door of his bedchamber, he suddenly rounded on them and unleashed a savage campaign of repression which continued intermittently till the end of the reign. The king's subjects were certainly puzzled by his behaviour, as were Protestant divines. Bucer told Luther in August 1530 that Francis was 'not far from the truth', yet a few years later Bullinger denounced him as the worst criminal who had ever sat on the French throne.[2]

Historians have not found the king's religious policy so disconcerting. They have explained its apparent inconsistencies as reflections of the king's easily impressionable character or unprincipled foreign policy. Francis, we are told, was 'weak, flighty and changeable: he was always won over by the last person who spoke to him and his clemency or intolerance was a faithful reflection of the influences under which he fell.'[3] One such influence was allegedly that of his sister, Marguerite d'Angoulême,

1. On 30 July 1540. The three reformers were Robert Barnes, William Jerome and Thomas Garrett and the three Catholics, Edward Powell, Richard Fetherston and Thomas Abel. See J. J. Scarisbrick, *Henry VIII* (1968), pp. 380, 383.

2. A.-L. Herminjard, *Correspondance des réformateurs dans les pays de langue française* (Geneva, 1868), ii, 271 (hereafter Herminjard); A. Bouvier, *Henri Bullinger* (Neuchâtel, 1940), pp. 201–2.

3. R. Hari, 'Les placards de 1534', *Aspects de la propagande religieuse* (Travaux d'Humanisme et renaissance XXVIII. Geneva, 1957), p. 81. (hereafter Hari).

who sympathised with the reform movement; another that of Anne de Montmorency, the grand master and later constable, whose name was a by-word for brutality, authoritarianism and orthodox reaction. Alternatively, it has been claimed that Francis subordinated his religious policy at home to the needs of his foreign policy. The correlation seems clear enough: between 1529 and 1532 he was anxious to win the friendship of the German Protestants; persecution of their French co-religionists, therefore, slackened while moderate reformers were encouraged. In 1533, on the other hand, Francis wanted to gain the friendship of Pope Clement VII; he, therefore, published two bulls against heresy and supported the Sorbonne in its fight against it. Then, in 1534, he met with disappointment in Rome, so he switched once more to the Lutherans and relaxed censorship of heterodox works. This had the effect of encouraging Protestant extremists to over-step the mark, hence the Affair of the Placards and the persecution that followed.[4]

The purpose of this study is not so much to refute these established interpretations, which may well contain a measure of truth, as to suggest other ways of looking at Francis's religious policy. To begin with, it was not as inconsistent as is commonly supposed. The Affair of the Placards, crucial as it was in the history of the French Reformation, did not cause a fundamental reappraisal of the king's attitude to heresy. The notion that he practised toleration before October 1534 and became a persecutor thereafter is an over-simplification. Francis had always been hostile to heresy and there was persecution in France long before the affair. There were burnings in various places from 1523 onwards, and it was in July 1528 that *l'estrapade* was first used. Instead of being burned at the stake, the victim was suspended over the flames from a gibbet and alternately raised and lowered by means of a pulley to prolong his agony.[5] In December 1527 Francis promised to deal with heresy in a manner that would show his subjects that he was 'the Most Christian King' not only in name but in deed; and, in the following year, his chancellor, Antoine

4. G. R. Elton, *Reformation Europe, 1517–1559* (1963), p. 119.
5. V.-L. Bourrilly and N. Weiss, 'Jean du Bellay, les Protestants et la Sorbonne', *Bulletin de la Société de l'Histoire du Protestantisme français*, 53 (1904), 114 (hereafter *BSHPF*).

Duprat, acting in his capacity of archbishop of Sens, prescribed draconian penalties for heresy at the synod of his province.[6]

But what precisely was heresy? Was it just Lutheranism or did it include evangelical humanism of the kind that had existed in France before Lutheranism first appeared there in 1519? As far as the Sorbonne or faculty of theology of the university of Paris was concerned the question did not even arise: orthodoxy began and ended with its own scholastic teaching. There was, therefore, no need to distinguish between Lutheranism and evangelical humanism; both were detestable. The point was clearly made by Noël Béda, the faculty's *syndic*: 'Luther's errors', he declared, 'have entered this [kingdom] more through the works of Erasmus and Lefèvre than any others'.[7] To a considerable degree, of course, he was right: no clear line of demarcation existed between Lutheranism and evangelical humanism; many scholars and preachers had a foot in both camps. Louis de Berquin, for example, was a disciple of both Erasmus and Luther. Without being a Lutheran, Jacques Lefèvre d'Étaples, the principal spokesman of evangelical humanism in France, came to share many doctrines with Luther.[8] There was, therefore, a certain ruthless logic about the Sorbonne's attitude.

Francis, however, could not be expected to endorse it. Since the beginning of his reign he had extended his patronage to humanism and had earned international acclaim for this. At the instigation of Guillaume Budé he had invited Erasmus to France in 1517 to take charge of a college devoted to the study of classical languages. Erasmus declined for personal reasons and little was done about the college, but the idea survived.[9] It reappeared in a watered-down form in 1530, when the king set up the *lecteurs royaux*, four Regius professorships—two in Greek and two in Hebrew. This was anathema to the Sorbonne because of the implication that the study of these languages was essential to a correct understanding of Scripture; in the faculty's judgement only the Latin Vulgate was respectable. But it was not only humanism that was well-

6. P. Imbart de la Tour, *Les Origines de la Réforme* (Paris, 1914), iii, 262–4 (hereafter I. de la Tour); A. Buisson, *Le chancelier Antoine Duprat* (Paris, 1935), pp. 293–8.
7. I. de la Tour, iii, 258 n. 2.
8. M. Mann, *Érasme et les débuts de la réforme française* (Paris, 1934), pp. 72–3.
9. A. Lefranc, *Histoire du Collège de France* (Paris, 1893), pp. 48–9; Erasmus *Opus Epistolarum*, ed. P. S. Allen (Oxford, 1913) ii, 454–8.

entrenched at court. Close links existed between the court and the *Cercle de Meaux*, a group of scholars and preachers who had gathered around Guillaume Briçonnet, bishop of Meaux and one of the main protagonists of the so-called *préréforme* in France. The most important member of the group was Lefèvre d'Étaples, the bishop's vicar-general; others were Pierre Caroli, Gérard Roussel, Guillaume Farel and Martial Mazurier. The main link between them and the court was the king's sister, Marguerite, who, in 1527, became queen of Navarre. In 1521, she sought Briçonnet's spiritual guidance and corresponded with him for about three years. Through him she became acquainted with Lefèvre's ideas; in return for his advice, the bishop expected Marguerite to win her brother's support for the cause of religious reform.[10]

Such was the background to the long struggle between the king and the Sorbonne over the persecution of heretics. This was not about whether or not to tolerate heresy (both sides would have ruled this out), but about its definition. Whereas the Sorbonne wanted to silence anyone who did not conform to its own narrow orthodoxy, Francis was more flexible. Thus, in June 1523 the Sorbonne was sternly rebuked by the chancellor for trying to examine Lefèvre's *Commentarii initiatorii* and ordered to submit any passages in the work which it deemed heretical to a royal commission.[11] In 1524 Francis told the parlement that Lefèvre was widely respected at home and abroad and forbade any discussion of his works; he also nipped in the bud an attack by the Sorbonne on Erasmus.[12] Marguerite explained to Briçonnet that her brother was determined to show that 'the truth of God is not heresy'.[13]

As long ago as 1914 Imbart de la Tour pointed out that the inconsistencies in Francis's religious policy were not due to any weakness of character but, on the contrary, to a firm resolve on his part to reconcile his patronage of humanism with the duty of defending the faith traditionally attached to his title of 'Most Christian King'.[14] One would like to believe this, but it is highly improbable that the king was consciously trying to protect

---

10. L. Febvre, *Autour de l'Heptaméron* (Paris, 1944), pp. 100–3.

11. I. de la Tour, iii, 228.

12. R. Doucet, *Étude sur le gouvernement de François Ier dans ses rapports avec le Parlement de Paris* (Paris, 1921), i, 344 (hereafter Doucet, *Étude*).

13. Herminjard, i, 78. She wrote this before 22 Nov. 1521.

14. I. de la Tour, iii, 237.

evangelical humanists while consigning Lutherans to the wolves. The ideological situation was far too confused in the 1520s to allow of such a distinction. As Lucien Febvre so aptly put it, this was an age of 'magnificent religious anarchy'.[15] What the king was in effect doing was to protect scholars and preachers attached to his court or with contacts there. Whether they were evangelical humanists or Lutherans was, it seems, immaterial to Francis; his prime concern was to protect the religious life of his court from interference by outside bodies. He may even have believed that a larger dose of evangelism was permissible there than in the kingdom at large. Be this as it may, it is difficult to avoid the conclusion that there was one law for the court and another for the country.

The Sorbonne's definition of heresy would not have mattered so much if the king had been able to impose his own more liberal view on the kingdom as a whole; but his control of the religious situation was less complete than is commonly supposed. The Sorbonne was, of course, the most prestigious theological faculty in Christendom and exercised a right of censorship over religious works. But this, in itself, would not have been of major significance if it had not been able to count on the active support of the parlement of Paris in the all-important matter of law enforcement.

Francis and the parlement clashed over many issues. They quarrelled over the Concordat of Bologna, fiscal expedients, the king's revocation of lawsuits to the *Grand Conseil* and religious persecution.[16] Although the parlement was the highest court of law in the realm under the king, it had over the years developed an identity of its own and an outlook which could be widely at variance with the king's wishes. This was true within the sphere of heresy jurisdiction, where the parlement could act on its own initiative. This needs to be underlined, for it is often assumed that it was invariably the king who tolerated or persecuted; in many instances the initiative lay not with him but with the parlement. Under French law heresy cases were of two kinds; *délits communs* and *cas privilégiés*. A *délit commun* was a matter for the local ecclesiastical court, but in a *cas privilégié*, which involved a breach of the peace, the parlement had the right to intervene as a court of first instance. Thus it was possible for the parlement to act swiftly on the doctrinal advice of the Sorbonne without waiting for a

15. L. Febvre, *Au coeur religieux du XVIe siècle* (Paris, 1957), p. 66.
16. R. J. Knecht, *Francis I and Absolute Monarchy* (1969), pp. 10–17.

royal directive.[17] The king would consequently find himself in
the position of either condoning what had been done in his name
or undoing this. The latter course of action would take the form of
a revocation to the *Grand Conseil*, a conciliar court which continued to follow the king on his progresses and was, therefore,
more susceptible to his control.[18] This is what happened in the
famous Berquin affair. Louis de Berquin belonged to that rare
species in sixteenth-century France: the aristocratic scholar. In 1523
his writings were examined by the Sorbonne and found to be
heretical; he was reported to the parlement and arrested on a
heresy charge. But Francis promptly revoked the case to the
Grand Conseil and Berquin was duly released.[19]

A disagreement between the king and the parlement was all the
more likely to happen when they were separated by a considerable
distance. The parlement was, of course, permanently fixed in
Paris, whereas the court remained peripatetic. Francis was a
relentless traveller; so much so that a Venetian ambassador complained that in the course of his entire embassy he was never able
to stay put for more than a fortnight.[20] Serious communication
problems often arose between court and capital. Even in the
sixteenth century France was a very large country; it normally
took six to eight days to travel from Paris to Lyons and from ten
to fourteen to Marseilles.[21] A crisis in Paris would have to be
dealt with immediately without waiting for royal instructions. It
follows that persecution in the capital might be initiated in the
king's name but without his knowledge.

Court and capital were never as far apart during the reign as in
1525 after the king had been defeated in Italy and taken to Spain as
a prisoner. For more than a year the kingdom was administered
from Lyons by his mother, Louise of Savoy, who needed the
parlement's help to organise the defence of northern France

17. R. Doucet, *Les Institutions de la France au XVI*e *siècle* (Paris, 1948), ii, 784–6;
G. Zeller, *Les Institutions de la France au XVI*e *siècle* (Paris, 1948), pp. 357–9.
18. Doucet, *Institutions*, i, 202–6.   19. Mann, op. cit., pp. 115–16.
20. N. Tommaseo, *Relations des ambassadeurs vénitiens sur les affaires de France*
(1838) i, 107–11.
21. R. Mousnier, *Études sur la France de 1494 à 1559* (Cours de Sorbonne, Paris,
1964) p. 11. In exceptional circumstances, of course, faster travel was possible.
Thus in July 1536 a *quartenier* of Paris undertook to carry the 'paquet de ville' to
Lyons within forty hours and to bring back the king's reply within the same
period. The municipal register described his feat as one of a 'diligence extraordi-
naire', M. Félibien, *Histoire de la Ville de Paris* (Paris, 1725), ii, 1002.

against a possible English invasion. Taking advantage of her weakness, the parlement submitted to her in April remonstrances which amounted to an indictment of royal policy during the first ten years of the reign. Though not mentioned by name, Francis was implicitly accused of protecting heretics. The remonstrances also embodied a programme of remedial action; the regent was asked to implement decisions by the parlement which the king had suspended, to prosecute all heresy suspects, even high-ranking churchmen (this was clearly aimed at Briçonnet) and to obtain papal permission for the establishment of a special court to deal with them.[22] Louise was unable to resist this pressure; she, therefore, applied to Pope Clement VII, who set up the *juges délégués*, a commission made up of two Sorbonnistes and two *parlementaires* with powers to deal with all heresy cases independently of the ecclesiastical courts.[23] This effectively put heresy jurisdiction under the direct control of the orthodox extremists.

The new machinery was immediately set to work against the *Cercle de Meaux*, and the king was prompted to make one of his rare interventions from captivity in the domestic affairs of the reign. He had doubtless been informed of the situation by his sister when she visited him in Spain. He ordered proceedings against Lefèvre, Caroli and Roussel to be suspended until his return, but the parlement instructed the *juges délégués* to press on regardless.[24] When the regent added her voice to her son's, she was rebuked by the parlement for inconsistently trying to obstruct the work of the commission she had helped to set up.[25] Despite the king's intervention, then, the *Cercle de Meaux* continued to be harrassed: Lefèvre, Roussel and Caroli were forced into exile, while Briçonnet earned the contempt of reformers by becoming rigidly orthodox.[26] Another victim of the captivity was Berquin: in January 1526 he was arrested for the second time and tried for heresy by the *juges délégués*. They abstained, however, from sentencing him when it became known that the king was on his way home.[27]

Francis's release from captivity in March 1526 brought the

22. Doucet, *Étude*, ii, 110.
23. *Ordonnances des Rois de France: Règne de François 1er*, (Paris, 1933), iv, 72–3 (hereafter *Ordonnances*).
24. Herminjard, i, 401–3.   25. Doucet, *Étude*, ii, 192–3.
26. Imbart de la Tour, iii, 250; Herminjard, i, 446.
27. Mann, op. cit., pp. 119–21; Doucet, *Étude*, ii, 199–202.

persecution to an end. Berquin was set free and the Meaux exiles came home: Lefèvre took charge of the royal library at Blois, Roussel became Marguerite's almoner and Caroli resumed preaching in Paris: what is more, the Sorbonne ran into trouble. The king instructed the parlement to ban the sale of Béda's *Annotationes*, a work in which Erasmus and Lefèvre were accused of every kind of heresy. Early in 1527 Francis abolished the *juges-délégués*.[28] These actions naturally created the impression abroad that the king was veering towards the Reformation. 'The King favours the Word' wrote Capito to Zwingli on 1 January 1527.[29] This, however, was a delusion. Francis was simply reasserting his authority after a concerted attempt by the Sorbonne and parlement to encroach upon it in his absence. His actions were part of an absolutist reaction after a period of royal incapacity; they need to be related to the *lit de justice* of December 1527 in which he forced the parlement to register an edict limiting its own powers.[30]

Contrary to what Capito imagined, Francis was not moving towards Protestantism. He favoured the Word to the extent of not being able to understand how a faith more firmly rooted in Scripture could be heretical, but he opposed any sort of dissent likely to disturb the peace. Thus, in June 1528 he reacted strongly to the mutilation of a statue of the Virgin and Child in Paris: he offered a substantial reward for information about the culprits, took part in a procession to the scene of the sacrilege and ordered a statue of solid silver to replace the damaged one.[31] This act of iconoclasm was the first of a series which may be taken as an indication that the French Reformation, at least at a popular level, was becoming more radical; for iconoclasm was an activity less typical of Lutheranism than of the so-called 'Radical Reformation'. It was the extremist, Karlstadt, not Luther, who, in 1522, called for the removal of all religious images; Luther believed that they could be 'useful and commendable as a remembrance and a sign'.[32] But the main point of difference between the moderates and the radicals was the doctrine of the eucharist. This was the

28. I. de la Tour, iii, 256–9.

29. 'Rex Verbo favet'. Herminjard, ii, 4.

30. *Ordonnances*, v, 81–3. See also Doucet, *Étude*, ii, 252.

31. *Le Journal d'un Bourgeois de Paris sous le Règne de François 1er*, ed. V.-L. Bourrilly (Paris, 1910), pp. 290–3 (hereafter *JBP*).

32. R. H. Bainton, *The Age of the Reformation* (Princeton, 1956), pp. 115, 117–18. See also my article in *History*, lvii (1972), 13–14.

issue over which efforts to bring about a Protestant union foun-
dered at the Marburg conference in 1529. Whereas Zwingli and
other Swiss reformers affirmed their sacramentarianism (i.e. their
view that the eucharist was a commemoration, not a sacrifice),
Luther clung at least to the real presence.[33]

These differences were echoed in France where the 1520s were
marked by a shift of allegiance among many reformers from
Luther to Karlstadt and Zwingli.[34] This was true, for example, of
Farel, one of the original members of the *Cercle de Meaux*. In the
early 1520s he rejected Lefèvre and Luther for Karlstadt and
Zwingli and in 1524 openly repudiated Luther's doctrine of con-
substantiation. His extremism also expressed itself in iconoclasm.
Though Farel worked mainly in Switzerland, he attached great
importance to the conversion of his native land and turned
Neuchâtel into a base for an evangelical offensive against it.[35]
This was to have dramatic consequences in the near future.

As the Reformation in France took a more radical turn, the
defenders of orthodoxy within the kingdom reacted vigorously.
They included the king, who had always opposed religious extremism particularly at a popular level. In December 1530 the
chancellor was instructed to appoint judges to try heresy cases
throughout the kingdom.[36] But the growth of radicalism did not
make Francis any more conciliatory towards the Sorbonne; if
anything, his relations with the faculty became more acrimonious
as it stepped up its efforts to control religious life at court. It
believed, not unreasonably, that heresy would never be stamped
out in the kingdom at large, whatever legislative action the king
might take, as long as it was allowed to flourish at court.

The king's protection, however, was not foolproof. His frequent absences from Paris meant that he was sometimes out-
stripped by events there, while sudden changes on the international
scene could inhibit his actions. Both factors contributed to the
tragic dénouement of the Berquin affair. In March 1528 his trial
was resumed before a commission of twelve laymen appointed by
the pope at the king's request. These judges, however, were soon

---

33. J. Atkinson, *Martin Luther and the Birth of Protestantism* (Harmondsworth,
1968), pp. 272–7.
34. I. de la Tour, iii, 466–72.
35. *Guillaume Farel, 1489–1565. Biographie nouvelle par un groupe d'historiens*
(Neuchâtel and Paris, 1930).
36. *Ordonnances*, vi, 135–6.

denounced as Lutherans by the Sorbonne and the ever-vacillating Clement was persuaded to revoke their powers. Francis protested vehemently to the papal legate; but after hearing that the French army in Italy had capitulated, he yielded to the pope. Berquin consequently had to face a hostile ecclesiastical tribunal. On 15 April he was found guilty and sentenced to life imprisonment. Instead of accepting this verdict, Berquin decided against the advice of all his friends to appeal to the parlement. Francis was then absent from Paris. The appeal was dismissed on 17 April, and on the same day Berquin was burned on the Place de Grève.[37]

This, however, was not a decisive triumph for the reactionaries. Skirmishing between the king and the Sorbonne continued well into the 1530s, but the essential nature of this conflict has often been misunderstood; it was concerned with jurisdiction, not tolera-tion. While the Sorbonne claimed the right to lay down the law in matters of faith, the king reserved this right to himself, particu-larly if his political interests were involved. This was clearly demonstrated in the matter of Henry VIII's divorce. The king of England, having decided to consult universities on the Continent about the validity of his marriage to Catherine of Aragon, ex-pected Francis, in return for substantial financial concessions, to put pressure on the French universities so that they should come out in support of his divorce. Most of them did, but the Sorbonne, at least its more extreme members, proved obstreperous as usual. A decision by the faculty in Henry's favour was challenged by Béda and his friends. Despite a stern warning from Montmorency, the syndic drew up a statement in support of the validity of Henry's marriage and persuaded fifteen colleagues to sign it. Guillaume du Bellay, who acted for Henry, was only able to overcome Béda's resistance by resorting to bribery and corrup-tion. In the end, the faculty voted in favour of Henry's divorce by a very small majority.[38]

Following this defeat the *Bédaistes* tried to discredit Guillaume's brother, Jean du Bellay, bishop of Bayonne and one of the king's most liberal councillors, by spreading a report that he had been charged with heresy in the parlement. The bishop complained to Francis, who demanded an explanation: how was it, he asked,

37. Mann, op. cit., pp. 144–8.
38. V.-L. Bourrilly, *Guillaume du Bellay, seigneur de Langey* (Paris, 1905), pp. 92–107.

that so serious a charge had been levelled at a member of his council without his prior knowledge? After considering the matter carefully, the parlement denied the report. This satisfied the king, but not the bishop, who requested an opportunity to clear himself. The matter was accordingly entrusted to the *Grand Conseil*, where presumably the bishop won his case, since in October 1531 he was sent to England as ambassador and in September 1532 became bishop of Paris.[39]

Another target of the extremists was Gérard Roussel, Marguerite de Navarre's almoner, who, in Lent 1531, was accused of preaching heresy in her presence at the Louvre. Francis, acting perhaps at his sister's instigation, summoned Roussel and ordered him in future to give advance notice to two reliable persons of whatever he intended to say in sermons before the queen of Navarre. There was no further trouble till Lent 1533 when Roussel was again accused of heretical preaching. A measure of professional jealousy doubtless animated his critics, for his popularity as a preacher was considerable. It reduced François Picart, one of Béda's friends, to despair: 'it's all up with us', he wrote, 'my chair is deserted. I am left with only a few old women. All the men go to the Louvre!'[40] No record exists of what Roussel actually said in 1533, but some of his audience were sufficiently shocked to complain to the Sorbonne. Six bachelors of theology were accordingly instructed to preach against Lutheranism in the capital, albeit without mentioning names, but they soon began to denounce Roussel and even the queen of Navarre. As public opinion in the capital reacted, Francis had to intervene: he set up a commission under the chancellor to look into the Lenten sermons and ordered the Sorbonne to submit to it evidence against Roussel. At this juncture the faculty backtracked: it informed the king that he had been misinformed. Francis nevertheless felt that he must act before leaving for the south of France to meet the pope. He decided that the heresy charge against Roussel could wait until his return, but that sedition needed his immediate attention. In practice this meant that Roussel was treated more leniently than his critics: both were silenced, but whereas the almoner was committed to Marguerite's sympathetic custody, his critics were banished more than twenty leagues from the

---

39. *BSHPF*, lii (1903). 114–20.   40. Herminjard, iii, 161

capital. Béda was also accused of stirring up trouble at the Sorbonne and humiliated by having his room searched for incriminating evidence.[41]

The king's action caused a storm of indignation in university circles and provoked an attack on his sister. In October students at the Collège de Navarre put on a play in which Marguerite was shown preaching heresy at the instigation of Roussel and tormenting anyone who would not listen to her. Although the play was soon withdrawn, it came to Marguerite's notice and the college was raided by the *prévôt de Paris*. The author was not found, but two senior members of the college were detained. How the affair ended is not known. Later in the month further offence was given to the king's sister, when her poem, *Le miroir de l'âme pêcheresse*, was included by the university of Paris in a list of suspect works. The king asked to know the reason for this, whereupon Nicolas Cop, the university's rector, called a meeting of all the faculties. He denounced the effrontery of those who had dared to impugn the honour of the queen of Navarre and urged his colleagues to dissociate themselves from the action of a few theologians. Finding itself isolated, the Sorbonne made an abject apology to the king.[42]

But the frequent skirmishing between the king and the Sorbonne implied no royal willingness to tolerate heresy. It was at Francis's request that on 30 August Clement VII drew up a bull intended to speed the procedure in heresy trials. On 10 November, after meeting the king at Marseilles, he drafted another containing special provision for the punishment of ecclesiastics. These bulls, however, were not published immediately; they were intended, it seems, as weapons for use only in an emergency. But this occurred sooner than expected.[43]

It was customary for the rector of the university of Paris to deliver a sermon on All Saints' Day in the church of the Mathurins, but that preached by Nicolas Cop in 1533 was not exactly conventional. Doctrinally it contained little that would have been surprising in a preface by Lefèvre; yet this was enough to upset the Sorbonne, which complained to the parlement. Before any

41. *BSHPF.*, lii (1903), 120–2, 193–204. See also Herminjard, iii, 52–61, 72–5.
42. Ibid., iii, 93–5; *BSHPF*, lii (1903), 204–13; P. Jourda, *Marguerite d'Angoulême* (Paris, 1930), i, 178–80.
43. I. de la Tour, iii, 530–1.

action could be taken, however, Cop called a general meeting of the university. His words, he claimed, had been misrepresented and the university's privileges flouted. He demanded that his critics be called to account, but, even with the backing of the arts faculty, he failed to get his way. For a moment it seemed as if Cop would obey a summons to appear before the parlement, but he suddenly vanished taking with him the university's seal. Three months later he turned up in Basle.[44]

The rector's flight, which was closely followed by that of his young friend, John Calvin, set off a wave of persecution. About fifty arrests were made by the parlement, and on 26 November the Sorbonne and parlement wrote to the king an alarming account of the growth of heresy in the capital.[45] The king appeared duly concerned. 'Nous sommes très-marris et desplaisans', he replied, 'de ce que en nostre bonne ville de Paris . . . cette maudicte secte hérétique Luthérienne pullule.'[46] He ordered publication of the two recent bulls against heresy and asked René du Bellay, the bishop of Paris's brother and vicar-general, to set up a commission made up of *parlementaires* to try those heretics already under detention.

The king's reaction is puzzling. Cop should have been in his good books considering that he had successfully defended his sister only a few weeks before. Nor was his sermon in any sense *avant garde*; it contained sentiments held by many people at court. Why then did Francis respond so favorably to the appeals of the Sorbonne and parlement? The answer normally given is that he was obeying the dictates of his foreign policy; that, having just concluded an alliance with the pope, he wanted to demonstrate his zeal for the faith.[47] But there is no reason to suppose that he viewed this alliance as an alternative to his friendship with the German Protestants which was equally important to his anti-Habsburg diplomacy. A more likely explanation of his conduct is that he was responding to a situation in the capital which had temporarily slipped from his control. The persecution, it should be emphasised, was initiated not by the king, who was in Marseilles at the time, but by the parlement aided and abetted by the

44. Mann, op. cit., pp. 164–6; F. Wendel, *Calvin* (1963), pp. 37–42.
45. *BSHPF*, lii (1903), 216–17.
46. Herminjard, iii, 114–18.
47. Hari, p. 82; see also Elton, op. cit., p. 214.

Sorbonne.[48] It would have been very difficult for Francis to resist their combined entreaties when he was unable to judge the Parisian situation for himself. There is evidence, moreover, that parlement and Sorbonne deliberately exaggerated the dangers of that situation in order to force the king's hand. René du Bellay refused to set up the commission ordered by the king, not only because he regarded it as an infringement of episcopal authority, but also because he felt that Francis had been misled. There was much less heresy in the capital, he explained, than the king had been led to believe and he denied a suggestion that his brother, the bishop, had been negligent in dealing with it.[49] It is significant that as soon as Francis was able to judge the real situation for himself, the persecution petered out. René du Bellay, far from incurring royal displeasure by his disobedience, as his friends had feared, was told that Francis wished him well. Roussel was cleared of the heresy charge that had been hanging over him, and Béda, after rashly attacking the *lecteurs royaux*, was convicted of *lèse-majesté* and banished for life to the Mont-Saint-Michel.[50]

The religious peace lasted till the Affair of the Placards in the autumn of 1534. On the morning of Sunday 18 October Parisians on their way to mass were startled to find that Protestant *placards* or broadsheets had been put up during the night in various public places.[51] Each placard consisted of a single printed sheet entitled *Articles véritables sur les horribles, grands et importables abuz de la Messe papalle*. This attacked the mass on four grounds: first, there has been only one sacrifice, that of Christ on the Cross, which, being perfect, is unrepeatable. Secondly, the mass implies Christ's real presence in the host, yet Scripture tells us that He is with God the Father till the Day of Judgement; since it is impossible for anyone to be in two places at once, the mass is clearly a lie and those who practise it liars. Thirdly, transubstantiation is a human invention contrary to Scripture. Finally, the eucharist is a commemoration, not a miracle and the mass, being contrary to Scripture, is nothing else than a lucrative fraud. The *Articles véritables*, in short, were a concise, lucid and uncompromising

48. *Catalogue des Actes de François 1er* (Paris, 1905), viii, 484.
49. *BSHPF*, lii (1903), 219–24.
50. Ibid., pp. 224–7; I. de la Tour, iii, 532; Herminjard, iii, 158–9.
51. The best modern account of the affair is in G. Berthoud, *Antoine Marcourt* (Geneva, 1973), pp. 157–222 (hereafter Berthoud). See also Hari, pp. 79–142 and *BSHPF*, liii (1904), 97–143.

statement of the sacramentarian doctrine.[52] The authorship of the placards was for a long time in doubt. Many contemporaries suspected Farel, but it is now known that the author was Antoine Marcourt, a Frenchman exiled in Switzerland, who in 1530 became the first pastor of Neuchâtel. He was also responsible for the *Petit Traité . . . de la sainte Eucharistie*, an elaboration of the doctrine outlined in the *Articles véritables*, which was published on 16 November 1534. Both works were printed at Neuchâtel.

The general reaction of Parisians to the discovery of the placards was one of dismay, indignation and alarm, feelings soon heightened by reports that identical placards had been found in the château of Amboise, where the king was in residence at the time, and in five provincial towns: Orléans, Blois, Amboise, Tours and Rouen. And the immediate sequel was a campaign of persecution more savage than any yet experienced by the French reformers. Following a wave of arrests the first sentences were passed on 10 November. A shoemaker's son, nicknamed 'the Paralytic', was burned on 13 November and on the following day, Jean du Bourg, a rich draper, suffered the same fate. By the end of the month four more dissenters—a printer, a weaver, a bookseller and a stone-mason—had been put to death. The persecution was accompanied by a wave of popular hysteria. It was said that the reformers were planning to sack the Louvre, to burn down all the churches in Paris and to massacre the faithful attending midnight mass.[53] Foreigners became highly suspect. A Flemish merchant was lynched by a mob shouting: 'He is a German. His death will gain us indulgences!' Englishmen too had to look to their lives.[54]

Francis, in the meantime, left Amboise and travelled back to Paris. On 9 December he wrote to Duprat from Bonneval as follows: 'Monsieur le légat, j'ay receu vos lettres du VII de ce moys e veu par icelles la diligence qui s'est faicte et faict chacun jour au faict des luthériens, dont j'ay été très aise et ne me scauroit

---

52. Hari, pp. 114, 119–20. Historians assumed for a long time that the text in Crespin's *Histoire des Martyrs* (1564 edn.) was authentic. In 1943 fragments of the original placards were found in the binding of a book at Berne municipal library. By piecing these together it has been possible to reconstruct the original text and show that Crespin's version contains interpolations and amendments of a later date.

53. *JBP*, pp. 379–80; Berthoud, pp. 181–7.

54. Herminjard, iii, 236 n. 5. See also Andrew Baynton's letter to Cromwell (Paris 1 Feb. 1535) 'the common people imagine that we and the Germans are all one, that is Lutherans'. *LP*, viii, 165 (SP1/89/f.137a).

on faire chose plus agréable que de contynuer, en sorte que ceste mauldicte et abhominable secte ne puisse prendre pied ne racine en mon royaulme. . .'[55] On 16 December Duprat sent the king a list of persons who were not to be allowed to escape and five days later Francis set up a special commission of twelve in the parlement to try suspects. His zeal in dealing with heresy earned him a special vote of thanks from the Sorbonne on 29 December.[56] On 13 January shortly after Francis's return to the capital, some copies of Marcourt's *Petit Traité* were found in the streets. This second 'affair', though less dramatic than the first, was in a sense more provocative, since it cocked a snook at the persecutors just as they were congratulating themselves on having stamped out the October 'plot'.[57] It was presumably this second affair rather than the first, which prompted Francis on the very same day to ban all printing till further notice and to order a procession for 21 January.[58]

This turned out to be one of the most spectacular demonstrations of orthodoxy ever seen in the capital. Never had so many shrines and relics been carried in procession before. They included the Crown of Thorns at the sight of which, we are told, 'people's hair stood on end'. But the central feature of the procession was the Blessed Sacrament which the placards had insulted. It was carried most reverently by Bishop du Bellay under a canopy borne by the king's three sons and by the duke of Vendôme. Francis walked immediately behind it, bareheaded, dressed in black and holding a lighted torch. Every now and then the procession halted and the host was placed on a wayside altar especially erected for the occasion. An anthem was sung and the king lost himself in prayer, a sight which allegedly drew tears from the spectators. Occasionally someone in the crowd shouted: 'Sire, faites bonne justice!', whereupon Francis made a sign indicating that he could be depended upon.[59] After a service at Notre-Dame, the king and queen were entertained to lunch at the bishop's

---

55. *BSHPF*, liii (1904), 117.　　56. Ibid., Hari, p. 107.

57. See the anonymous letter written in Paris on 25 Jan. 1535 probably to John Longland, bishop of Lincoln, in *The Athenaeum* No. 2761 (25 Sept. 1880), p. 401. Also Berthoud, pp. 187–9.

58. *BSHPF*, liii (1904), 118. The ban on printing was not registered by the Parlement. It was lifted on 26 Feb. 1535. Archives nationales, X^{1a} 1538, f. 113.

59. Among several contemporary descriptions of the procession one of the fullest is in *Cronique du Roy Françoys premier de ce nom*, ed. G. Guiffrey (Paris, 1860), pp. 114–21. The best modern account is in Berthoud, pp. 190–5.

palace. Then, in the presence of a large and distinguished crowd, Francis made a speech urging his subjects to denounce all heretics, even close relatives or friends.[60] The day ended with the burning of six heretics. Many more, however, were to suffer the same fate before the persecution ended in May. Meanwhile other repressive measures were taken. On 24 January a royal proclamation called on seventy-three 'Lutherans' who had gone into hiding to give themselves up within three days under pain of death. They included some famous names, notably Pierre Caroli and the poet, Clément Marot.[61] On the 29th another edict made harbourers of heretics liable to the same penalties and offered informers a quarter share of their victims' property.[62]

Why did Francis react so violently to the Affair of the Placards? The traditional answer is that he had been enraged at the discovery of one of the placards on his bedchamber door. This rests on more or less contemporary evidence, though this is far from unanimous about details. Crespin states that the placard was found at the Louvre, de Bèze gives the location as Blois; both mention the bedchamber door, but another source, Fontaine, states that the placard was found 'en la tasse du Roy, où il mettoit son mouchouër'. Florimond de Raemond describes how a certain Guillaume Feret, valet to the king's apothecary, threw Protestant articles of faith into the 'cabinet du Roy' and planted 'des petis billets, dans la nef, dont on le servoit à table'. Nearly everyone mentions the king's anger. Crespin states that Francis 'vomited rage through his eyes and mouth', and de Bèze writes that he determined there and then to 'tout exterminer'. Fontaine says that the king after having the placard read to him, 'entra en un zèle incroyable'.[63] A distillation of these stories has found its way into most modern textbooks. 'It seems characteristic of the superficiality of Francis', writes A. G. Dickens, 'that a personal affront should have decided his policy.'[64]

60. The actual text of Francis's speech has not survived. Its gist, however, is known thanks to several contemporary accounts. See Berthoud, p. 196.

61. For the full list see Hari, pp. 104–6.

62. *BSHPF*, liii (1904), 129.

63. J. Crespin, *Histoire des Martyrs* (1554); T. De Bèze, *Histoire Ecclésiastique* (1580), S. Fontaine, *Histoire catholique de nostre temps* (1558) and F. De Raemond, *Histoire de la naissance, progrez et décadence de l'hérésie de ce siècle* (1647). The relevant passages are quoted by Hari, pp. 84–8. Also Berthoud, p. 181.

64. A. G. Dickens, *Reformation and Society in sixteenth-century Europe* (1966), p. 98.

Superficial Francis may have been, but it is difficult to believe that only the personal affront provoked the persecution. That at least one placard was found in the king's apartments at Amboise is almost certain, for the martyrs of 1535 included a chorister of the royal chapel, who had allegedly introduced placards into the château while the king was residing there.[65] But was this in itself a crime of sufficient gravity to justify a violent and protracted campaign of repression in the capital? Intrusions on the king's privacy were not unknown. Unauthorised persons drifted in and out of his apartments with ease; so much so that he once complained of thefts from his wardrobe and chapel.[66] In November 1530 three armed strangers were found in his bedchamber at the Louvre, yet his only reaction on this occasion was an injunction to the parlement to be more vigilant in the streets of Paris at night.[67] Given these circumstances, the king's alleged rage in October 1534 is difficult to explain; indeed nothing in his behaviour suggests such an outburst. Instead of rushing back to the capital he travelled there at a most leisurely pace.[68] Could it be that too much significance has been given to the placard on the king's bedchamber door? Contemporaries doubtless welcomed it as a conveniently succinct explanation of the affair's extraordinary aftermath; but the historian needs to probe further.

If he discounts the traditional explanation of the persecution what alternative is there? Can it be that Francis was responding to the international situation? This is even less likely, for the persecution was an appalling embarrassment to him in his dealings with the German Protestants. The election of the Emperor Charles V's brother, Ferdinand, as King of the Romans, in January 1531 and the opposition this had aroused among the German princes had given Francis a splendid opportunity of interfering in the Empire's domestic affairs. He had succeeded in forming an anti-Habsburg coalition of princes, but its effectiveness had been hampered by religious differences among its members. Hence his decision, in 1534, to work for a reunion of the churches. He sent

---

65. *JBP*, p. 384. He was allegedly sent to Paris by the king and burned at the 'carrefour du Gros Tournois' on 13 March 1535.

66. *Ordonnances*, vi, 122–3.

67. Arch. nat., Registres du Parlement, X^{1a} 1536, f. 68 v.

68. Francis left Amboise on 20 Oct. He stayed at Châtellerault from c. 7 until 22 Nov. and at S. Germain-en-Laye from 20 Dec. to 3 Jan. *Cat. Actes de F. 1er* viii, 487.

Guillaume du Bellay to Germany and Switzerland and entered into negotiations with some of the leaders of the Reformation, notably Melanchthon and Bucer. Du Bellay led them to believe that his master's motives were essentially religious and invited them to send their views in writing to Paris on the feasibility of a doctrinal compromise. By late summer Melanchthon and Bucer had replied in a most encouraging way. As long as the preponderant role of faith was recognised, Melanchthon was sure that a mutually satisfactory doctrine of justification could be worked out. The mass, he admitted, presented a more difficult problem, but a synod ought to be able to solve it.[69] Francis's policy, therefore, seemed on the verge of success, when the Affair of the Placards upset all his plans. The persecution badly damaged his reputation beyond the Rhine. Imperial agents pointed to the shameful contrast between his treatment of his fellow Christians and his friendly reception of Turkish ambassadors. On 1 February Francis defended himself in a manifesto addressed to the Imperial Estates. He had done nothing wrong, he claimed, in negotiating with the Turks; the king of the Romans had set him the example and Christendom needed peace. As for the persecution in France, it had been political, not religious; he had punished sedition as the estates themselves would have done in similar circumstances. He denied that there were any Germans among the victims: 'à vostre nation est libère en France de faire ce qui est libère à mes propres enfans.'[70]

But whatever excuses the king might offer in a futile effort to regain the confidence of the German reformers, he could not disclaim responsibility for the persecution in France. What is far from clear, however, is the precise nature of that responsibility: did Francis actually unleash the persecution, as is generally stated, or did he merely give his approval to measures taken by others in his name? There is, in fact, no archival evidence connecting the start of the persecution in Paris with any incident at Amboise.[71]

69. Bourrilly, *G. du Bellay*, pp. 123–36, 149–77, 179–81; J. V. Pollet, *Martin Bucer; études sur la correspondance* (Paris, 1962), ii, 492–7.

70. Bourrilly, op. cit., p. 191. For the full text in Latin see Herminjard, iii, 249–54.

71. A letter written by the king to the *Bureau de Ville* from Pontlevoy, near Blois, on 19 Oct. and delivered on 26 Oct. makes no mention of the affair. *Registres des délibérations du Bureau de la Ville de Paris*, ed. A. Tuetey (Paris, 1886), ii, 194.

When the municipal government (*Bureau de Ville*) met on 19 October it was in response to a call from the parlement; its registers do not mention the king. It was the parlement which ordered the search for culprits and a general procession on 22 October.[72] Francis, as far as is known (unfortunately the parlement's registers for this period have a hiatus), did not react officially until he wrote to the chancellor on 9 December, nearly two months after the event. Thus, it seems that it was the Affair of the Placards, as manifested in Paris, rather than the personal affront to the king which provoked the persecution in the first instance, and that this was set in motion by the parlement, as in the autumn of 1533 following Cop's sermon. On this occasion, however, the king had called a halt to it after returning to the capital. Why did he not do the same in January 1535? The answer surely depends on a correct assessment of the Protestant challenge. The placards were quite different from Cop's sermon; they were not a moderate statement addressed to a learned audience, but a violent attack on a fundamental tenet of the faith directed at all the king's subjects. The manner of their distribution and display may well have shocked public opinion: introducing one into the king's apartments was an impertinence; displaying others in five towns on the same night pointed to the existence of a well-organised clandestine movement. But the message of the placards was far more important than the method of their dissemination: it clearly exemplified the radicalism towards which the French Reformation had been moving since the mid-twenties. Its language, moreover, was exceptionally abusive even by sixteenth-century standards. Thus, transubstantiation was denounced as 'un horrible et execrable blasphème', an 'idolatrie publique' and the 'doctrine des diables', while priests were condemned as 'misérables sacrificateurs', 'faux antechrists', 'loups ravissans', 'brigans', 'paillardz' and 'ennemys de Dieu'.[73]

Nothing could have suited the Sorbonne and the parlement better. For years they had been trying to silence evangelism only to meet with repeated obstruction from the king; now they had him in their power. He could not dispute the seriousness of the offence committed by the reformers; nor could he stem the tide

---

72. Ibid., ii, 192–3.
73. Opinions differ on this point. Compare Hari, pp. 120–1 with Berthoud, p. 218.

of popular hysteria which it had provoked. Embarrassing as the persecution was to his foreign policy, it could not on this occasion be unwound. Had Francis attempted this, his credibility as the Most Christian King would have suffered irreparable damage. Finding himself without room to manoeuvre, he chose the only sensible course which was to identify himself publicly with the persecution, hence the gigantic procession and slogans in praise of the king's faith associated with it. He was doubtless confirmed in his decision by the second 'affair' of 13 January.

The Affair of the Placards has been rightly regarded as a watershed in the history of the French Reformation, though usually for the wrong reasons. It did not lead to a change of royal policy from toleration to persecution. Toleration before October 1534 had been strictly selective; only scholars and preachers connected with the court had enjoyed the king's protection; no toleration had been shown to heretics in general, particularly disturbers of the public peace. The placards were significant because they revealed the existence within France of a well-organised group of radical dissenters whose sacramentarianism was offensive to both liberal and reactionary opinion. By appealing directly to the man-in-the-street, Marcourt and his associates forced the king of France to endorse a campaign of persecution which previously he might have been tempted to mitigate. The placards marked the end of Lucien Febvre's 'long period of magnificent religious anarchy' when, in the absence of any clearly formulated confessions of faith, it had been virtually impossible for anyone with evangelical leanings to draw the line between orthodoxy and dissent. Marcourt showed that such a line did exist, and those Frenchmen who had been content so far to follow a middle path in religion were now forced to take sides. Fear of persecution also compelled moderates to reconsider their position, for the repression of 1535 was not limited to sacramentarians; any dissenter risked the stake.[74]

Whatever impact the placards may have had on Francis's personal convictions, they certainly simplified his task of government by dispelling the religious mists which in the past had so often clouded his relations with the parlement and the Sorbonne. He

74. See the letter from J. Sturm to Bucer (Paris, 10 March 1535) in which he writes: 'Nihil interest inter Anabaptistam, Erasmianum, Lutheranum; omnes sine discrimine coërcentur et educuntur; nemo tutus nisi Papista.' Herminjard, iii, 273.

did not immediately abandon his efforts to reach an understanding with the German Protestants, nor did he stop patronising humanists, but he no longer found it as necessary to defend preachers accused of heresy or to shield individuals from the normal processes of the law. French Protestantism, it has been said, was transformed by the Affair des Placards into a 'religion for rebels'; as such it had to be stamped out.[75] Henceforth crown, parlement and Sorbonne united in a common struggle against a heresy which everyone could recognise.[76]

75. Berthoud, p. 219.
76. This paper is based on one delivered on 3 July 1975 to the Anglo-American conference of historians at the University of London.

VII

Victim or Spendthrift? The Bishop of London and his Income in the Sixteenth Century

GINA ALEXANDER

In July 1558 Edmund Bonner, bishop of London, wrote: 'I do spende a greet deale moor than is my lyveload, wherin thoughe I doo playe the foole, yet suche is the place that I am in that I can not otherwise doo'.[1] He was stating not only his own financial problems but those of most Tudor bishops. Bonner, Ridley and Grindal held the see of London from 1540 to 1570, and during that period suffered a continuously diminishing real net income. Royal depredations made serious inroads into the wealth of many Tudor bishops, but they do not provide the sole explanation for the poverty of the bishops of London.

Rapacity of the crown was, however, the major cause for the reduced income of other bishops. Henry VIII's exchanges with Cranmer probably reduced his income at Canterbury by about 8 per cent. The main spoliation at Coventry and Lichfield occurred between 1537 and 1547 and may have reduced the gross revenues of the see by 25 per cent. Even more dramatic was the plunder of York, for between 1542 and 1545 two archbishops reduced the income of their see by 50 per cent. Under Edward VI the greed of crown and courtiers continued to wreak havoc with episcopal income: in the first years of his reign the revenues of the see of Lincoln were more than halved as a result of exchanges with the crown and at Bath and Wells the income of the see in 1550 was 30 per cent of what it had been in 1539. Some bishops were spared: Canterbury and York suffered no further depredation under Edward, and Ely too was unscathed. Mary's reign provided a breathing space: at York there was even restitution and at

1. Inner Temple Lib., Petyt Ms. 538/47 f. 3.

Chester a substantial grant. However, on Elizabeth's accession, Grindal and at least ten other bishops were forced to exchange lands with the crown to their detriment.[2]

Royal behaviour in London was in marked contrast to that in many other sees. Henry VIII was relatively gentle with Bonner, and Ridley was remarkably lucky under Edward. Although Grindal was the chief victim in London of royal greed, his cash income was not reduced.

Until 1545 the temporalities of the see, listed by the receiver-general as twenty-four manors, had been virtually unchanged since the thirteenth century. Ten of the manors were in Essex, three in Hertfordshire and nine in Middlesex, with one manor in Sussex and one in Surrey. Except on the manors of Fulham and Hadham, little of the demesne was still 'in hand'. By the fifteenth century the bishops of London had given up direct management of their estates almost entirely, and at the beginning of the six-teenth century episcopal manors were either leased in whole or in part to farmers, or were rented to copyholders and free tenants whose rents were collected by the bishops' bailiffs.[3] The pattern of diocesan temporalities was to change out of all recognition as a result of the crown's actions between 1545 and 1562, although the cash income of the bishops of London was to remain remark-ably constant.

Bonner's first exchange with Henry VIII in 1545 did not greatly reduce the income of his see. Bonner granted the crown three manors in Essex and one in Sussex in exchange for two in Worces-tershire, one in Gloucestershire and one in Hereford. The value of the four manors lost by Bonner was much the same as that of those gained. Those lost had yielded an average annual net cash

2. F. R. H. DuBoulay, 'Archbishop Cranmer and the Canterbury Tempor-alities', *EHR*, 47 (1952), 34; M. R. O'Day, 'Thomas Bentham: a Case-Study in the Problems of the Early Elizabethan Episcopate', *Journ. Eccles. Hist.*, 23 (1972), 140. Dr O'Day has amplified her conclusions in correspondence. C. Cross, 'The Economic Problems of the See of York', *Land, Church and People*, ed. J. Thirsk (1970), pp. 72–3, for York and Lincoln; P. M. Hembry, *The Bishops of Bath and Wells 1540–1640* (1967), pp. 106, 116, 254; F. Heal, 'The Tudors and Church Lands: Economic Problems of the Bishopric of Ely during the Sixteenth Century', *EcHR*, Ser. 2, 26 (1973), 202–3; F. Heal, 'The Bishops and the Act of Exchange of 1559', *Hist. Journ.*, 17 (1974), 239–40. C. Haigh, 'Finance and Administration in a new diocese: Chester', *Continuity and Change* (1976), ed. O'Day and Heal, p. 155.

3. I am grateful to Mrs Pamela Taylor for explaining the changes in the management of the temporalities in the middle ages.

income, excluding sales of timber, averaging £114 before 1520 and amounting to £126 in 1527. Including the timber, these four manors were given a gross valuation of £145 in the *Valor Ecclesiasticus* and of almost £152 in 1544.[4] The four manors granted by Henry VIII to Bonner in 1545 were valued at that time at almost £155, including £26 a year for the timber. Their cash value was £111 in 1550, and over £152 in 1556 when timber on one of the manors had been sold.[5] Bonner also granted Henry VIII two other Essex manors, Crondon and Chelmsford, in 1545. He received no compensation at all for these lands which contributed 4 per cent of his gross income: they were valued at nearly £50 per annum in 1535 and £53 in 1546. Their net cash yield, averaging £43 a year between 1527 and 1539, was 5 per cent of the bishop's net cash income in those years.[6]

The next exchange of London lands with the crown—a much more advantageous one to the diocese, though not to the church as a whole—occurred a few days after Nicholas Ridley had been translated from Rochester in April 1550 to take the place of the deprived Bonner. Four valuable London manors were granted to the crown and immediately passed to three courtiers, Sir Richard Rich, Lord Wentworth and Sir Thomas Darcy. In return Ridley received fourteen manors in Middlesex, Hertfordshire, Essex and Warwickshire, lands in Uxbridge and London and three rectories. The property transferred to London at this time had belonged to the diocese of Westminster until its surrender to the crown by Thirlby on 30 March 1550, except for the manor and rectory of Rickmansworth which had belonged to the monastery of St Alban's.[7] The lands granted by Ridley to the crown had been valued between £438 and £480 in 1527, 1535 and 1550, although their average annual cash yield in 1527 and between 1535 and 1539 was £377. The gross value of the property granted to Ridley was estimated at £527 in 1550 and at £555 in 1556 and the cash yield to the receiver-general in 1556 was £477. As well as this cash income, increased by over 25 per cent, Ridley received

4. London Guildhall Lib., Ms. 10123/1–3; *Valor Ecclesiasticus*, i, 356; E318/721/1–2.

5. Ibid., 3, 9–15; SC6/Edw VI/306/2d.; SC6/PM/194/1d.2.

6. *Valor*, loc. cit.; SC6/Hen. VIII/903/20; London Guildhall Lib., Ms. 10123/3; St Paul's Lib., Box B/94 Ms. 227/3.

7. E318/1685/1; E305/G 25; *CPR, 1550–1553*, p. 15; *CPR, 1549–1551*, pp. 262–3, 404, 423.

rents in kind of thirty quarters of grain and 244 quarters of malt from his new manors, and a reduction of his tenth from nearly £112 to £100 a year.[8] Royal generosity to the diocese of London was at the cost of the extinction of the diocese of Westminster; nevertheless Ridley's acquiescence in the crown's demands in 1550 strengthened the financial position of the see.

The most fundamental change in the composition of London diocesan revenues, a change which also had far-reaching effects on the value of those revenues, occurred at the beginning of Elizabeth's reign, between 1559 and 1562. In exchange for eleven manors (valued at £388, including timber sales), Grindal received six rectories yielding annually £100 and tenths from the dean and chapter of St Paul's of £288, a total equalling the estimated value of the manors he had lost. He also secured a release from his own tenth of £100 a year.

Although much less severe than Grindal might initially have feared, this exchange of 10 February 1562 had important long-term effects. In the first place, the commissioners' valuation of the eleven London manors surrendered to the crown was an underestimate. In 1556, for example, Bonner's receiver had taken over £561 in rents and sales of wood from these eleven manors, i.e. over 50 per cent more than the royal commissioners' valuation. In the second, Grindal suffered in the long term from the nature of the revenues he received, namely, the tenths paid by the dean and chapter of St Paul's.[9] The six rectories, although all leased to farmers when Grindal acquired them, did at least allow the possibility of entry fines when in due course the leases fell in and the rectories were leased anew, albeit at about the old rents.[10] But the tenths were a fixed monetary charge owed by the chapter to the crown (and thence diverted to the bishop) which could in no way be improved. They were therefore particularly vulnerable to inflation: and they contributed 25 per cent of the entire revenue accounted for by the bishop's receiver-general after 1562. In the short term Grindal may not have been seriously affected by the substitution of a fixed cash income for manorial revenues. In the

8. E318/1685; SC6/Edw. VI/306; SC6/PM/193.
9. *CPR, 1560–1563*, pp. 306–8; Heal, 'Act of Exchange', p. 239; SC6/PM/194/1–2.
10. St Paul's Lib., Box B/94 Ms. 232/2d.; St Paul's Lib., Registrum Nowell, i, ff. 272, 338.

long term the exchange meant a serious erosion of the real income of his see.

New royal taxation may have had a greater effect on episcopal income than exchanges of temporalities with the crown. From 1535 these temporalities, like those of most other clergy in England, were subject to first-fruits and tenths. Bonner was slow to pay off his first-fruits: in 1554, fourteen years after his translation to London, he still owed £125 when Queen Mary released him of all debts to the crown. Ridley too found it difficult to pay his first-fruits quickly: £100 was still owing after his death. Similarly Grindal had only paid £254 of his first-fruits at the end of 1562. In the first half of his episcopate Bonner had to find nearly £112 a year for his tenth and Ridley had to pay £100, but these payments were probably also frequently delayed. Bonner, for instance, was at least a year late in paying the tenth due at Christmas 1554.[11] Grindal was spared this burden after 1562. The paucity of the evidence about these payments and the dilatory way in which they seem to have been paid make it impossible to estimate exactly how they affected the bishops' net cash income each year. Nevertheless it is clear that first-fruits were an onerous burden and that, between 1535 and 1554, payment of the tenth further reduced the bishops' disposable income.

Although the bishops of London's losses were not as great as those of some of their contemporaries, they did not escape scot-free the effects of royal greed. Bonner's income probably declined by about 5 per cent after 1545, but Ridley's advantageous exchange five years later restored the level of episcopal income. Nevertheless, the value of the temporalities to the bishops was reduced in the short term by royal taxation and in the long term by the nature of the income diverted to the see in 1562.

A more detailed analysis of the income of the bishops of London can be made from their receivers-general's accounts. Fifty different accounts have survived for the sixteenth century and it is possible to have a clearer idea of the changes in episcopal income in this see than in many others. The receivers were responsible for most of the revenues from the farmers and bailiffs of the episcopal manors. Those cash rents which were handed directly to the bishop and the rents in kind given to the clerk of the household were also noted by the receiver-general. The receiver did not

11. E337/2/45; *CPR, 1553–4*, p. 120; E334/4/48; E334/7/86; SC6/PM/194/3.

normally record fines on new leases paid to the bishop or the cash the bishop received from sales of timber.

From the receiver-general's accounts can be extracted figures for the gross value of the episcopal estates, the total receipts of the receiver-general and the amounts of cash either assigned by him directly to the bishop, or spent by him for the bishop. The gross values of the estates, as calculated by the receivers, are distorted by their inclusion of arrears. Even after arrears are removed, the gross value is still an illusory figure, for it includes rents which had been remitted and court fines imposed but not collected. The total receipts of the receivers are also deceptive as a guide to the value of the see, since receivers included in their total of receipts cash which had not in fact been received and did not include other sums (for instance, arrears from preceding years) which they did receive. The figures of the bishops' cash receipts are also an incomplete statement of their income as they do not include a cash equivalent of rents in kind or a record of extra revenues paid to the bishops personally. Each of these three sets of figures, set out in full in Table 1, has therefore certain disadvantages, but used together they clarify the financial position of the bishops of London.

The uneven nature of the evidence between 1518 and 1559 makes it impossible to compare *in detail* episcopal income immediately before the three exchanges of 1545 and 1550 with the revenues immediately after them. However, we can draw some broad conclusions about the impact of all the exchanges with the crown on the level of episcopal income. The average gross annual value of the see was £1281 between 1515 and 1518. Despite all the vicissitudes between 1545 and 1562 the average gross annual value of the see between 1564 and 1569 was £1335 and in the 1570s £1385. Before 1520 the bishop's average annual net cash receipts were £1003, between 1563 and 1567 £1065 and between 1571 and 1580 £1154. Before 1520 the receiver-general's annual nominal net profits were on average about 80 per cent of the gross value of the see. In the 1560s this figure had risen to 85 per cent and in the 1570s to 92 per cent. Similarly the bishop's cash receipts were 76 per cent of the total gross value of the see before 1520, but had risen to 82 per cent in the late 1560s and to 83 per cent in the 1570s. The bishops of London's cash income had therefore not suffered—in absolute terms—as a result of the

Table 1. Income and Inflation

Date (year ending Michaelmas)	The gross value of episcopal properties (excluding arrears from previous years)	Receiver-general's nominal net profits of manors (excluding arrears from previous years)	Cash assigned by receiver to and for bishop (including arrears paid to bishop)	Cash receipts adjusted for inflation[1]
	£	£	£	£
1515	1284[2]	1015	1135	1060
1516	1242	1062	880	800
1517	1264	902	833	750
1518	1338	1132	1166	1005
1527	1369	997	966	657
(Valor	1214	1119)		
1535	—	955[3]	(848)	(647)
1536	—	952	(848)	(517)
1537	—	926	(848)	(547)
1538	—	973	(848)	(614)
1539	—	1070	(848)	(576)
1550	—	1114	776	296
1556	1642[4]	1420	1072	289
1559	—	1299[5]	685	268
1560	1101	848	733	276
1561	—	898	770	272
1562	—	1184	958	360
(1562)	—	(1760)[6]	(1533)	(576)
1563	—	1145	1025	—
1564	1395	1166	1177	—
1565	—	1127	1032	355
1566	1299	1109	1130	394
1567	1311	1118	1026	364
1569	1365	1212	1073	389
1571	1374	1270	1217	459
1572	—	1256	1205	446
1573	1380	1279	1216	444

Table 1 (cont.)

Date (year ending Michaelmas)	The gross value of episcopal properties (excluding arrears from previous years)	Receiver-general's nominal net profits of manors (excluding arrears from previous years)	Cash assigned by receiver to and for bishop (including arrears paid to bishop)	Cash receipts adjusted for inflation[1]
	£	£	£	£
1574	1358	1147	1086	290
1578	1418	1310	1061	302
1579	1383	1277	1153	353
1580	1402	1292	1131	331

[1] The real value of the bishops' net cash income has been estimated in inverse proportion to the movement of the Phelps Brown and Hopkins's composite consumables' index, base 1450.

[2] All figures are given to the nearest £.

[3] I am grateful to Mrs Pamela Taylor for drawing my attention to the draft summary accounts for 1535 to 1539. The bishop received £4240 in five years. I have taken an average. The figures in col. 4 are speculative. St Paul's Lib., Box B/94 Ms. 227.

[4] The figures for 1556 are distorted. The gross value of the see was inflated by £280 of unpaid fines: SC6/PM/193/11. The receiver's profits included £136 in entry fines and sales of wood and £32 repayment of subsidy: SC6/PM/194/2d.

[5] In 1559 one half-yearly account was made for Bonner and a second for the Queen. Bonner received £180 and Grindal eventually received £505. The accounts do not reveal how much went to the Queen: St Paul's Lib., Box B/91 Ms. 229, Box B/94 Ms. 231.

[6] In 1562 Grindal received £576 for tenths for 1560 and 1561. The figures in brackets include the backpayments: St Paul's Lib., Box B/94 Ms. 232/2d.

depredations of the crown. On the contrary, it had grown slightly.

Comparisons of gross and net cash receipts lead to two further conclusions. In the first place they cast doubt on the value of the *Valor Ecclesiasticus* as a guide to episcopal income, at any rate in London. The *Valor* estimated the gross values of the manors of the diocese in 1535 at nearly £1214, a conservative figure compared to the calculations of the receivers between 1515 and 1518, and in 1527. The commissioners responsible for the London *Valor* also concluded that, after the deduction of fees and expenses, the bishop had 'clear' over £1119, or 92 per cent of the gross, and calculated the tenth owing to the crown accordingly. However, in the five years before 1535 for which records are extant the receivers' receipts were an average of 78 per cent of the gross value of the see and the bishops' net cash receipts were 76 per cent. In the five years immediately after 1535, Stokesley's average annual income was only 75 per cent of the *Valor*'s figure of 'clear' income and presumably only about 70 per cent of the gross value of the see. At no time before the 1570s did the receiver-general account for as high a proportion as 92 per cent, and the bishop's net cash receipts, even then, only rose to 83 per cent of the gross value of the see. The *Valor* may be an adequate guide to the amount of money the bishops ought to have received, but it overestimated by between 15 per cent and 20 per cent the 'clear' value of the bishop's cash receipts.

The second conclusion to emerge from these figures is that despite variations in income from year to year, the Elizabethan bishops were taking a higher proportion of the gross cash value of the see than their pre-Reformation predecessors. The rise in the gross value of the see from before 1520 to 1580 was about 8 per cent, the rise in the receiver's nominal receipts was about 10 per cent, while the rise in the bishop's net cash income was about 15 per cent.

The rise in the receiver's receipts and the bishop's income occurred even though the bishops made few attempts to adjust existing rents. They did, however, spur on their receivers and seneschals to chase arrears, seek out forgotten rents and to take greater profits from manorial courts. Unpaid rents from the current and previous years could depress the bishop's income markedly. In 1549–50 unpaid rents totalled over 15 per cent of the receiver's total receipts, and these unpaid debts, combined with a charge of £54.10.0. for the expenses of Bonner's household, made Ridley's cash position unusually difficult in his first year at London. Grindal also began his episcopate with a drastically reduced income. All claims to arrears were abandoned at the beginning of an episcopate, and moreover until the crown completed its exchange, Grindal's nominal income was only three-quarters of what it was to be after 1562.[12] By contrast, when the

12. SC6/Edw VI/306/2d.; *APC, 1547–1550*, p. 422; St Paul's Lib., Box B/94 Ms. 231. See F. R. H. DuBoulay, 'A Rentier Economy in the later Middle Ages: the Archbishopric of Canterbury', *EcHR*, Ser. 2, 16 (1963–4), 437.

receiver was able to make a determined effort to clear arrears, as in 1514-15, 1517-18 and 1565-6 both the receiver-general's receipts and the bishop's own cash income were noticeably improved. A particularly conscientious official could also make an improvement in the bishop's income by seeking out forgotten rents. In March 1569/70 Grindal specifically acknowledged the pertinacity of his deputy receiver-general, William Marshall, in securing rents from Bishop's Stortford.[13]

Income also rose when manorial courts were held and fines imposed and collected. Manorial court profits varied considerably, but obviously the failure to hold a court would depress the bishop's income. When the seneschal was particularly active court fines would increase significantly; for example, amercements, entry fines for copyholds and heriots collected at Hadham during 1559-60 totalled £46 instead of the usual pound or two, and at Harringay during 1570-1 reached £23 instead of the usual few shillings. Bonner himself was probably personally responsible for imposing the extraordinary fines of £160 and £120 on two men in the manorial court at Fulham in 1556. But any hopes he may have had of thereby increasing his income were vain. Instead of paying, one of his tenants sued him in chancery and later had his fine reduced to £3.6.8. by Grindal's officials.[14]

The bishops could secure a higher proportion of the income from their estates by reducing the fees and expenses of the central officials and cutting down on repairs. The receiver was responsible for payments for certain extra repairs, such as those to the seawall at Clacton and the bridge at Walthamstow in 1527 and the repairs to the bridges at Bishop's Stortford in 1578, and it may have been beyond the power of the bishop to curb the incidence of such expenses.[15] More could be done when the bishop or his collector was directly responsible for repairs. During the 1560s all the profits from the tenements around St Paul's were used for the repairs to the cathedral, which was in urgent need of a new lead roof. The repairs were either completed or abandoned and in the 1570s the bishop received an average of £69 a year from these rents.

13. St Paul's Lib., Registrum Nowell, i, f. 348.
14. SC6/Eliz/1458/4d.; London Guildhall Lib., Ms 10123/5, f. 90; SC6/PM/193/11, C1/1418/29-30, SC6/Eliz/1458/7d.
15. London Guildhall Lib., Ms. 10123/3,f. 35; Ms. 10123/8, f. 28v.

Up to this point we have been considering the receivers' and the bishops' cash receipts. However, rents in kind were also a major source of income accounted for by the receiver-general. Before 1550 the bishops of London had no specified rents in kind, but in the exchange of 1550 Ridley had acquired the rectory of Ashwell and the manors of Stevenage and Greenford and thereby augmented his cash income by annual rents of 244 quarters of malt and thirty quarters of grain. In 1552 Ridley substituted a rent of twenty quarters of wheat for a cash rent of £7 a year for lands in Fulham.[16] Some time before 1556 a similar substitution was made: twenty-one quarters of grain to be paid instead of £8.9.2. for tenements on the demesne at Fulham. This change from cash rents to rents in kind was similar to the 'new' leases being made at this time by Sir Thomas Smith, who proved a far-sighted landlord when provost of Eton. Ridley could only effect marginal change in the value of his diocesan revenues, but in Fulham at least he augmented the value of his temporalities by increasing the proportion of rents in kind, particularly important in a period of rapid inflation.[17]

It is clear that despite inevitable arrears these rents were a very important addition to the bishop's cash income. Bonner seems to have received most of his rents in kind in the famine year of 1556 but the receiver also bought a further seventeen quarters of grain at £1.7.2. a quarter. He may have been lucky to do so when the general average wheat price for that year was over £1.11.0. a quarter. In 1556 the rents in grain were probably worth over £90. In that year the bishop accepted £43 in lieu of arrears of forty-one quarters of malt.[18] At this rate of £1.0.11. a quarter his rents in malt from Stevenage and Ashwell were worth over £255. Although the tables recording the fluctuations in grain prices are some guide in estimating the value of the bishops' rents in kind, their cash values cannot be tabulated exactly because we do not know what sort of grain and malt was delivered to the bishop's household or the exact prices he paid in any year except 1556. If the bishop received all the rents in kind due to him, they were the

16. St Paul's Lib., Registrum Sampson f. 249v; SC6/PM/193/11d.

17. M. Dewar, *Sir Thomas Smith* (1964), pp. 69, 185; and see P. Bowden, 'Agricultural Prices, Farm Profits and Rents', *The Agrarian History of England and Wales*, iv (1967), ed. J. Thirsk, p. 683.

18. SC6/PM/194/2-2d.; W. G. Hoskins, 'Harvest Fluctuations and English Economic History, 1480-1619', *Ag. Hist. Rev.*, 12 (1964), 36, 45.

equivalent of a cash income of at least £125 and, in a year of dearth, of more than £300.

In other dioceses, as well as the rents in kind accounted for by the receiver, further rents in kind were payable to the bishop personally. Indeed, in the diocese of Ely the bishop could rely on produce from his demesne not only to supply his household but also to give him a cash profit.[19] The bishops of London had no such valuable demesne lands. Of the forty-eight properties outside the city of London which at one time or another between 1540 and 1570 belonged to them, on only three were demesne lands reserved for the bishop's own use.

Bonner may have lived at Fulham, but the lands of the demesne still 'in hand', and not let, were worth only £1.6.8. a year. At Hadham perhaps thirty-one acres, together with the manor house, were reserved for the bishop. The bailiff there repaired the house, manured the fields and saw to the haymaking on the bishop's meadows. Grindal may have been able to maintain his household from the produce of the manor when he visited Hadham but he probably did not receive substantial provisions from the manor when he was resident in London: in 1565 he leased the watermill at Hadham for a rent which was to be paid in wheat if he were at the manor but otherwise in cash.[20] It is thus unlikely that demesne produce significantly reduced the costs of any Tudor bishop of London. Bonner certainly had to spend cash on provisions: in 1556 his old friend, Thomas Sherle, and the receiver-general spent £78 on grain, cattle and sheep for the use of the household.[21]

Besides receiving rents in kind which the receivers noted in their accounts, the bishops of London also had an income from entry fines and sales of timber. Except in 1556 this income rarely came to the attention of the receivers, and may indeed be described as 'private' income. Unlike fines for entry into copyholds which were determined in the manorial courts and therefore accounted for by the bailiffs to the receiver, entry fines for leases by indenture were negotiated with the bishops and paid to them personally. Although about 170 episcopal leases have survived for the period 1540 to 1570 none of them gives a figure or a rate for the entry fine. Nor is it possible to guess the amount of the entry fines from

19. Heal, 'Ely', pp. 208–9, 216.
20. SC6/PM/193/11; St Paul's Lib., Registrum Nowell, i, f. 144.
21. SC6/PM/193/18; SC6/PM/194/2d.

the incidence of leases because they were for varying terms of years and for properties of greatly differing value. Another difficulty in arriving at an estimate of the value of the entry fines is that when leases were granted to relatives and friends the entry fines may have been waived or reduced. However, two unrelated pieces of evidence hint that entry fines for leases on episcopal lands were substantial. In 1539 the bailiff of Greenford paid the last abbot of Westminster £100 as a fine for the renewal of his lease for property for which he paid £8 a year and thirty quarters of corn. In 1556 the receiver-general noted payments of £30 in fines to alienate and enter into a lease at Knowle in Warwickshire. This was perhaps only part payment, as the lease was not signed until after the end of the accounting year. Nor do the accounts refer to any other fines for leases by indenture, although at least seven other leases were made by the bishop in the year ending Michaelmas 1556.[22] Such fragmentary evidence forbids firm conclusions, but it provides an indication of a significant income from entry fines.

There is rather more evidence about the cash which the bishops received from sales of timber. Bonner sold wood in 1541 for a total of £60 and in 1547 for £30. Ridley in 1551 made two sales which yielded £86. In 1556 the receiver noted income from three timber sales which totalled £106, and Bonner also made another timber sale of £40 which was not recorded by the receiver.[23] We do not know whether these sales diminished the capital value of the see. Of the seven manors from which Bonner and Ridley had made a profit on timber, two were taken by the crown in 1559. Grindal sold timber in 1560 and 1566 but as he sold it by the row or acre felled we cannot tell how much cash he received.[24]

1555–6 is the only year in which some figures have survived in the receiver's accounts of the bishop's 'private' income. In that year Bonner's receipts from entry fines and sales of wood were over £176, more than 14 per cent of the receiver's total receipts and over 16 per cent of the bishop's own recorded cash income. 1556 was a year of exceptionally bad harvests and high prices, and the bishop and the receiver may have tried to tap all possible sources of revenue. Cash payments to the bishops for entry fines

22. C1/1078/24; SC6/PM/194/2; St Paul's Lib., Registrum Sampson, ff. 239v, 331v–339.
23. Ibid., ff. 105v, 182v, 230, 239v, 333v; SC6/PM/194/2.
24. St Paul's Lib., Registrum Nowell, i, ff. 66, 175v.

and sales of wood could be a considerable addition to the cash income they were assigned by the receivers.

Although the gross value of the see and the bishops' net cash income increased in the sixteenth century, and although the bishops' rents in kind and 'private' cash income were substantial, their income did not rise in real terms. On the contrary, they suffered painfully from the effects of inflation. In the absence of any household accounts it is impossible to separate how much the bishops spent on food from their spending on luxuries and manufactured goods. We have already shown that the bishops of London, unlike bishops in other parts of the country, were not able to live on the produce of their demesne lands and were forced to spend a considerable proportion of their income on food. The separate indices of the prices of foodstuffs and industrial products cannot, therefore, be used in estimating the real value of the bishops' income. Indeed, the real value of the bishops' net cash income cannot be calculated exactly, although it is possible to draw some tentative conclusions by comparing the table of net cash income in inverse proportion to the movement of the Phelps Brown and Hopkins's composite consumables' index.[25]

The figures in column 4 of Table 1 suggest that between 1563 and 1569 the bishop's net cash income may have been worth, in purchasing power, approximately 40 per cent of what his predecessor had received between 1515 and 1518. It is conceivable that the Elizabethan bishops' rents in kind and unaccounted entry fines and profits from timber sales augmented his income by as much as £350 a year. Even so, when Grindal's net cash income in the late 1560s is increased by this amount, his real income was probably worth less than 60 per cent of what his predecessor had received before 1520. The improvement in real income in the early 1570s had evaporated by 1580. In that year the bishop's cash income was probably worth only 37 per cent of what it had been sixty years before. In the unlikely event that his 'private' income added 15 per cent to his cash receipts and that his rents in kind were worth £300, his total income was still probably worth less than half his predecessor's cash receipts in 1518. Finally, it must be

25. E. H. Phelps Brown and S. V. Hopkins, 'Seven Centuries of the Price of Consumables compared with Builders' Wage Rates', *Economica*, n. s., 23 (1956), 312. See also their 'Wage-rates and Prices', *Economica*, n.s., 24 (1957), 306.

remembered that, even if the decline in the real income of the bishops of London was not as severe as has been suggested, it was a decline at a time when some lay landlords were increasing their cash income from leasehold tenures and entry fines by at least 50 per cent, and thereby maintaining their real income.[26] Bonner's complaint that he was hard up was an understatement.

The rigidities of leasehold and copyhold tenure on their manors made it difficult for the bishops to improve the long-term profitability of the see. They had little opportunity to take profits from direct farming and seemed able to change only a fraction of their cash rents into rents in kind. The bishops, faced with this difficult financial situation, compounded their problems by their own actions. Like many other Tudor bishops, such as Warham of Canterbury or Goodrich of Ely, they were more concerned with their families.[27] As bishop of London for sixteen years, Bonner had more chance than Ridley to milk the see for the benefit of his relatives.

In a lease which confirmed the grant of a house in Fulham to his mother, sister and niece, Bonner declared that he was 'straightlie bounde by goddes lawe to take care of all thoes that be myne and specially of thoes that be of the same house whereof I am'. Bonner made at least thirty-two leases for properties worth more than £5 a year. Of these, nineteen leases and reversions were made to his relatives and friends and none was for a term of less than forty years. He showed particular favour to his two nephews, Thomas Parsons and Philip Mountjoy, to Philip's son William, and to his friends the Lechmere brothers, involving them closely in the management of the episcopal estates as well as giving them property. Apart from granting one lease to Somerset for lands in Fulham worth £6.8.4. for 200 years, Bonner seems to have preserved his estates from predators among the nobility.[28] He himself was the predator, establishing his family's fortunes at the expense of the diocese and preventing his successors from renewing leases or from levying entry fines.

26. A. Simpson, *The Wealth of the Gentry, 1540–1640* (1963), p. 207; E. Kerridge, 'The Movement of Rent, 1540–1640', *EcHR*, Ser. 2, 6 (1953–4), 23–5.
27. F. R. H. DuBoulay, 'Who were Farming the English Demesnes at the End of the Middle Ages', *EcHR*, Ser. 2, 17 (1965), 451–2; Heal, 'Ely', p. 211.
28. St Paul's Lib., Registrum Sampson, ff. 165, 200.

Bonner enabled his relatives to take the profits from direct farming and he also gave them a share in the future value of the properties. In 1546, for example, Bonner leased the manor house at Stepney to Parsons for just under £20 a year to hold from 1568. Stepney was surrendered to the crown in 1550 but in 1564 Parsons was able to sell his rights in the reversion for a 'compotente somme of money'. In 1587 Edmund Lechmere received £120 for his share in the reversion of the manor of Fering which Bonner had granted him in 1556 to hold from 1604.[29]

Bonner did suffer one setback. In 1545 he granted the reversion of the manor of Southminster for forty-one years from 1573 to Parsons and his sisters for their 'prefermente and advauncement'. Southminster was one of the four manors surrendered to the crown in 1550. Despite Mary's confirmation of the lands Ridley had received from the crown, Bonner made strenuous efforts in 1555 and 1558 to get Southminster back, arguing 'I never did any acte wherby in lawe I have foregone theym'. Bonner may have been anxious not only to secure the income from this valuable manor for himself but also to ensure his nephew's rights. To no avail. On Elizabeth's accession a private act of parliament confirmed the grant Ridley had made of these manors to the crown.[30]

Bonner blatantly justified the favours he lavished on his family. Ridley tried to be more discreet. In 1551 he leased the parks of Ridmerley and Bushley in Worcestershire to his secretary George Carr who then conveyed the lease, through assignees, to Ridley's sister and brother-in-law. Ridley's affection for his sister could not be concealed for long: on his reinstatement Bonner ignored Ridley's lease and made his own disposition of the parks. These conflicting family ambitions resulted in a dispute which was aired in the parliament of 1559, considered by the court of requests and by king's bench and by chancery between 1559 and 1563, by the privy council in 1591, and finally resolved by statute in 1593.[31]

Nor was Grindal immune from the temptations offered by the temporalities of the see. Grindal's reputation at York was of a man

29. St Paul's Lib., Registrum Nowell, i, f. 104; Hereford and Worcestershire Rec. Off., Lechmere Ms 705: 134 BA 1531/7 (ii).

30. St Paul's Lib., Registrum Sampson, f. 148v; *CSP Span.*, xiii, 134; Inner Temple Lib., Petyt Ms. 538/47 f. 3; House of Lords Rec. Off., 1 Eliz. 1 cap. 25.

31. St Paul's Lib., Registrum Sampson, f. 251v; *CJ*, i, 55; *LJ*, i, 577; C1/1397/1, Req 2/36/52/1, C78/27/17/18–22; *APC*, *1590–1591*, pp. 292–3; *APC*, *1591*, pp. 52–3, 60–61, D'Ewes, *Journal*, pp. 491, 496, 500–501.

greedy for the welfare of his family. In London, before he was prevented by act of parliament from making leases of over 21 years,
he signed five leases in 1560 for terms between 55 and 70 years.[32]
At the beginning of his episcopate he may have attempted to
change some of the tenancies-at-will and copyhold tenures at
Hadham to leaseholds, possibly in order to exact entry fines.[33]
But Grindal had little room for manoeuvre. He found that, of the
seventeen manors remaining to the see, Bonner had made leases
or reversions on seven of them, six to relatives, which would preclude any major alteration of tenure or tenant until 1589 at the
earliest.[34] Three other manors were encumbered by long leases
made by the abbot and bishop of Westminster. The seven other
properties were administered for the bishop by bailiffs who collected rents from free and copyhold tenants. Difficult as Grindal's
situation was, he might nevertheless have tried to take a new look
at the management of the lands and revenues of the see, possibly
pursuing much more vigorously Ridley's precedent of changing
cash rents to rents in kind. Grindal's doctrinal position differed
radically from Bonner's, but there was little to choose between
them, or Ridley, in their approach to the temporalities.

What final conclusion can be drawn? First of all, it is clear that
the bishops of London had escaped the crown's plunder of episcopal wealth relatively unscathed. The crown was partly responsible for the difficulties of the bishops of London, but the
income of all bishops and higher clergy was diminished by royal
taxation. Unlike Bath and Wells, York, Lincoln or Coventry and
Lichfield, the revenues of London were not depleted by Henry
VIII or Edward VI. If Grindal suffered at the beginning of
Elizabeth's reign so did at least ten other bishops. He retained the
same cash income and avoided paying such rents to the crown as
were imposed on the bishops of Durham and Winchester.[35]
    The receiver-general's accounts show beyond all doubt that the
cash income of the bishop of London improved between 1520 and

32. C. Hill, *Economic Problems of the Church* (1956), p. 19; St Paul's Lib., Registrum Sampson, ff. 393v, 394, 401v, 402v, 405.
    33. E.g., ibid., ff. 404, 406.
    34. Ibid., ff. 146, 109v, 166, 296, 348, 350. The crown also found that on nine
of the manors surrendered to it in 1559 Bonner's leases would run until between
1587 and 1655.
    35. Heal, 'Act of Exchange', p. 240.

1580. And yet Bonner's complaint had substance. We may conclude with some confidence that the real income of the bishops of London was drastically reduced not by the direct action of the crown but by inflation. The bishop could no longer maintain his 'place' or show that hospitality and liberality which was expected of him. Finally, neither Bonner, Ridley nor Grindal made any serious attempt to find long-term solutions to their problems. In this analysis of the economic problems of the diocese the role of bishops may seem relatively minor, but their actions made a difficult situation worse. All three bishops looked to their own, and Bonner, in particular, took both present and future income of the see for his family at the expense of his successors.[36]

36. I am grateful to my husband for helping me with this paper.

VIII

Episcopal Palaces, 1535 to 1660[1]

PHYLLIS HEMBRY

'It standith stately'—Leland's view of an episcopal palace reflected an aspect of Tudor England where the numerous residences
of the bishops were almost as familiar a part of the scene as the
monastic houses. Major episcopal palaces were imposing piles of
masonry flanked, like Durham, by the cathedral, but most were
only fortified manor-houses such as the modest red-sandstone
Bosbury in Herefordshire. Spread the length and breadth of the
land, from defensive Norham guarding the border for the bishop
of Durham against the Scots to Egloshayle in Cornwall, a retreat
of the bishops of Exeter, there were still about 177 habitable homes
for twenty-one English and Welsh bishops, compared with 825
monastic buildings when the Reformation parliament met. Today there are forty-three episcopal palaces among forty-two
bishops, Canterbury alone having two.[2]

The principal palaces, of which a bishop might have more than
one, were frequently situated on a hill or an artificial mound,
both for grandeur and defence. Beaudesert in Staffordshire had a
view of nine counties and Bishop Auckland, one of the favourite
castles of the bishop of Durham, was on a hill, as were Bishop
Middleham in Yorkshire, Blockley in Worcestershire, and
Bishop's Castle in Shropshire which, in Leland's words, was 'set
on a strong rock'. Only the exceptions were on low ground, like

---

1. The main sources for this study are *VCH*; N. Pevsner *et al.*, *The Buildings of
England* (Harmondsworth, 1951–74); S. Lewis, *Topographical Dictionary of England*
(1840) and *Topographical Dictionary of Wales* (1840); W. Camden, *Britannia*, ed.
R. Gough (1789); J. Leland, *Itinerary*, ed. T. Hearne (Oxford, 1769); *Valor
Ecclesiasticus*, ed. J. Caley and J. Hunter (1810). I am grateful to Mr P. A. Faulkner
for a helpful discussion of this subject, and to Mr H. A. Hanley and Mr K. C.
Newton the county archivists of Buckinghamshire and Essex for answering
queries.

2. A. G. Dickens, *The English Reformation* (1964), p. 51; *Daily Telegraph*, 4 Dec.
1974.

Bishop's Stortford in Hertfordshire, placed to command the ford over the Stort, and Sleaford in Lincolnshire, protected by a surrounding stream from a cut in the fen.

There were about 1000 deer parks in England and many of these were episcopal. Bishops may well have had parks in manors where they had no palaces, but it would be a fair assumption that all their homes were in a parkland setting. The bishop of Hereford had parks at Ross, where in the fourteenth century there were at least 800 deer, and at Prestbury, which was invaded in 1516 by poachers who hunted the deer with bows and arrows and killed two keepers. Moats were another common feature of these 'palaces', underlining their defensive and exclusive position and contributing to the drainage of the site. The moat still exists at Wells in Somerset, as do the outlines of the deep but empty one at Sherborne in Dorset. Other moated sites included Eccleshall in Staffordshire, Hartlebury in Worcestershire and Riccall in Yorkshire, where the magnificent manor-house was surrounded by a triple moat.[3]

The major residences at least were nearly always on a river, as Maidstone was on the Medway, Newark on the Trent, and Stockton on the Tees, and so flooding was one of their hazards, as Bishop West of Ely found in 1520 when stranded at Somersham in Huntingdonshire. The countryside was inundated, so that he could leave only by boat. Five hundred men were working on the banks which were in imminent danger of collapse, and a hundred more stood by to ring the bells for night alarm. Waterways had been an important consideration in the building of these palaces to ease the transport of bulky and heavy materials. Rivers also solved the problems of sanitation and, however unhygienically, sometimes of water supplies, and provided routes for the ferrying of household provisions, and visitors, servants and messengers. The first stage of many an episcopal journey must have been by boat. Wolsey was not the only ecclesiastic with a home, Hampton Court, on the Thames: the bishop of Salisbury also had, in Leland's words, 'a fair old house of stone' at Sonning, from which he made the last lap of his journeys to London.

The main clutch of a bishop's residences was within his diocese,

3. T. Allen, *A new and complete history of the county of York* (1828–31), ii, 357; *Diocese of Hereford, Extracts from the Cathedral Registers, 1275–1535*, ed. E. N. Dew (1932), pp. 68, 143.

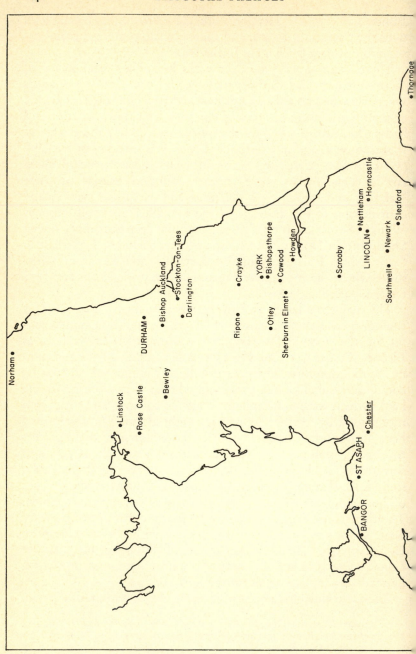

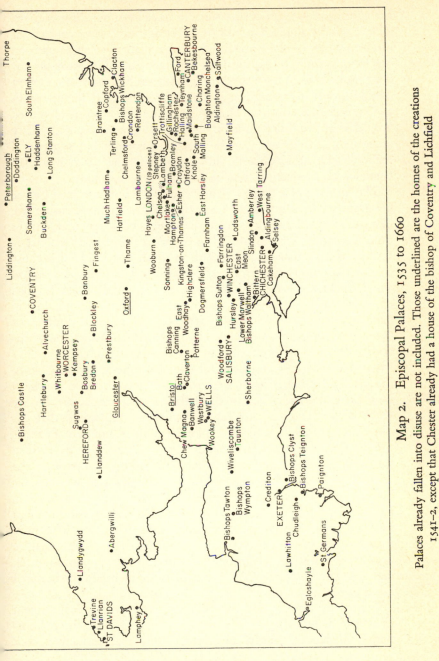

Map 2. Episcopal Palaces, 1535 to 1660

Palaces already fallen into disuse are not included. Those underlined are the homes of the creations 1541–2, except that Chester already had a house of the bishop of Coventry and Lichfield but some homes seem at first sight to have been puzzling outliers. These, usually modest mansions, were administrative centres for distant estates, or they provided a convenient overnight base on the long journey to London which faced the bishops of the far west and north. The bishop of Exeter toiling up from Devon could sojourn at Farringdon and his neighbour of Bath and Wells at Dogmersfield, both in Hampshire. The first stop of Hereford would be at Prestbury under the lee of the Cotswolds, and of Ely at Somersham. When Carlisle reached his plain but substantial manor-house at Horncastle in Lincolnshire he must have reflected with satisfaction that his journey was half done.

The location of a bishop's palaces was often determined by the geographical distribution of his estates. Those in an extensive see, like Lincoln, were widely scattered over several counties, but in other cases they were confined to one shire. There was a concentration of episcopal landed wealth in south-east England because of the proximity of the richest bishoprics, Canterbury, London and Winchester—and Chichester. Out of a total of 168 English episcopal palaces forty-four were in the south-east, notably in Kent, which was endowed with the astonishing number of seventeen, but Hampshire came close with eleven. When the south-west with its conglomeration of twenty-five is added, as well as Middlesex with five and London with the nineteen town houses, the preponderance of episcopal homes, ninety-three, in southern England is marked. Clearly the balance of episcopal wealth lay south of the Thames, although it must be emphasised that the discussion here is of habitable episcopal homes, not of manors.

The third largest concentration of palaces was in eastern England, especially in Essex, where the bishop of London held seven. By contrast the seven northern counties had only twenty between them: Yorkshire boasted eight, but there was none in Lancashire. Eight west midland counties had twenty, and ten east midland ones were the least favoured part of England with only thirteen palaces. There was none in Bedfordshire, Leicestershire or Nottinghamshire. The four Welsh bishoprics, the poorest of all, had but nine houses in Wales, but three of them also possessed a London residence; only St Asaph did not.

Canterbury was by far the best endowed, with a magnificent choice of twenty-one homes. Of these, three (Canterbury, Lambeth and Knole) might be termed principal residences, but

Charing, Croydon, Otford and Saltwood were hardly less important. Archbishop Cranmer's 'great exchange' with Henry VIII, by which he was deprived of eight of these homes, seems the more rational in the light of this extraordinary total. Next were Winchester with fifteen, Exeter with fourteen, and London with twelve. Exeter's wealth, which included eight palaces in Devon, seems to have been an undue accumulation for a bishopric of the middle rank. There followed Lincoln, with eleven; York, Ely, and Bath and Wells, ten; Norwich, nine, Durham and Coventry and Lichfield, eight; Hereford, Salisbury and Worcester, seven; Carlisle and Chichester, six each; and Rochester, with only four.

All the English and Welsh bishops except St Asaph had a London palace. A metropolitan base was a necessary adjunct of their office, for most of them were frequently involved in the affairs of state. Their London homes were often called 'inns', not to be confused with taverns, and several, such as Bath Inn, Chester Inn (belonging to Coventry and Lichfield), Worcester Inn, and the homes of Durham, Norwich, Llandaff and Carlisle were in the Strand. Salisbury Place, the most important house in Fleet Street, was the grandest, but Ely Inn was also part of a large episcopal estate in Holborn with an orchard and garden where roses could be gathered by the bushel. Winchester House in Southwark was a sumptuous home with gardens of sixty or seventy acres and a large landing place called the Bishop of Winchester's Stairs.[4]

Medieval bishops had been even better endowed. At least twenty palaces were out of use by Tudor times and had fallen into ruin, so there were about two hundred in the later middle ages. The bishop of Salisbury in particular was worse off, having lost three of his Wiltshire homes: Devizes, which was to have been his premier palace, was already in decay, Edington had been destroyed during Cade's rebellion in 1450, and Woodford was pulled down between 1535 and 1539. The bishop of London had abandoned his hunting lodge at Hornsey, a moated, square building with a drawbridge where Henry Tudor had met a deputation of

4. J. Stow, *A survey of London*, ed. W. B. Wheatley (1956), p. 212; Marjorie B. Honeybourne, 'The extent and value of the property in London and Southwark occupied by the religious houses *etc.*' (London Univ. M.A. thesis, 1931). Southwark was, of course, part of the diocese of Winchester.

London citizens in 1485. About fifteen years later the site was reputedly rifled for stone to build the parish church.[5] Archbishop Islip, when faced by the ruin of Wrotham by pestilence, had the palace there pulled down in 1352 and the materials carted to Maidstone to complete a new building begun by Archbishop Ufford.[6]

Some retrenchment in resources was logical by the sixteenth century: castles in England had become 'relics of a lawless past'. They were anachronisms in view of advances in military technology, except those newly built for specific purposes. Even the more modest mansions of the bishops had to be repaired, maintained and guarded. The crown had a similar problem with its enormous collection of obsolescent castles. Lord Treasurer Winchester in 1561 conducted a survey of superfluous buildings, and in 1609 the exchequer again reviewed sixty crown castles, all of which, with a few exceptions, were found to be 'very ruinous' and 'utterly decayed'. There was no need to level the site of an abandoned episcopal home: the shaped stones and the roofing materials were so valuable that the plundering locals took their share. Nature, with the nettles and bushes, did the rest.[7]

Reduction by the bishops was, however, on a comparatively small scale and was more than off-set by the staggering amount of new building of a more domestic kind on which they embarked on the eve of the Reformation. Of forty-one cases of work on palaces in the fifteenth and early sixteenth centuries, thirty-one, that is, about 75 per cent, can be attributed to the years 1470–1535, so almost a sixth of the episcopal homes were being improved at this period. Despite earlier Lollard criticisms of episcopal wealth, and obviously confident of the morrow, bishops put in hand what in total amounted to a massive investment of labour and materials. Most of this activity was in the form of embellishments or additions to existing buildings and it amply supports Professor Du Boulay's description of the fifteenth century as 'an age of improvement'. As he has shown, the receivers' accounts for the

5. J. H. Lloyd, *The history, topography and antiquities of Highgate* (1888), pp. 36–7. I am grateful to Prof. R. B. Pugh for this reference.

6. F. R. H. Du Boulay, *The Lordship of Canterbury* (1966), p. 239; S. Bagshaw, *History, Gazeteer & Directory of Kent* (1847), i, 52.

7. H. M. Colvin, 'Castles and Government in Tudor England', *EHR*, 83 (1968), 225ff.

Canterbury estates are full of details of repairs: judging by the visible evidence, this must have been so in other episcopal estates.[8]

The erection of a gatehouse was a typical improvement, as at Slindon in Sussex, Cawood in Yorkshire and Sonning in Berkshire, where excavations in 1916 revealed evidence of a late fifteenth-century gatehouse as well as an earlier great hall. Sonning was not the only home even at this late date to have such a fundamental unit as the great hall built: so did Hartlebury in Worcestershire and Norham in Northumberland which had other improvements. At Rose Castle in Cumberland, the chief residence of Carlisle, a tower and a chapel were constructed *c.* 1488 and a second tower in 1522–4. Bishop's Waltham in Hampshire had buildings thought to be the bakehouse and brewhouse added in the late fifteenth century.

Nor was the activity, of which these are but a few examples, only that of patching and enlargement. The number and scale of entirely new building projects suggest an episcopate confident in its resources and sure of its destiny. For five hundred years the manor-house at Downham in Cambridgeshire had been a main Ely residence, but by 1356 it was ruinous. Bishop Alcock (1486–1500) decided to reconstruct a two-storeyed palace in red brick with blue brick diapering and stone dressings, and he was simultaneously rebuilding his principal palace, Ely, in the same idiom. Alcock's contemporary, Rotherham of York, made a new range at Bishopsthorpe using the same kind of red brick with vitrified diaper patterns. He added to the monumental palace at Southwell, and he had already left his mark as bishop of Lincoln (1471–80) when he substantially altered the hall at Newark and began an extensive building programme, carried on by his successors, at Buckden.

The bishops seem to have emulated each other in the grandiose scale of their building: master masons' plans and costs must have occupied much of their thoughts. Waynflete of Winchester about 1475–80 erected the three-storeyed Esher Place, and may have established the fashion for red brick with blue brick diapering, since his venture was earlier than those of Alcock and Rotherham. He also added the tower to Farnham in Surrey. Sherburne of Chichester (1508–36) improved the manor-house at Cakeham and built or enlarged that nearby at Selsey.

8. Du Boulay, op. cit., p. 239.

The pattern for new building on a truly palatial scale had been set by the primate of all England himself when Bourchier bought the manor of Knole in 1456, patched up the old manor-house, and also embarked on the fashioning of a great palace of Kentish ragstone. He apparently started on this house almost immediately, for by 1467 it was sufficiently finished for repairs to the roofs to become necessary and the building of a new tower to be put in hand.[9] His successors, Morton and Warham, also spent considerable sums there. Perhaps because Knole was constructed in the now old-fashioned ragstone rather than brick, Warham embarked on the extravagance of another building enterprise only three miles away at Otford. There he had inherited the manor-house repaired by Archbishop Dene (1501–3), parts of which were uncovered in an excavation in 1974. Warham destroyed nearly all of it and erected a palace of brick, which was in use by 1518. He called it his power-house, and well he might for it cost £33,000 and was said in its heyday to have rivalled Hampton Court. To Erasmus, who visited him at Otford, Warham said with feeling, 'stones are heavy carriage, as I know to my cost when I want them for building purposes'. The primate had over-reached himself: his fine new houses excited the envy of Henry VIII, who later demanded both, although Cranmer strove to retain Knole. Ralph Morice, one of Canterbury's estate wardens, was present when Henry debated their respective merits: the king preferred Knole for its more wholesome position and decided that he would occasionally stay there while his household lay at Otford. So the archbishop lost both homes.[10]

Yet Warham was but aping Archbishop Morton, the master builder of all bishops. For fourteen years he was the most important subject in the kingdom and his building activities were commensurate with his power. He had, while bishop of Ely, rebuilt the ruinous Wisbech Castle and what was later known as the 'old palace' at Hatfield. Now he improved Croydon, a favourite summer residence, and also repaired Maidstone; he was responsible for almost all of Ford, much of Lambeth, and some work at Aldington Park and Canterbury. His contemporary, Richard Fox,

9. P. A. Faulkner, 'Some Medieval Archiepiscopal Palaces', *Arch. Journ.*, 127 (1970), 140ff.

10. C. Hesketh, 'The Manor House and Great Park etc. at Otford', *Arch. Cant.*, 31 (1915), 1–24; C. P. Ward, 'Emergency Excavations at Otford Palace, 1974', *Arch. Cant.*, 89 (1974), 199–203; DuBoulay, op. cit., p. 324.

who promoted the work on the great kitchen of Durham and the extension of its great hall, was said to have been 'a good surveyor of works'. The same might be said of Morton.

Outclassing all episcopal building was Thomas Wolsey's great enterprise at Hampton Court. No other house then built in England, except perhaps Otford, was of the scale of this new palace of the archbishop of York. Some 2500 artisans and labourers were employed in its construction. Chalk was carried from Taplow and Windsor and timber from Reigate, lime came from Lime-house and bricks from the kilns at Battersea. The moat, one of the last to be dug in England, enclosed extensive gardens and mazes, and the parks were some 2000 acres.[11]

Of the materials for these palaces brick had suddenly become the most prestigious. South-east of the belt of oolitic limestone running from Dorset to the North Riding bricks and tiles were displacing the traditional timber and thatch of many homes. As we have seen, English bishops were pacemakers in the employ-ment of bricks two or three decades before they came into general use about 1500, but generally speaking building materials were still, because of their weight and bulk, drawn in from compara-tively short distances of ten or twelve miles.[12] The extensive quarries of Kentish ragstone in the episcopal manor of Boughton Monchelsea supplied the material for the building of Knole. The bishop of Exeter owned large limestone quarries at Bishop's Teignton where he had a mansion and at Chudleigh, the site of a sumptuous palace. Hereford had been able to build his manor-house of limestone at Prestbury in Gloucestershire from the near-by quarry in the Cotswolds.[13] In default of stone, timber had to be employed, as at Scrooby in Nottinghamshire, where York had 'an ancient abode of splendour and hospitality' built nearly all of timber.[14]

The functions for which an episcopal palace was built were manifold: it had to be a stately residence, worthy of an occupant who played a major part in the life of the nation. Defence, Mr

11. C. H. Ferguson, *Naked to mine enemies: the life of Cardinal Wolsey* (Boston, 1958), pp. 221–7.
12. *The Historical Geography of England before 1800*, ed. H. C. Darby (Cambridge, 1936), p. 343.
13. H. E. O'Neil, 'Prestbury Moat, A Manor House of the Bishops of Hereford', *Trans. Bristol and Glos. Arch. Soc.*, 75 (1956), 14.
14. F. and J. White, *History, Directory and Gazeteer of Nottingham* (1844), p. 649.

Faulkner has argued, was a less important consideration for ecclesiastics protected by their rank, and so the domestic demands of
their private palaces were paramount over the military. Despite
the prevalence of moats, massive curtain walls, and imposing,
deterrent gateways, it was only in exceptional cases that bishops'
homes had a military role. The outstanding example of a defensive stronghold is Norham in Northumberland, which the
bishop of Durham held as an outpost against the Scots. Even as
late as the sixteenth century embrasures for artillery were added to
its defences. These were not superfluous, for just before the
battle of Flodden in 1513 the fortress was attacked and taken by
the Scots. A similar target of the Scots was Rose Castle in Cumberland, the principal residence of Carlisle, who kept a garrison
there. The Scots sacked it repeatedly, killing his deer and empty-
ing his fishponds.

A bishop's palace, then, was both a noble home and sometimes
a fortress: it was also the background for religious ceremonies. In
1381 Archbishop Courtenay received the *pallium* in his manor-
house at Croydon.[15] The ordination of priests frequently took
place wherever the bishop happened to be residing: in the case of
the Elizabethan Bishop Barnes of Durham this was at Durham,
Stockton or Bishop Auckland, where he chiefly lived and where
he died.[16] So an episcopal palace had to be adapted to ritual and
ceremony, with space for long processions and large assemblies
and sufficient chambers to serve as robing rooms. The palace was
also a judicial and administrative centre: the bishops held ecclesiastical courts in their larger residences and some contained prisons
for convicted clerics, as did the palaces at Ross, Wells and Banbury,
which Leland described as 'a terrible prison'. Other palaces were
the nuclei from which groups of episcopal estates were run:
Taunton Castle was such a focus for the bishop of Winchester's
outlying estates in west Somerset.[17]

The constable or keeper of an episcopal palace was a man of
great responsibilities in arranging ceremonies and hospitality: at
Lincoln in 1535 Robert Smythe was paid £3.0.10. a year for this
post. John Wilcox at Exeter had the more generous wage of £8

15. Faulkner, op cit., p. 135.
16. 'The Injunctions and other Ecclesiastical proceedings of Richard Barnes,
bishop of Durham (1577–87)', ed. J. Raine, *Surtees Soc.* 22 (1850), xcviii ff.
17. *The Medieval Customs of the Manors of Taunton and Bradford on Tone*, ed.
T. J. Hunt (Somerset Rec. Soc., 66, 1962), p. xxi.

as well as 8s for every person committed to the bishop's prison, and he was allowed the occupation of a house. The duties of the keeper included the reception of guests who might arrive daily with their parties: in the mid-fourteenth century Archbishop Stratford of Canterbury had important visitors on twenty-six out of forty days.[18] The scale of hospitality at Otley in the next century is indicated by the annual purchase of four score tuns of claret. Entertainment ranged from the reception of monarch and retinue, as when Henry VII and Prince Arthur first met Catherine of Aragon at the bishop of Bath and Wells's palace at Dogmersfield in Hampshire in 1501, to dining local justices, as did the Elizabethan Bishop Freake of Norwich in his manor-house at Ludham.[19]

Much of the pageant of Tudor and Stuart history was played out in episcopal palaces, especially those on the routes to the continent or the north. Henry VII was feasted at York in 1487 and Margaret Tudor was there in 1503, having first been received at Scrooby in Nottinghamshire, and she passed on to Durham on her way to Scotland to marry James IV. Archbishop Morton entertained Henry VII in 1507 at Charing in Kent and Henry VIII and Queen Catherine also slept there, after Otford, with a retinue of five thousand in 1520 on their way to meet Francis I at the Field of Cloth of Gold. Many were the visits to Bishop's Waltham of Henry VIII, Wolsey (who held it briefly as bishop of Winchester, 1529–30), and Thomas Cromwell. The agreement between Charles V and Henry VIII, known as the Treaty of Waltham, was signed there in 1512. The palace at Canterbury was the scene of a splendid state occasion in 1520 when another treaty was under negotiation with Charles V, who attended a ball and danced with Queen Catherine, and in 1544 Henry dined at Ford in Kent with Cranmer.[20] The Surrey palaces, easy of access from the capital, were particularly favoured by royal visits. Henry VIII was at Farnham twice in 1531, Mary was entertained there by Bishop Gardiner on her way to Winchester to marry Philip of Spain, and Elizabeth I was often a guest.

The dissolution of the monasteries destroyed many former

18. REQ 2/14/75; Du Boulay, op. cit., p. 259.
19. A. Hassell Smith, *County and Court, Government and Politics in Norfolk, 1558–1603* (Oxford, 1974), p. 226.
20. S. Bagshaw, *Kent*, ii, 57–8.

centres of hospitality: the only buildings of sufficient scale to accommodate the court on progress now were the crown castles, but some of them were ruinous, and the noble and episcopal palaces. The bishops' homes, on which on the eve of the Reformation so much had been lavished in improvements and new building, were desirable places in which to stay. Elizabeth certainly thought so: in 1573 alone, in addition to visiting Farnham, she was entertained by Archbishop Parker at Canterbury, she was at Croydon in Surrey for a week, and at Mayfield in Sussex, which belonged by then to the financier, Sir Thomas Gresham. She was the guest of Bishop Bullingham at Hartlebury in Worcestershire, and even the minor episcopal homes received royal visits. She was entertained by Bishop Cox of Ely at Long Stanton in 1564, and in 1578, during the episcopate of Aylmer of London, the manorhouse of Much Hadham in Hertfordshire stirred into activity when she arrived and held a privy council attended by such notabilities as Lord Treasurer Burghley and the earls of Leicester and Warwick.[21]

By the time Elizabeth was journeying round the bishops' homes some fundamental changes had occurred. This is not the place to enlarge on the general impact of the Reformation on the episcopate but it certainly affected the palaces. There was, first, the great debate on the amount and kind of ecclesiastical wealth to confiscate. It is now well known that the discussion in the 1530s ranged around schemes to confiscate both monastic and also cathedral, that is episcopal and capitular, endowments, or, alternatively to take the surplus wealth of the bishops and trim the rest to an agreed figure for each see. In the event both wholesale and partial seizure was abandoned, but unofficially and intermittently well into Elizabeth's reign pressure was put on the episcopate to part with manors outright or on lease to the crown or its favourites.[22] In some bishoprics the result was a dramatic loss of wealth: few if any bishops escaped, but Barlow's surrenders at Bath and Wells, Ponet's at Winchester, and those of Holbeach at Lincoln were outstanding. Nor were bishops themselves always innocent. Carew, the historian of Cornwall, described Veysey's conduct at Exeter as an anticipation that cathedral churches would

21. *APC 1577–78*, p. 324.
22. Du Boulay, op. cit., p. 317; P. M. Hembry, *The Bishops of Bath and Wells, 1540–1640* (1967), pp. 59–61, 74.

not long survive the suppressed monasteries; so he gave or leased all away and left a pittance to his successors.[23] The seizure of episcopal estates inevitably involved a loss of bishops' palaces. Veysey gave up thirteen and kept only one, but in anticipation of this event he had already built a brick house for himself, called More Hall, at Sutton Coldfield, where he died.

The episcopate as a whole suffered a marked reduction in the number of its homes and the process of depletion went on until the end of Elizabeth's reign when in 1600 she acquired Somersham from Ely. Some homes confiscated in the mid-century were afterwards recovered: Bath and Wells had lost his splendid palace at Wells to Protector Somerset and had to take refuge in the dean-ery, but his successor retrieved it, just as Winchester repossessed Bishop's Waltham. When all the movements of property had settled down it was clear that none of the principal palaces (ex-cluding Bishopsthorpe, which had been sold to Walter White) had been lost.[24] The secularisation of episcopal homes, marked though it was, left the bishops with their key palaces, but apart from the London properties, where exchanges for other premises were sometimes involved, at least sixty-seven out of 177 had been granted away or almost permanently leased out by the end of Elizabeth's reign. Although the crown had made important gains, such as Banbury (from Lincoln) and Norham (a sacrifice from Durham), the courtiers were most prominent in the roll call of the new owners. Lord Chancellor Audley added to his Essex estates Lambourne and Terling, taken from Norwich. Sir Thomas Wriothesley was building up a complex of ex-monastic estates in Hampshire, including Titchfield (which became his main seat) and so the acquisition of Dogmersfield from Bath and Wells and Farringdon from Exeter followed. Richard, 1st Lord Rich, after he became the chancellor of the court of augmentations, gained Braintree and Chelmsford near his Essex seat of Leighs, and Thomas Cromwell took North Elmham and Mortlake. The mortification of the episcopate in seeing courtiers moving into their homes was underlined when Sir William Paget acquired the mansion of Beaudesert from Coventry and Lichfield and adopted the title Baron Paget of Beaudesert, and John Russell, 1st earl of

23. R. Carew, *The Survey of Cornwall* (1769), p. 81.
24. T. Allen, op. cit., i, 476.

Bedford, lord keeper of the privy seal, as well as robbing Lincoln of Wooburn, took Bishop's Tawton and Bishop's Clyst from Exeter and renamed the later palace Bedford House.[25]

Some uneasiness about this secularisation of episcopal estates is revealed in the action of Sir William Petre, who acquired the manor and park of Crondon in Essex which the bishop of London had kept in demesne for domestic needs. Petre did well out of this estate. In 1548 alone his *ménage* consumed one stag, thirteen bucks and five does, mostly from Crondon Park. Although he denied that he was under any obligation of conscience or law to make redress, nearly a quarter of a century later he made a deed of gift of £100 to the dean and chapter of St Paul's specifically in relation to Crondon so that future bishops could use the income for household provisions and hospitality.[26]

It was time to call a halt: by 1559 the process of secularisation had gone far enough. To secure the new Protestant regime bishops had to stay in their dioceses and attend to their responsibilities and so their homes had to be safeguarded. The act by which Elizabeth I acquired the right of the crown to seize episcopal manors during a vacancy and to have long leases of bishops' estates, a valuable source of patronage for the monarch, significantly exempted any of the mansion houses commonly used as a dwelling by any archbishop or bishop or any demesne lands held with them for the maintenance of hospitality and good housekeeping.[27]

So the first generation of Elizabethan bishops soon repaired to their diocesan homes. By the summer of 1561 letters, some of complaint, came flooding back to the council. Pilkington of Durham, deprived of Norham Castle, which had gone to the crown, asked for a warrant for thirty barrels of salmon from its lessee. None was perhaps louder in his complaints of depredation than Berkeley at Wells, who was left with only eight manors, and of these three which had mansion houses, Banwell, Westbury and Wiveliscombe, were leased out. He was now reduced to only one dwelling, the palace at Wells, and that had been left rifled and

25. W. White, *History, Gazeteer and Directory of Devonshire* (1850), p. 202; REQ 2/14/75; S. R. Gammon, *Statesman and Schemer: William, First Lord Paget—Tudor Minister* (Newton Abbot, 1973), p. 114. I am grateful to Dr G. A. Alexander for the Chelmsford reference.

26. F. G. Emmison, *Tudor secretary: Sir William Petre at court and home* (1961), pp. 133, 137, 285–6.

27. 1 Eliz. c. 19.

ruinous by his Catholic predecessor, Bishop Bourne, so that he had to fell sixty-one trees for timber for its repair.[28]

Yet, despite the exempting clause in the act of 1559, such were the financial needs of the crown that the plunder of the bishops' homes went on. The crown took and held some, like Sonning in 1574, which in 1610 became part of the endowment of the prince of Wales, and Somersham in 1600. To name but a few among the Elizabethan courtiers, the earl of Leicester appropriated Prestbury in Gloucestershire, Sir Thomas Sackville began his family's long association with Knole, Sir Thomas Gresham lorded it at Mayfield and often entertained the queen there, and Lord Norreys acquired Dorchester near his home at Rycote. The culmination came when Sir Walter Raleigh, seeking a west country base for his power and thwarted in his attempt to deprive Bath and Wells of Wiveliscombe, in 1592 took that proud outlier of the Salisbury estates, Sherborne Castle in Dorset. More significant still for the future was Sir Robert Cecil's acquisition in 1607 of the bishop of Ely's old palace at Hatfield, which had been a crown possession since 1549.

Another way in which bishops' homes were affected by the Reformation was that they now had to house families. It is unlikely that the households of medieval bishops contained any women: none is mentioned in the will of Bishop Rich of Chichester (d. 1253), who left bequests to his entourage.[29] Now in Edward VI's reign the clergy were allowed to marry, and, rather grudgingly, again by Elizabeth I, and so accommodation had to be found for wives and children, and sometimes for in-laws as well. No doubt the majority of episcopal wives were devout women who behaved with decorum, and the great complex of chambers and antechambers in the major palaces easily absorbed them. One gets teasing glimpses of them, as when Bishop Parkhurst of Norwich died at his country seat at Ludham in 1575, and among the inventory of his goods were those of his wife, including gowns, gorgets, a mantle, a petticoat and a hood of cloth; also three lady's saddles and their harness, and a petticoat of his daughter Anne. We also see Mrs Cox managing her husband's dairy at Ely and driving hard bargains over episcopal cheese and butter, and the termagant Mrs Freake of Norwich, whom the

28. *CSP Dom.*, *1547–80*, pp. 172, 176; SP12/6/27; SP12/137/33.
29. 'Will of Richard de la Wych', ed. W. H. Blaauw, *SAC*, i (1848), 177–83.

servants called 'Mrs Busshopp'.[30] Mrs Bullingham at Gloucester emerges cajoling her husband into granting her scheming brother John Marrow a lease of the Vineyard, the only habitable home remaining to the see, the palace in Gloucester being described as 'a very vast, melancholic, decayed and ruinous house'.[31]

The case of Gloucester raises a further problem arising from the Reformation: that of providing homes for the incumbents of the new bishoprics created in 1541–2. For Bristol, Chester, Gloucester and Peterborough there was a ready-made solution: the abbot's lodging of a suppressed monastery was made over as the new bishop's palace. That at Chester, thereafter known as 'the old Bishop's Palace', had been the lodging of the abbots of St Werburgh and was an extensive mansion of local red-sandstone. It was not the most attractive of residences, gloomy and rambling, and brewing and malting in nearby buildings created a serious nuisance, of which Bishop Bridgeman complained in 1638. The original endowment of the new see had included a country retreat for the bishop, the manor and house at Weston in Derbyshire, but the first bishop, John Bird, in 1547 granted away all the property of the see except the palace in Chester.

At Peterborough, where there had been a Benedictine abbey, John Chambers, the last abbot, became the first bishop, and his lodging was renamed the bishop's palace.[32] Another adapted Benedictine house was St Peter's at Gloucester where the first bishop, John Wakeman, inherited sumptuous lodgings which he repaired and furnished. He had also been endowed with the Vineyard House at Over, to the west of Gloucester, a favourite residence of many bishops for its rural delights and its convenience of being close to the city.[33] At Bristol the abbot's lodging of the Augustinian abbey was taken over. When the see of Oxford was founded in 1542 it was fixed at Osney Abbey and the last abbot, Robert King, became the first bishop. The intention was that his

30. E135/25/31; F. O. White, *Lives of the Elizabethan bishops of the Anglican church* (1898), p. 152.

31. Ibid., pp. 92, 194; F. D. Price, 'Bishop Bullingham and Chancellor Blackleech: a diocese divided', *Trans. Bristol and Glos. Arch. Soc.*, 91 (1972), 193.

32. J. H. E. Bennett, 'The Old Bishop's Palace, Chester', *Chester and N. Wales Archit., Archeol., and Hist. Soc. Journ.*, n.s. 37 (1948) pt. 1, 69–106; W. Whellan, *History, Gazeteer and Directory of Northamptonshire* (1849), pp. 672, 676.

33. I am indebted to Dr P. E. Chandler for the use of his notes on the Old Bishop's Palace, Gloucester.

palace should be at Gloucester Hall, but the see was removed to St Frideswide's Priory (Christ Church) at Oxford in 1545. The bishopric was kept vacant for twenty-one years, 1568 to 1589, and it was left to Bishop Bancroft to provide a suitable episcopal residence at Cuddesdon where he held the parsonage. In 1636, finding it 'mean and ruinous', he was licensed to build a house on the glebe-land, and Charles I in encouragement allowed him to take fifty timber trees from the forest of Shotover and excused his first fruits of £343.7.11½.[34] The result was 'a fair house of stone' with a chapel and a surrounding garden and orchard.

Bancroft was not the only early-Stuart bishop involved in building projects. Elizabethan bishops, apart from Parker, who repaired the palace hall at Canterbury, had been more concerned with the recovery of their endowments and the impact of inflation on costs. There is some evidence that it was now the custom of bishops to demand £400 from the executors of their predecessors by way of dilapidations. Berkeley at Wells was not the only one who moaned on this score: Cheyney at Gloucester in 1563 was equally vociferous about the great cost of running a household 'in this dear world'. When Barnes took over at Durham in 1577 he complained that Pilkington had allowed the manor-house at Stockton to go to ruin and that its repair would cost about £1600. Freake of Norwich tried to recover from Parkhurst's estate for decay at Ludham and Norwich.[35] Sometimes a long vacancy, as followed the death of Cox of Ely (1581-1601), led to the neglect of episcopal buildings: in 1588 it was estimated that £400 or £500 would be needed to repair Somersham. Apart from questions of cost, insecurity about its possessions undoubtedly deterred the Elizabethan episcopate from further building, except of personal homes such as the moated manor called Edwin's Hall at Woodham Ferrers built by Sandys of York about 1576, and the fine new house which Bishop Godwin of Wells built for his son Thomas at Towerhead in Banwell.[36]

Not until after 1604 was a halt called to the alienation of episcopal lands by an act that forbade their transfer even to the king. With the new monarch came a new security for the bishops, whose possessions were to be protected from diminution 'for the better

34. *CSP Dom.*, *1636–37*, p. 507.
35. Hassell Smith, op. cit., p. 213.
36. W. White, *History, Gazeteer and Directory of Essex* (1863), p. 474.

maintenance of God's true religion, keeping of hospitality and avoiding of dilapidations'.[37] Now better defended, the bishops resumed their building activity, but in a much lower key than the expansion of the late fifteenth century. At Chester, Lloyd built a timber-framed house, perhaps again as a personal venture; Andrews of Ely spent considerable sums on the repair of Downham, and £2000 at Wisbech, which was in need of repair after use as a prison for Catholic recusants, and his successor continued his work. Jegon of Norwich lost the greater part of his house at Ludham in 1611 by fire, but he kept the house in commission, for he appointed a keeper there in 1614 and his successor Harsnett undertook the cost of rebuilding.[38] The greatest enterprise at this time was probably at Buckden, where Chaderton (1595–1608) had allowed the palace to go to ruin. Bishop Williams spent lavishly on the buildings and constructed fishponds and gardens and a raised walk between two rows of trees in the neglected grounds. He also restored Lincoln, deserted since the Reformation, using materials from Nettleham, which had been abandoned for about sixty years and which he pulled down about 1630.[39]

By the time Williams moved on to York in 1641 the situation was grim for the bishops, who were under attack by the Root and Branch movement. When civil war broke out in 1642 their palaces became prime targets of the parliamentarians, and the ensuing devastation was catastrophic for them. At least nineteen major residences and five minor ones were reduced to ruin or very badly damaged. When Bishop's Waltham was destroyed in 1644, a cavalier wrote 'Waltham House in ashes': Bishop Curll escaped from there in a dungcart. The episcopal homes of York suffered badly: Southwell was demolished, as well as Cawood, which was forsaken for Bishopsthorpe, now regained as the official residence. In 1646–7 the Commons ordered that Crayke Castle, another York home, should be rendered untenable and deprived of a garrison. Stockton, belonging to Durham, commanded the passage of the Tees and was completely destroyed in 1652. Rose

37. 1 Jas.1.c.3; C. Hill, *Economic Problems of the Church. From Archbishop Whitgift to the Long Parliament* (Oxford, 1956), pp. 31–2.

38. *Extracts from the two earliest minute books of the dean and chapter of Norwich Cathedral, 1566–1649*, ed. J. F. Williams and B. Cozens-Hardy (Norfolk Rec. Soc., 24, 1953), p. 46.

39. J. W. F. Hill, *Tudor and Stuart Lincoln* (Cambridge, 1956), p. 123.

Castle in Cumberland was burnt. Waller blew up Farnham and occupied the habitable parts as his headquarters 1643–4. He dismantled more of it afterwards and also besieged Chichester. Eccleshall was so damaged that it had to be rebuilt in 1695 before the bishops of Coventry and Lichfield could live there, St Asaph was used as a tavern, and at Exeter (twice besieged) the palace was used first as a barracks then for a sugar-refining business until the Restoration, when it was repaired at great expense. Lincoln was used as another barracks and timber that Bishop Williams had intended for the construction of a library was commandeered for fortifications.[40] Hartlebury, Peterborough and Wells all suffered great damage, as did Gloucester, which by 1647 was 'very ruinous and not habitable'. Of the less important homes the newly-built Cuddesdon was 'scorched' by Colonel William Legge in 1644 to prevent parliamentary occupation, Bekesbourne in Kent was almost entirely pulled down, as was Ford to the south in 1658.[41] Bishop Wren was in 1642 the last occupant of Downham, which fell into disrepair and was not used by later bishops. Alderman Pack, the grantee under the Commonwealth, pulled down many of the buildings at Buckden, undoing Bishop Williams's recent work, so that at the Restoration Bishop Hacket could deplore the dreadful waste with the cry: 'What remains of all this cost and beauty? All is dissipated, defaced and pluckt to pieces to pay the army. . .'

The cost of all the necessary rebuilding at the Restoration was immense. At Lichfield, whose cathedral area had suffered more severely than any other, Bishop Hacket spent £20,000 on repairs and his successor then began on the palace in 1687. Rose Castle had £1000 spent on it; Norwich, which had been let off in tenements, was refurbished at great expense, and at least £10,000 was expended at Farnham. Bishop Saunderson set about the urgent rebuilding of Buckden, for, at his successor's arrival in 1663, it was still the only habitable episcopal dwelling. When in 1668 Cosin of Durham drew up his account of rebuilding his two castles at Durham and Bishop Auckland and the house at Darlington it came to not less than £17,000. The chapel at Auckland alone cost £6000.[42]

40. W. White, *Devonshire* (1850), p. 75; J. W. F. Hill, op. cit., pp. 123, 163.
41. S. Bagshaw, op. cit., ii, 223, 233.
42. *The correspondence of John Cosin, D.D.*, (ii) (Surtees Soc., 55, 1870), p. 171.

The church had been restored and episcopal possessions had been reclaimed from the parliamentary purchasers, but the piles of ruinous masonry and the ravaged deer parks surrounding them were a mute testimony of the fate of bishops' palaces since Wolsey had completed his proud building of Hampton Court.

IX

The East and West in Early-Modern London

M. J. POWER

The expressions 'east end' and 'west end' of London raise stereo-types in our mind which derive their force from the present physical character of the two areas.[1] The contrast between White-chapel Road in the east and Strand in the west, Cable Street and Piccadilly, Wapping and Westminster, is stark and reflects com-plex differences in wealth and use. The origins of such differences lie in their initial pattern of settlement before 1700.

Both areas underwent development in the second half of the sixteenth century, which created the first suburban sprawl, a phenomenon vividly described by John Stow in his *Survey* of 1598. This trend continued in the seventeenth century, plotted on the increasingly sophisticated maps of London drawn by William Fairthorne (1658), Wenceslaus Hollar (1658), and Ogilby and Morgan (1681–2). The reason for this growth was first explored by late-seventeenth-century statisticians who demonstrated that expansion was due not to a natural increase in the indigenous population, but to a steady and massive immigration, a theme elaborated by modern historical demographers. E. A. Wrigley suggests that some 8000 migrants entered London each year be-tween 1650 and 1750 and not only made up for the natural de-crease of the resident population, but also accounted for the actual increase in total population, from 200,000 in 1600 to 575,000 in 1700.[2] Such growth was viewed with considerable misgiving by the City government. There was good reason for concern. Not only was the fear of plague justified (the great attacks of 1603,

1. My grateful thanks go to my wife, Marjorie, and to Jennifer Kermode, for reading and making helpful suggestions on an earlier draft of this paper.
2. See especially essays of John Graunt and Sir William Petty in *A collection of the yearly bills of mortality from 1657 to 1758 inclusive* (1759); E. A. Wrigley, 'A simple model of London's importance in changing English society and economy, 1650–1750', *Past and Present*, 37 (1967), 44–6.

1625 and 1665 spread from the suburbs), but there were real problems in governing a metropolis which grew each year by a number greater than the population of most provincial towns.

This study describes the resulting suburban environment in the most conspicuous areas of growth between 1550 and 1650, the east and west ends. Were these suburbs as congested as the large number of immigrants might lead us to expect? Did growth affect all suburbs in a similar fashion, or did distinct economic and social groups settle in different areas? N. G. Brett-James attempted to answer some of these questions but his analysis does little more than establish when building took place in various suburbs.[3] Closer study of the physical development of a few areas has been undertaken by the *Survey of London*, but little attempt has yet been made to compare the results of such work for different areas. We have remarkably little data for differentiating the kinds of houses built in the developing suburbs of seventeenth-century London, for distinguishing wealthy from poor areas, or for drawing conclusions about the conditions of life in each district. Yet such investigations are important to the study of growth in a city renowned not only for its size and vigorous growth, but also for the diversity of its physical and social composition.

I. EAST- AND WEST-END HOUSING

Lack of evidence prevents a thorough assessment of the physical characteristics of all the building in the east or west end, but for certain areas parliamentary surveys allow us a unique insight into local conditions and enable distinctions to be drawn not only between the two suburbs but between neighbourhoods. All land confiscated from the crown or the church by Parliament was surveyed in the late 1640s or early 1650s so that it could be sold at its true value, and the particular use of such surveys for our enquiry lies in their detailed description of the size and value of houses. In the east end, land surveyed included the Tower Liberty and Shadwell; in the west end, surveys were made of parts of Piccadilly, Long Acre, Strand, High Holborn and Westminster. This last formed an urban settlement which differed from the rest

3. N. G. Brett-James, *The Growth of Stuart London* (1935) (hereafter Brett-James).

of the western suburbs, and, as we shall see, had various distinctive characteristics of its own.

Most of these areas were built up for the first time during the century before 1650. Stow described the Tower Liberty, surrounding the fortress, as 'greatly straitened by encroachments (unlawfully made and suffered) for gardens and houses . . . whereby the Tower ditch is marred'. This building may have taken place in the 1580s when Mr Heming, a tenant of the gentleman porter of the Tower, was throwing up 'alehouses and houses of suspicious resort' by Tower Hill.[4] Stow himself had seen the elm trees of Shadwell, a riverside hamlet of the large parish of Stepney, displaced by small tenements, but such building must have been thinly scattered, for most of the housing there was built later, in the 1630s and 1640s.[5]

Such piecemeal development also characterised much of the west end. Piccadilly was still an unnamed expanse of green fields when Stow wrote, for he makes no mention of it. Robert Baker, a tailor, began its development with Piccadilly Hall after 1612. Other grand houses were added, Shaver's Hall in 1635, for example, but the area was not intensively built up until Colonel Thomas Panton began development after the Restoration.[6] Likewise Stow makes no mention of Long Acre, which was laid out by Sir William Slingsby in 1615 and built upon in the 1620s and 1630s.[7] Strand, in contrast, was an already old-established street when Stow was writing. It linked the City and Westminster and was graced by great houses, the Savoy, Somerset House, Essex House, Arundel House, Bedford House and Cecil House, a place for 'gentlemen and men of honour'. There were lesser buildings too. One terrace of houses surveyed in 1650 fronted Somerset House and was probably erected soon after 1549, after that whole area was levelled by Protector Somerset to build his new palace.[8] High Holborn, too, saw development before 1600. Stow described 'many fair houses built and lodgings for gentlemen, inns

4. J. Stow, *A Survey of London*, ed. C. L. Kingsford (1908) (hereafter Stow), i, 129; *Analytical Index to the Remembrancia*, ed. W. H. and H. C. Overall (1878) (hereafter *Remembrancia*), pp. 429, 434.

5. Stow, ii, 71; M. J. Power, 'The urban development of East London, 1550–1700', (London Univ. Ph.D. thesis, 1971), pp. 136–40.

6. C. L. Kingsford, *The Early History of Piccadilly, Leicester Square and Soho* (1925), pp. 71, 79–85.

7. *Survey of London*, ed. F. H. W. Sheppard, xx, 125; Brett-James, p. 161.

8. Stow, ii, 93, 97.

for travellers and such like'.[9] Many gaps were filled in during the busy building period between 1600 and 1650. In New Palace Yard, part of Westminster, building development was complete before Stow wrote, all being 'replenished with buildings and inhabitants'.[10]

Table 1. Housing Characteristics derived from Parliamentary Surveys, 1650–1

	No. of houses	Rooms per house	% in multi-occu-pation	% with gardens	Value per room £ p.a.	% shed houses	% brick houses
EAST END							
Tower Liberty	217	5.2	0.5	12.9	2.20	15.3	8.8
Shadwell	701	3.7	0.0	39.4	1.03	6.4	8.7
Total	918	4.0	0.1	33.2	1.40	8.4	8.7
WEST END							
Piccadilly*	45	5.0	0.0	97.8	1.90	0.0	60.0
Long Acre**	255	6.1	24.3	20.8	1.50	3.6	72.2
Strand†	34	10.7	26.5	47.1	2.70	5.4	5.9
High Holborn‡	114	9.9	21.9	71.1	1.40	1.1	63.2
Total	448	6.7	21.4	42.9	1.60	2.2	63.6
WESTMINSTER							
New Palace Yard	22	4.3	13.6	31.8	3.70	38.9	9.1

*Several parcels of land and buildings around the present Circus.
**The present street from Mercer Street to Drury Lane.
†A group of houses on the south side of the street fronting Somerset House.
‡Several parcels of land and buildings on the south side of Holborn near Lincoln's Inn Fields.

Both the older and newer areas came to the attention of the parliamentary surveyors in 1650 and 1651 after the land had been confiscated from the crown or, in the case of Shadwell, from the dean of St Paul's. Table 1 shows the result of this scrutiny.[11] The

9. Ibid., 87; *Survey of London*, v, 15–16.
10. Stow, ii, 102; Brett-James, pp. 140–1.
11. The parliamentary surveys used were: St Paul's Cathedral Library, press E, drawer 5, Shadwell; E. 317 Middlesex 94, St Botolph and St Peter near the Tower; E. 317 Middlesex 73, Piccadilly; E. 317 Middlesex 51, Long Acre; E. 317 Middlesex 81, Strand; E. 317 Middlesex 25, High Holborn; E. 317 Middlesex 63, New Palace Yard, Westminster; S. J. Madge, *The Domesday of Crown Lands* (1938), gives an account of the methods of the parliamentary surveyors.

east end stands out as less grand than the west. Houses were smaller there, overwhelmingly of two storeys or less (89 per cent), averaging 4.0 rooms compared with 6.7 in the west. Moreover, more than 90 per cent were built of 'timber and Flemish wall' or timber and boards rather than brick. Perhaps because the houses were small they were almost invariably in single occupation, unlike in the west. The growing east-end population was perhaps absorbed by the building of houses very close together, for few had gardens attached, especially in the Tower Liberty, where the inhabitants could have obtained some relief by escaping to the large open spaces of Little and Great Tower Hill. The impression of dense, small-scale housing is strengthened by a relatively large percentage of shed dwellings, 8.4 per cent compared with 2.2 per cent in the west. A shed was described in 1637 as 'a leaning to something to bear up the roof', in other words a penthouse. John Stow himself makes the point about the size of houses near the Tower and evidently had mixed feelings about this type of development. He talks of the area being 'pestered with small tenements', yet evokes a much cosier image by writing of the 'homely cottages' there.[12]

Though both east-end areas had small houses, property values varied markedly; Tower houses were valued at an average of £2.20 per room, Shadwell's houses at only £1.03 per room. The low value of property in Shadwell is what we might expect. Yet the Tower area, physically not so different, was valued at an even higher rate than most west-end areas. It is certain that property values rested not only on the size of the house but also on the desirability of its location. The Tower Liberty was immediately adjacent to the City of London, and an ideal residential location for those with business at the Tower itself, or on the busy section of the river there. The Tower wharf was an important loading and unloading quay, and nearby, to the east and west, lay St Katharine's wharf and the quays of the City. Shadwell was close to the river but, being more than one mile from the City, was away from the hub of commercial activity.

The housing in the west end was very different from that in the east, and in the west itself there was considerable variation within its borders. On the whole houses were considerably larger than in the east, for instance in Strand and High Holborn, two major

12. *Survey of London*, xx, 126; Stow, i, 124.

thoroughfares, where some 64 per cent of the houses were of three or four storeys. A much greater percentage of them were built of brick (63.6 per cent against 8.7 per cent in the east), especially along Piccadilly, Long Acre and High Holborn. It is significant that these areas were mainly built up in the early-seventeenth century, when house walls were coming to be built exclusively of brick.[13] In earlier developments such as Strand, the Tower Liberty and New Palace Yard in Westminster, timber-framed housing with an infill of 'Flemish bond' was still usual. A higher proportion of west-end houses were in multi-occupation (21.4 per cent against 0.1 per cent in the east), an indication of pressure on accommodation, yet shed dwellings were uncommon. All this suggests a rather grander, more substantial and more desirable physical environment than in the east. That it was also more open is shown by the greater proportion of gardens in the west, 42.9 per cent against 33.2 per cent. In view of these facts, it is a little surprising that the overall value of accommodation in the west end, £1.60 per room, was only marginally higher than in the east, £1.40 per room, and the only west-end area which was significantly higher was Strand.

Strand was the busiest and most socially desirable of the four west-end areas, besides being strategically positioned between the City and Westminster by the Thames. Some 76 per cent of the houses were three- or four-storeyed, and an unusual double-banked structure with a range at the front and another at the rear made these dwellings the most impressive houses surveyed in the sub-urbs. The street was one of the grandest in the capital, and the area near Somerset House was its most elegant stretch, 'both for the largeness of the street, and the ability of the inhabitants who drive a considerable trade, being so near the court'.[14] Strand apart, the other three areas were not nearly so impressive. Picca-dilly, unlike its three west-end neighbours, had small one- and two-storeyed houses (91 per cent of the total) rather like those in the east, all in single occupation. Pressure on accommodation was

13. Proclamations in 1605 and 1630 encouraged building with brick; Brett-James, pp. 81, 108–9. Elsewhere the use of building materials depended on local availability. In King's Lynn, for example, brick was the rule by the early seventeenth century, but in Exeter wood persisted until much later; V. Parker, *The Making of King's Lynn* (1971), p. 102; D. Portman, *Exeter Houses 1400–1700* (1966), pp. 56–9.

14. J. Stow, *A Survey of London*, ed. J. Strype (1754) (hereafter Strype), iv, 101.

evidently not as intense as elsewhere in the west. It is true that almost all Piccadilly houses had gardens attached, an exceptional attribute in any suburban area at the time. Some of them were elaborate and beautiful oases: Captain Geer's Shaver's Hall, a large mansion of twenty-five rooms, stood in three-and-a-half acres of ground, with tennis courts, bowling alleys, a banqueting house and other garden rooms. Other houses, though smaller in scale, boasted courtyards and stables. Piccadilly must have been the greenest of suburbs, with frequent mews adding to the open character of the place. Inhabited sheds were unknown. All these features made it an apparently most attractive area and resulted in a valuation higher than Long Acre or High Holborn. Yet it was not without its critics. In 1637 it was observed that 'every mean courtier' was erecting a house 'in every corner of the mews fit only for stables'. Hedge Lane was described by Strype as a place of no great account for buildings or inhabitants, and Shag Lane was 'meanly built, neither are its inhabitants much to be boasted of'.[15]

The western suburbs lowest in value, Long Acre and High Holborn, had two common characteristics, a high proportion of brick houses and multi-occupation. Houses in Holborn tended to be larger (60 per cent were three- or four-storeyed compared with 44 per cent in Long Acre), and gardens were more common, yet the value of property in each was low. Neither boasted the elegance of Strand or the rural aspect of Piccadilly. Long Acre, while being built up in the 1620s, became 'so foul and noisome as is both impassable for His Majesty . . . and is otherwise so offensive as is not to be suffered'. In a report to the privy council in 1638 Inigo Jones referred to the 'pestering of such places with alleys of mean houses', and it was even argued by the churchwardens of St Clement Danes in 1631 that 'the building of houses there is a greater nuisance and inconvenience to the public than the placing of a laystall [a waste tip]'. Yet such disadvantages did not prevent Oliver Cromwell, John Taylor the water poet, Major-General Skippon and other notables from residing in the street in the 1640s.[16]

High Holborn, too, had its drawbacks. Though a broad handsome street, it was considered by Strype 'not over well inhabited',

15. Brett-James, p. 177; Strype, vi, 646–9.
16. Brett-James, pp. 161–4; *Survey of London*, xx, 126.

and though flanked by Great Queen Street and Lincoln's Inn Fields, both of them aristocratic quarters, it was also adjacent to humbler residences in Newton Street, Little Turnstile and such 'ordinary places'.[17] Given these drawbacks, not even pressure on accommodation raised the value of rooms in Long Acre and High Holborn. Table 1 shows clearly that, far from being a homogeneous area, the west end contained a variety of distinct kinds of urban environment.

Westminster stands apart in physical character as well as distance. Its most distinct characteristics were an extremely high valuation, higher than any other area, and an extraordinarily high percentage of shed dwellings. The location of New Palace Yard, described by Strype as 'well inhabited', so close to the court at Westminster, goes a long way to explaining the high valuation. The sheds suggest a considerable number of poor people, servants perhaps to their more fortunate neighbours, and many more of these servitors were accustomed to an even lower level of accommodation, inhabiting cellars according to a report on the plague of 1665.[18] Westminster society seems to have been mixed. A further significant aspect of Westminster houses was the prevalence of multi-occupation in small timber-framed houses (some 78 per cent of houses were of two storeys or less). Though multi-occupation was more common in Long Acre, Strand, or High Holborn, there the houses were much larger. The combination of small houses and multi-occupation in Westminster must have led to severe overcrowding, and, taken together with the percentage of shed houses, suggests that pressure on accommodation was intense.

Physically, then, the west end, though hardly uniform, tended to be grander and more spacious than the east end, and Westminster was in a class of its own, with its small houses, cramped and crowded. Another side to the physical environment can be seen by examining evidence of use of buildings. By definition houses are residential, but the extent to which they accommodate other activities is made clear in Table 2.[19] The percentage of dwellings used as taverns, shops or workshops brings out further distinctions between the suburbs. There is an obvious concentration of industry in the east. Though Long Acre and High Holborn har-

17. Strype, iv, 76–7.   18. Strype, vi, 640; Brett-James, pp. 359–60.
19. Sources as for Table 1.

Table 2. Use of Houses for Taverns, Shops and Industry

	% of houses used for taverns	% of houses used for shops	% of houses used for industry
EAST END			
Tower Liberty	3.2	9.7	5.55
Shadwell	6.2	7.8	3.9
Total	5.7	8.3	4.4
WEST END			
Piccadilly	8.8	0.0	0.0
Long Acre	4.7	6.6	2.3
Strand	8.8	91.1	0.0
High Holborn	5.2	10.5	2.6
Total	5.6	13.4	2.0
WESTMINSTER			
New Palace Yard	13.6	13.6	0.0

bour some crafts, these are unmatched by any in Piccadilly, Strand or Westminster. The industrial character of the east was hardly pervasive: 4.4 per cent of dwellings pressed into use as workshops did not make the area an industrial suburb, and one wonders about the appropriateness of the term industrial to describe such small enterprises. Nevertheless both the Tower Liberty and Shadwell were distinctly more industrial in character than the west, which, on average, had crafts in only 2 per cent of dwellings. The Tower Liberty's industry was mainly metallurgical, with three smiths' forges and a bellfounder's. Shadwell's industry was influenced largely by the proximity of the Thames, with its ship-building and fitting; there were five ropemakers and ten timberyards, two of which were owned by shipwrights. Crafts in the west end were more varied: Long Acre boasted various brewhouses, a smith's forge, a stone-cutter's yard and a timberyard, High Holborn a smith's forge, a chandler's workshop and a tanner's shed. With the sole addition of the windmill at Piccadilly these businesses were the sum of industrial premises mentioned in the surveys of the west end.

What it lacked in industry, the west end appears to have made up in shops; 13.4 per cent of dwellings had shops, compared with only 8.3 per cent in the east. This big difference is explained by the existence of a large shopping centre in Strand, evidently the seventeenth-century equivalent of contemporary Oxford Street. Almost all the thirty-four houses situated on the plot surveyed contained shops (91.1 per cent), including two saddlers, two shoe-makers, two cutlers and two chandlers, a sempster, a goldsmith, a tailor, a spectacle-maker, a confectioner, an apothecary and a milliner. This list suggests a concentration of specialist shops catering for the 'carriage trade' characteristic of a central shopping district. Strype commented on 'the ability of the inhabitants who drive a considerable trade'. Among them were the young freemen of the Goldsmiths' Company who had migrated from Gold-smiths' Row in Cheapside. Trade was further encouraged by the building of exchanges, like the one erected on the site of Durham House in 1608, which seriously worried traders of the Royal Exchange in the City, who feared its competition.[20] Strand was ideally placed to serve the fast-developing west end, with its high percentage of wealthy residents.[21] Their attention would, no doubt, have been beguiled by the array of signs which graced the shop fronts: the *Three Bells*, the *Sugar Loaf*, the *Gun*, the *Prince's Arms*, the *Golden Lion*, the *Three Pigeons*, the *Feathers*, the *Golden Fleece*, the *Three Pattens*, the *Golden Ball*, the *Plough*, and the *Bird in Hand*.

Though the concentration of shops in Strand might suggest that the west end was a busy shopping area, the surveys of the other three west-end locations do not support this supposition. High Holborn, a major thoroughfare like Strand, did not have shops of either the same quality or quantity. They amounted to only 10.5 per cent of the dwellings, a mundane collection of grocers, chandlers, smiths, shoemakers, and the like. Long Acre, with a yet smaller percentage of shops (6.6 per cent), contained an equally prosaic selection. Piccadilly, as befitted a rural suburb, had no shops at all. If we ignore Strand, the west end seems little more orientated towards shopping than the east end. The Tower Liberty (9.7 per cent shops) and Shadwell (7.8 per cent shops), had proportionately as many shops as west-end areas, Westminster rather more (13.6 per cent), though the character of the shops differed greatly. Those in the east were the usual provisioners to be found in most neighbourhoods: bakers, grocers, butchers,

20. Strype, iv, 101; *Remembrancia*, pp. 105–6, 109, 519–20.
21. See p. 172.

tobacco stores. In Westminster residents were also served by a
watchmaker and a scrivener.

Taverns, as Table 2 shows, were common everywhere, averaging one to every eighteen houses, both in the east and west ends.
The high percentage in New Palace Yard (13.6 per cent of houses)
is probably a reliable indication of how common drinking places
were in Westminster. An act of 1585 setting up a court of burgesses
for Westminster allowed sixty taverns in St Margaret's parish
(which included New Palace Yard), and only twenty each in the
parishes of St Martin-in-the-Fields (which included Long Acre),
and St Clement Danes with St Mary Savoy (which included
Strand).[22] Moreover, Westminster taverns were very large,
dominating surrounding dwellings; the *Bear* boasted twenty-one
rooms, for example. Large taverns were occasionally found in the
east end, too. The *Angel* (twenty-one rooms) near the Tower, or
the *Queen's Head* (sixteen rooms) in Shadwell, dominated their
streets, dwarfing other buildings. These grand places were untypical. More common were the humbler drinking places located
in the ground-floor rooms of small terraced houses, especially in
Shadwell. West-end taverns were usually larger, in keeping with
the size of houses there. A hostelry must have been a drinking
palace indeed to command attention in an area such as Strand, in
the company of enormous private houses like Northumberland
House, Buckingham House or Somerset House. In Piccadilly one
such establishment did stand out. Simon Osbaldeston's 'entertainment centre', Shaver's Hall, was described by the earl of Clarendon as 'a fair hall for entertainment and gaming, with handsome
gravel walks . . . upper and lower bowling greens, whither very
many of the nobility and gentry of the best quality resorted both
for exercise and conversation'.[23] Although the suburbs differed
widely in their physical characteristics, the one common factor
seems to have been the ubiquitous tavern, an obvious concomitant
of the precocious growth of the brewing industry in seventeenth-
century London.

2. SOCIAL DISTINCTIONS IN THE EAST AND WEST ENDS

Suggestive as such comparisons about the physical size and use of
houses may be, they depend upon surveys of seven small districts,

22. Brett-James, p. 131.   23. Ibid., 181–2; C. L. Kingsford, op. cit., 79–81.

containing only five per cent or so of the houses in the eastern and western suburbs; this may give a misleading impression of the overall character of each area.[24] It is possible to put the figures derived from the parliamentary surveys into context by analysing the hearth tax statistics for the entire eastern and western suburbs in 1664. First imposed in 1662, the hearth tax was a levy on householders based on the number of hearths in the household. The units used were different from those of the parliamentary surveys, that is, hearths and households instead of rooms and houses, but the difference between them would have to be very great to make them valueless.[25] Table 3 sets out information from the hearth tax which shows a gratifying similarity between characteristics of the areas included in parliamentary surveys and the three wider districts of which they formed parts.[26] The contrast between east and west is confirmed. Just as in the parliamentary surveys houses had been smaller in the east than in the west (4.0 against 6.7 rooms per house), so, over the whole east end, the number of hearths per household, 2.7, was much lower than the overall west-end average of 5.5. Westminster enjoyed housing (4.3 rooms per house or 4.2 hearths per household) neither as grand in scale as that of the west end nor as mean as that of the east.

The average number of hearths in the west end was boosted by the size of the town palaces of its wealthiest residents, especially in the parishes of St Clement Danes and St Mary Savoy (Strand) and the Thames-side liberty of the duchy of Lancaster. The earl of Northumberland's house, visually striking and clearly engraved on Ogilby and Morgan's map of London of 1681–2, contained sixty-seven hearths.[27] The duke of Buckingham's had sixty, the duchess of Somerset's fifty-nine, and that of Edward Hyde, earl of Clarendon and lord chancellor, forty-one. Just to the north, Inigo Jones's piazza at Covent Garden was another area of large households: the earl of Bedford, owner of the land, counted fifty-nine hearths in his large house on the south side. This was the

24. 1388 houses are listed in the parliamentary surveys compared with 27,221 households in the 1664 hearth tax for the east and west ends.

25. In the 1670s, 121 families (households) lived in every 100 houses in the City wards without the walls: P. E. Jones and A. V. Judges, 'London population in the late-seventeenth century', *EcHR*, 6 (1935–6), 53–4.

26. Greater London Council Record Office, Middlesex division: MR/TH 4 Tower division; MR/TH 2 Holborn division; MR/TH 7 Westminster division.

27. See also J. Summerson, *Architecture in Britain, 1530 to 1830* (edn 1970) (hereafter Summerson), pp. 84–5.

first of the London squares, an early experiment in town planning, graced on the north and east by 'stately buildings for the dwelling of persons of repute and quality, their fronts standing on pillars and arches of bricks and stone rustic work, with piazzas or walks like those of the Royal Exchange in London and imitating the Rialto in Venice'.[28] The inclusion of Jones's St Paul's church made the square one of the showpieces of London in the mid-seventeenth century. In St Clement Danes, the Inns of Court were conspicuous institutions, accounting for very large numbers of hearths: Lyon's Inn forty-six, New Inn sixty-five, Clement's Inn one hundred and fifteen. These Inns and great households were exceptionally large, but throughout the west end were many households of twenty or thirty hearths.

The four east-end areas show a striking similarity in household size, Spitalfields, a new development built in the 1640s, '50s and '60s, being the only part where the average number of hearths was distinctly higher than the norm. In the west end, too, there is a remarkable consistency in the number of hearths per household, with the exception of St Paul Covent Garden and the duchy of Lancaster Liberty, both markedly above the norm for the reasons described above, and St Giles-in-the-Fields, rather below average. St Giles was on the periphery of the built-up area of London, and thus less desirable, being some way from either Westminster or the City.

The difference in average household size between east and west suggests very different societies inhabiting both areas. This conclusion is reinforced when we take account of the distribution of the rich and the poor in each area. Taking the elite first, the proportion of titled people, nobility or gentry, listed as householders in the hearth tax (see Table 3), was 0.1 per cent in the east, 3.9 in the west and 3.2 in Westminster. The landed classes had no desire to live in the east end, a conclusion which becomes inescapable when it is realised that two-thirds of the 0.1 per cent of upper-class householders there were absentee landlords, in contrast with the overwhelming majority of landowners in residence in the west. The latter were not evenly distributed, as Table 3 shows; St Paul Covent Garden and St Andrew Holborn had a high percentage of titled folk. St Mary Savoy and St Clement Danes, the

28. Brett-James, p. 175; Summerson, pp. 134-7; *Survey of London*, xxxvi, 25-34, 64-80.

Liberty of the Rolls, and St Giles had a low percentage, the first two monopolised by lawyers and the latter too far out to be desirable.

The statistics in Table 3 obscure the large extent to which the distribution of the aristocracy and gentry was restricted almost exclusively to a single street or square within a given district. Almost half the 7.6 per cent in the parish of St Paul Covent Garden, for example, lived around the piazza. Lincoln's Inn Fields, in the parish of St Andrew Holborn, provides an even more striking example of this concentration. It was a new development, like Covent Garden, laid out by William Newton in the late 1630s and '40s.[29] A total of twenty-one peers and forty-two gentlemen, most of the landed people in the parish, lived around the Fields by 1664. They formed a titled enclave outnumbering the less exalted inhabitants, and, to match the social tone of the square, its residents had large households, averaging 10.9 hearths. One advantage of such new, planned environments for their wealthy residents was that they gathered together similar social groups and excluded the poor. Strype observed of the Covent Garden piazza, for example, that it was 'well inhabited by a mixture of nobility, gentry and wealthy tradesmen . . . scarce admitting of any poor, not being pestered with mean courts and alleys'.[30]

Some indication of the whereabouts of the disadvantaged can be gained if we accept the percentage of non-chargeable households in each area as a measure of the proportion of poor. The non-chargeable category included those who paid no tax or poor rate, those occupying a house worth less than £1 per annum, charitable institutions and industrial hearths; and with few falling into the last two groups, the vast majority of non-chargeable households were poor.[31] In this respect Table 3 reveals another disparity between east and west. Some 51.9 per cent of east-end households were in the non-chargeable category, compared with only 18.0 per cent in the west end. Whitechapel and Shoreditch stand out as the east-end areas with the largest percentage of poor; at the other extreme were the parish of St Paul Covent Garden,

29. *Survey of London*, iii, 7–10; Summerson, pp. 162–4.
30. Strype, vi, 661.
31. C. A. F. Meekings, *The Surrey Hearth Tax of 1664*, Surrey Rec. Soc., 17 (1940), xii–xiii.

Table 3. Household Characteristics derived from
the Hearth Tax, 1664

	Situation of parliamentary survey areas	Total house-holds	Hearths per house-hold	% titled people	% non chargeable	% empty house-holds
EAST END						
Shoreditch		1438	2.6	0.1	59.4	2.2
Spitalfields		948	3.2	0.0	45.0	0.6
Whitechapel		2482	2.4	0.2	70.1	5.8
Riverside*	(Tower Liberty) (Shadwell)	10545	2.7	0.1	47.2	5.3
Total		15413	2.7	0.1	51.9	4.9
WEST END						
St Martin-in-the-Fields	(Piccadilly) (Long Acre)	3072	5.0	3.7	19.3	1.0
St Paul Covent Garden		485	7.7	7.6	10.1	2.3
St Mary Savoy (Strand) and St Clement Danes		1008	5.9	1.0	4.2	0.7
Duchy of Lancaster		522	6.3	3.8	2.3	0.0
St Andrew Holborn	(High Holborn)	1834	5.7	6.8	23.7	1.6
Rolls Liberty**		292	5.9	2.1	9.9	1.4
St Giles-in-the-Fields		1524	4.8	2.2	26.9	3.4
Total		8737	5.5	3.9	18.0	1.6
WESTMINSTER						
St Margaret†	(New Palace Yard)	3071	4.2	3.2	47.6	1.2

*Includes Tower Liberty, the Minories, St Katharine's, East Smithfield and Stepney: Wapping (and Wapping in Whitechapel), Shadwell, Ratcliff, Lime-house, Poplar and Blackwall.

**Included in Holborn division hearth tax, though strictly speaking was in Farringdon Without ward of the City.

†Omitting Kensington and Knightsbridge.

St Mary Savoy and St Clement Danes, the duchy of Lancaster and Rolls Liberties. These were the areas closest to the City to the east and west respectively. Moving westward through St Clement Danes and the City to Whitechapel, the traveller would have been in no doubt that he had passed from a grander western suburb to a poorer eastern quarter. Westminster, once again, is a hybrid. Mixed with the notable proportion of gentry and aristocracy there was a high proportion of people at the opposite end of the social scale. The high percentage (47.6 per cent) of poor accords with the large number of shed dwellings observed earlier in New Palace Yard. The country's elite lived in close proximity to humble folk.

3. A 'FAYRE' WEST END, AN 'UNSAVERY' EAST END

The marked difference between the east and west ends causes one to wonder why people settled in the east at all, though, of course, the desirability of a location is only one, and not necessarily the most potent, force attracting migrants to different suburbs. That Westminster and the west end attracted great numbers is clear enough from the accommodation crisis they were suffering in the mid-seventeenth century. The high rents in Westminster (£3.70 per room per annum), the degree of multi-occupation of houses (13.6 per cent of houses: see Table 1) and the very low percentage of households left empty (1.2 per cent: see Table 3) are strong indications of this crisis. The same must be said about the west end, for, though it lacked the high rent of Westminster (being only £1.60 per room on average), it had an even higher degree of multi-occupation (21.4 per cent), and a similarly low proportion of empty households (1.6 per cent). In sharp contrast the east-end figures all suggest that the scramble for accommodation was less intense: low rent (£1.40 per room), the almost complete absence of multi-occupation (0.1 per cent) and a high proportion of empty households (4.9 per cent) indicate a suburban area where the supply of housing was well ahead of the rate of population increase.

The reasons for this contrast between east and west are unclear. In both ends of London the population was increasing very rapidly in the early-seventeenth century and pressure on accommodation should have been equally evident. The type of person attracted to each area obviously differed greatly. In the west—by the late sixteenth century—parliament and the Inns of Court were drawing great numbers of gentry, lawyers, government servants and men of affairs, and a large service population of shopkeepers and the like to support them. In the east we find a more homogeneous society of mariners, craftsmen, sailors' victuallers, almost all moderately humble working people.[32] It surely was true of the gentry and many other immigrants who settled in the west that they aspired to a size and style of house and environment which was more costly and took longer to build, and created a housing shortage as a result. The humbler craftsmen and mariners who moved into the east may have been content with small, cramped accommodation.

The impact of these distinct communities on the physical aspect of the two suburbs was evident from an early date. The tone of John Stow's description of them in 1598 changes sharply as he moves from east to west. In the east his description is full of censure: tenements are 'small and base', cottages 'filthy', streets 'pestered with tenements'. Whitechapel Road so depressed him that he thought it 'no small blemish for so famous a city to have so unsavery and unseemly an entry'. In sharp contrast is his attitude to the west end. Houses are invariably 'fayre', often 'for gentlemen'. Such terms are not used to describe only the great houses of Strand, but are applied to the terraces of less remarkable dwellings along the principal streets of the west end and Westminster.[33] While this dichotomy between a 'fayre' west and an 'unsavery' east is not completely reflected in our examination of the two areas fifty years later, the physical and social distinctions were still strong enough to show that east- and west-end development continued along divergent lines in the early-seventeenth century.

The advantages of living in the west end are underlined by the apparently greater healthiness of its residents. Surviving evidence allows only the comparison of the numbers of burials and baptisms as an indicator of health. Crude as such statistics may be the results are suggestive. Stepney's burials were 50.5 per cent more numerous than baptisms in the early-seventeenth century, Whitechapel's burials 58.9 per cent above its baptisms, while comparable

32. M. J. Power, op. cit., ch. 6.
33. Stow, ii, 71, 72, 74, 87, 88, 98, 101.

figures for St Martin-in-the-Fields were 39.4 per cent, and for St Margaret Westminster, 35.8 per cent.[34] Other factors may explain the difference: west-end residents were perhaps more likely to retire to the country to die, for example; a higher percentage of the western population may have been of child-bearing age than

Table 4. The Incidence of Plague in East and West
from Bills of Mortality

| | % of plague deaths of total deaths | | | |
	1603	1625	1636	1665
EAST END				
Shoreditch	*	70.5	52.9	73.0
Whitechapel	*	68.7	60.0	80.9
St Katharine by the Tower	*	74.5	55.1	62.9
Stepney	96.6	*	48.0	76.6
Total		70.2	53.8	76.4
WEST END				
St Martin-in-the-Fields	*	66.2	34.6	60.0
St Mary Savoy	93.7	70.4	50.9	65.3
St Clement Danes	*	58.8	24.9	66.9
St Andrew Holborn	*	74.7	46.5	78.4
St Giles-in-the-Fields	*	71.0	49.6	72.2
Total		68.7	41.8	69.1
WESTMINSTER				
St Margaret	87.3	*	39.9	73.7
LONDON AND SUBURBS	85.5	65.3	44.5	70.5

*No figures are available.

in the east. But the contrast between the figures is great enough to suggest that the east-end environment made some contribution to the higher ratio there of burials to baptisms.

Weight is given to this conclusion by a study of how plague afflicted the suburbs (see Table 4).[35] In every major seventeenth-

34. *Register of St. Martin-in-the-Fields*, ed. T. Mason and J. V. Kitto, 2 vols. (1898, 1936); *Memorials of St. Margaret's Church Westminster, the Parish Registers*, ed. A. M. Burke (1914), xviii–xx; St Dunstan Stepney and St Mary Matfelon Ms. registers at Greater London Council Record Office.

35. Statistics computed from *A collection of the yearly bills of mortality from 1657 to 1758 inclusive* (1759).

century outbreak the east end apparently suffered more severely than the west end or Westminster. Westminster seems to have been the most lightly affected, except for the plague of 1665, when it suffered more than the west end. The grimmest statistics come from the parishes of Whitechapel and Shoreditch in the east. They were noted by Gregory King as parishes with very heavy mortality.[36] St Andrew Holborn and St Giles-in-the-Fields were the western parishes worst affected, and significantly they were the west-end parishes most notable for their high proportion of poor people (see Table 3). Some relationship between disease and poverty is evident and these figures further emphasise the different nature of the eastern and western suburban communities.

More work on the wealth of the suburban areas of London might add some refinements to our understanding of their differences, but from this survey of the east and west ends in the mid-seventeenth century it is very clear that in terms of their physical environment, the wealth, status and quality of life of their residents, they were different worlds. In a century of rapid growth after 1550 London suburban expansion took two very distinct paths.

36. D. V. Glass, 'Gregory King's estimate of the population of England and Wales, 1695', *Population Studies*, iii (1949–50), 350.

X

Antwerp and London: the Structure and Balance of Trade in the 1560s

BRIAN DIETZ

While concentration and specialisation were the fundamental characteristics of English commerce throughout the sixteenth century there was a slight but significant change in development from about 1550. Until then the trend towards both had quickened, especially in the export trade—where the 'natural' monopoly of cloth had grown at the expense of wool and the more artificial monopoly of London was extended at the cost of the outports. Parallel and related to this, metropolitan trade itself was increasingly concentrated along the Antwerp axis. From about mid-century some, if not all, of these trends were reversed. Cloth held its monopoly but its range, which had previously been narrowed by the eclipse of worsteds, was slowly widened by the advance of the 'new draperies'; and, if London's dominance was apparently undisturbed, her own markets were diversified and extended. Tentative steps to outflank the great commercial base on the Scheldt by developing other, more distant markets were indeed taken in the 1550s. The decisive impulse in this direction, however, was the collapse of the base itself in 1568, when Elizabeth's seizure of the Spanish pay ships in December provoked the second and, as it proved, decisive trade embargo of the decade. Thus, in the years immediately preceding this irreparable break in the axis, the pattern of English trade, though already in transition, was confined and specialised to perhaps a unique degree. For this reason the decision to replace the particulars of account in 1564 by the far more detailed and informative port books was a fortunate coincidence, as is the fact that, while many of the London series have been lost and are in other respects imperfect or incomplete, three survive which offer an exceptionally full view of the Antwerp trade in this rare and brief period of comparative calm and stability. Two were among the first books to be issued by Lord Treasurer Winchester late in 1564 for use the following Easter term (and in time, therefore, to record trade a few months after the lifting of the earlier embargo which had been imposed in the Low Countries in November 1563). These are the controller's account of the petty custom on denizen exports and the surveyor's parallel record of exports by aliens.[1] The third book is unique. In one volume are contained the controller's accounts of the subsidy of tonnage and poundage inwards on native and Hanse goods in what proved to be the last full year of trade with the Low Countries.[2] This year cannot, of course, be called 'typical'; nor could it be said that commerce was restored to 'normal' in 1565. The extraordinary fluctuations in trade between London and Antwerp in the mid-sixteenth century make distinctions between normal and abnormal, typical and untypical, too superficial to have much meaning. Nevertheless, for these last few years of un-interrupted intercourse between two of the great centres of European commerce the port books provide a uniquely detailed record of the commodity exchange and the role of individual mer-chants, and also permit some insight into the question of the balance of trade.

Such claims obviously imply a confidence in the customs officials and their accounts which may need some defence. As the question of their reliability and accuracy has been much debated, comment will be confined to two aspects that have a special relevance.[3] One concerns the relationship of the Merchant Ad-venturers to the government and its own members. For a com-pany heavily dependent on official support, it was hardly in its

1. E190/2/1; 1/4. Exports for the year from Michaelmas 1564 can be measured by adding totals from the particular of account of the petty custom to Easter 1565. E122/89/8. Alien and Hanse shipments are included but not destinations or types of cloth. The document itself is imperfect and a number of items are illegible. Total shipments were 75,384 cloths, of which English merchants owned 52,282 and aliens 12,048.

2. E190/4/2, which is calendared in *Port and Trade of Early Elizabethan London: Documents*, ed. B. Dietz, (Lond. Rec. Soc., viii, 1972).

3. The author's views are presented in the introduction to the above volume. See also D. Woodward, 'Sources for Maritime History, III: The Port Books of England and Wales', *Maritime Hist.*, iii, 2 (1973). The London books are discussed by N. J. Williams in *Lond. and Middlx. Arch. Soc. Trans.*, xviii, pt. 1 (1955), 13–26.

interests to condone evasion by individual and competing members; nor was it in its power, even if it were in its interests, to practise such deceits corporately. Arguably, therefore, the Fellowship's own jealously-guarded jurisdiction and close supervision of shipments supplemented the checks and controls of the crown's own officials, as they had at an earlier period.[4] The second question, which has an obvious bearing on customs' evasion as well as wider implications, is: what proportion of *real* commodity values were these duties? On imports, excepting wine (which generally paid a specific duty), the charge was five per cent of the valuations as revised in the new Book of Rates of 1558. Winchester's revision seems on average to have more than doubled the official values, but evidence of wholesale prices paid by merchants suggests that a more realistic assessment should have been upwards by a further quarter or more.[5] English factors at Danzig in 1557 and 1558 were quoting prices which were consistently higher than the new valuations by this proportion. Pitch, for example, was valued at £2 the last but in Danzig cost around £3.5.0.[6] Agents at Antwerp four years later also reported grocery prices well above the official valuations.[7] No firm conclusions can be drawn from such a small sample of commodities which in the Book ran to over a thousand. The data, however, suggest that the merchants whom the lord treasurer must have consulted over such a wide range of wares aimed for the best terms possible from a government which, though intent on increasing revenue, lacked the expertise and perhaps the disposition to drive too hard a bargain. The Book of Rates is best seen perhaps as a compromise between the queen's representatives, who achieved a substantial upward revision from a very low base, and the merchants who exploited their expert knowledge of prices, measures etc. to keep the real cost to the importer of the *ad valorem* duties at one or two per cent less than the

4. P. Ramsey, 'Overseas trade in the reign of Henry VII', *EcHR*, Ser. 2, 6 (1953), 176.

5. T. S. Willan, *Tudor Book of Rates* (Manchester, 1962), p. xxviii.

6. W. Sharpe, 'Correspondence of Thomas Sexton, merchant of London, and his factors in Danzig, 1550–1560' (London Univ. M.A. thesis, 1952), *passim*. See also H. Zins, *England and the Baltic in the Elizabethan Era* (Manchester, 1972), pp. 304–5.

7. Correspondence of George Stoddard's factors SP46/13/110–43. V. Vasquez de Prada gives textile prices which also suggest substantial undervaluations, although problems of correspondence between units of measurement and currency make comparisons uncertain. *Lettres Marchandes d'Anvers* (Paris, 1960), pp. 304–5.

official rate of 1s. in the £.[8] Was the specific duty on cloth, the only one of importance in the Antwerp trade, also a compromise? For this familiar domestic product the government had less need to rely on information from interested parties and the raising of the rate to 6s. 8d. on the notional short cloth or cloth of assize was unquestionably steep. Yet evidence of prices, although fragmentary and relating to an article which varied widely in quality and cost within as well as between the different types, indicates that the burden of the specific duty, while not directly related to values, was consistent with the official rate of the *ad valorem* duties. Over a range of woollen cloths 6s. 8d. represented between three to eight per cent of their cost to the merchant.[9] In no sense could these duties be considered either protective or a strong inducement to evasion. Furthermore, if the rates were roughly equal, there are no obvious grounds for believing that the official accounts will be more or less accurate as between imports and exports. For both they obviously understate: the assumption, however, of this discussion is that they do so evenly and not to an extent that invalidates any statistics that can be compiled from them.

EXPORTS

The export registers cover a period of five months from late April 1565 to the end of September. The data extracted from them are presented in Table 1 to show how cloth exports were distributed among markets and between native, alien and Hanse merchants. Over a full year the seasonal changes in the pattern of sailings from the Thames are unlikely to have a serious effect on these results. French ports, especially Bordeaux, probably received more cloths in the winter months when the first vintage was collected, while the Baltic, being a summer voyage, would

8. Recommendations put to the Royal Commission on the Exchanges in 1564 urged that poundage on imports should be exacted according to their true value. Six years later a list showing market and official values of a wide range of commodities indicates that the 'true' rate of poundage was only about three per cent. *Tudor Economic Documents*, ed. R. H. Tawney and E. Power (1924), iii, 359; Willan, *Rates*, p. xliv.

9. Ibid., pp. xv–xviii. Further evidence for this estimate was found in HCA 13/16ff. 203–4, *John Isham. Mercer and Merchant Adventurer*, ed. G. D. Ramsay, (Northampton Rec. Soc. 1962), pp. 32–3 and O. de Smedt, *De Engelse Natie te Antwerpen in de 16e Eeuw*, ii (Antwerp, 1954), 350.

take proportionately less. Consignments for Antwerp apparently passed through the customs from December onwards in anticipation of the end of the restraint.

Table 1. London Cloth Exports, Easter to Michaelmas
1565 (to the nearest shortcloth)

Destination	Denizen	Alien	Hanse	Total	%
Antwerp	28519	3492	1675	33686	65.8
Russia	596	—	—	596	1.2
Danzig	1446	—	1531	2977	5.8
Hamburg	96	3	2530	2629	5.1
Emden	2436	—	—	2436	4.8
Holland	73	80	1753	1906	3.7
France	1328	17	—	1345	2.6
Spain	4641	40	—	4681	9.2
Portugal	33	4	—	37	0.1
Barbary	890	—	—	890	1.7
Total	40058	3636	7489	51183	100.0

These figures call for little comment. Antwerp's supreme importance in the export trade, especially for English merchants, is confirmed and the more recent and distant markets are seen to be peripheral economically as well as geographically. Emden, where the Adventurers had moved their staple the previous year, had clearly lost its rival attractions and, despite the considerable investment there of capital and effort, one company, represented by the mercer and alderman, William Allen, was responsible for almost all the cloth shipments in 1565. Three years later even his interest seems to have gone. That the Adventurers should hurry back to Antwerp when the embargo was raised was in no way surprising. With few exceptions they were specialists in the one market and rarely traded cloths elsewhere. Fewer than thirty Adventurers shipped cloths to other ports (mostly in Spain) and three only exported to more than two markets. The advice given later to their famous member, Lionel Cranfield, not to have 'too many irons in the fire' would have been familiar and generally accepted.[10] The alderman, whose business interests ranged from Morocco through Spain and France to the Low Countries, Germany and Russia, was quite exceptional. More typical were

10. R. H. Tawney, *Business and Politics under James I* (Cambridge, 1958), p. 67.

Allen's fellow mercers and Adventurers, John and Henry Isham. Both kept close to the well-charted channels of traffic and spread their investment not by diversifying markets abroad but by buying land and lending money at home.[11] In one respect only were they unusual, and even there the departure from the norm was towards yet more specialisation. This was in their preference for the cheaper northern kerseys over the superior and more popular southern variety, as well as over the conventional broadcloth. Together they shipped more than a quarter of the Adventurers' northern kerseys in 1565. Most were presumably destined for Italy in return for the fustians and silks that were the staple of their import trade. Kerseys were also the Italian merchants' speciality. Overall, however, the port books confirm the dominance of the West Country broadcloths. Sixty-five per cent of the cloths shipped to Antwerp were Gloucesters or Wiltshires, the remainder being made up in roughly equal quantities of dyed Suffolks, which sold better in the Baltic, and cloths from the south-eastern cloth-producing counties. Broadcloths of all kinds outnumbered the cheaper kerseys and dozens by about three-to-one, a ratio which had seemingly changed little for a generation or more.[12] By the end of the century the redirection of London's trade and the growth of the 'new draperies' had depressed the sales of the cheaper cloths even further.[13]

If the Ishams held aloof from the search for new and wider markets they nonetheless prospered. Indeed, their careers testify to the economic advantages of specialisation, although it must be said that the reverse of the coin was shown when John virtually retired from trade after his familiar Antwerp market closed. But by then he could afford retirement, for he and his brother had joined the ranks of that small, powerful and wealthy elite which dominated London's overseas trade. Probably not many more than fifty active merchants comprised this elite and while its composition obviously changed its exclusiveness was remarkably constant. In 1535 seventeen Adventurers, or thirteen per cent of all traders, had owned almost half the cloths shipped from London for the summer market.[14] Thirty years later fifteen per cent, with

11. *Isham* (ed. Ramsay), Introduction.
12. Smedt, *Engelse Natie*, ii, 427–30, 433.
13. L. Stone, 'Elizabethan Overseas Trade', *EcHR*, Ser. 2, 2 (1949) App. ii.
14. Smedt, *Engelse Natie*, ii, 427–30.

mercers particularly prominent, owned exactly half the cloths that
were shipped over the five-month period; and in the full year
from September 1564 almost half of all the exports by English
merchants were owned by forty-six. A half-century later the
pattern of distribution was much the same.[15] Complaints then
that the Fellowship was 'the spring of all monopolies . . . engross-
ing the grand staple commodities of cloth into so few men's
hands' reflected not a new phenomenon but a more openly
critical attitude towards it.[16] In William Cecil's time such concentration had official if not wider support. It was the young and
inexperienced 'unable and unsufficient merchants' rather than the
monopolists or 'engrossers' who attracted his disapproval.[17]

Unpopular with the government also, though for different
reasons, were London's foreign businessmen. Many were indeed
small 'in-and-out' traders, often shipmasters trading for themselves in a few cloths or tuns of beer; but their casual intrusions
were a minor irritant when compared with the permanent presence of the very 'sufficient' and experienced communities of
foreign merchants who were so fiercely condemned in the early
years of Elizabeth's reign.[18] Although the Hanse was the first to
be attacked, the Steelyard men do not appear to have been serious
competitors in the Antwerp trade itself. Extravagant claims were
made that they 'coloured' their trade by using English agents, but
such charges were part and parcel of the xenophobic campaign
against them.[19] If the practice was so common, why did one Hanse
merchant, Gawen van Alden, declare nearly 900 cloths for Antwerp in 1565? Altogether more convincing was the objection that
their cloth shipments to Hamburg competed strongly with the
Adventurers in vital German markets. Even in imports there was
an element of competition with the shipment of cheap linens
('soultwich' and 'middlegood'), flax and other wares. More substantial as well as direct, however, was the competition from a

15. A. Friis, *Alderman Cockayne's Project* (Copenhagen–London, 1927), pp. 77–
78, 93.
16. From the Free Trade Bill of 1604: *CJ*, i, 218.
17. Memorandum by Cecil in *Tudor Economic Documents*, ii, 45–7. More than
half the Adventurers in 1565 might have fitted Cecil's description with 116 out of
215 English merchants shipping fewer than 100 cloths each.
18. This concerted attack by the crown and the Adventurers is a main theme
of G. D. Ramsay, *The City of London in International Politics at the Accession of
Elizabeth Tudor* (Manchester, 1975).
19. SP12/60/97.

dozen or so Italian businessmen who dominated the aliens' trade. In 1564/5 seven Italians shipped half the cloths in the alien account: the Venetians Placito Ragossini, Innocento Lucatelli and Antonio Donato; Ambrogio Ferrari of Milan; Michel and Paulus Fortune of Florence; and from Florence also the ubiquitous Roberto Ridolfi, who was agent for various Italian firms—including the Cavalcanti, whose London branch he took over in the 1560s.[20] In the absence of any record of their import trade it can only be surmised that they were no less active there; and that was the point on which English hostility and dissatisfaction were focused. As Table 3 reveals, in the four years from the re-opening of the Scheldt in 1565 aliens paid never less than a third of all poundage, and much of this was presumably charged on shipments from the Low Countries.

IMPORTS

The high degree of specialisation and concentration by and among merchants and in the export trade generally is not found with the same consistency in the record of imports. On the one hand, the tendency towards oligopoly is if anything even more apparent with a mere thirty or so merchants accounting for half the Antwerp trade; on the other, the port book shows that the Adventurers all had a much wider range of both goods and markets. About one in four (or one in three if Bergen-op-Zoom is thought of as anything more than a commercial suburb of Antwerp) imported from other markets as well as their staple. Canvas from Rouen supplemented, and in a few cases dominated, the trade of drapers, skinners and ironmongers; and the grocers, who seem to have been more prominent as importers than exporters, shipped oils and fruit in quantity from Spain. Even those who did not extend their markets had to deal in a much wider variety of wares. Most had the speciality associated with their company, but only the mercers were able to keep strictly to it; and demand for their silks and fustians was such that they were also the staple commodities of leathersellers and haberdashers, although most included linen, dyestuffs and metalware in their imports from the Low Countries. Grocers were more eclectic still. Foodstuffs, drugs and

20. HCA13/16, ff. 279, 286.

hops were their stock-in-trade but most made part of their return in other commodities such as linen, although this, with household fabrics, was more the speciality of skinners and drapers. As is well known, the overseas trading companies' lines of demarcation had clearly become blurred, if not wholly erased by this period.

This evidence of the particular merchant's activities and experience would imply two important general features of the import trade which seem to contrast markedly with the pattern for exports: one is the reduced role of Antwerp in providing returns for cloth, the other the much wider range of goods that the single export commodity secured at the mart itself. Both trends can be measured from the port book, although it is essential to note that the results relate only to the native and Hanseatic trade. The value of London's imports from all markets in 1567–8 has been estimated at £165,722, of which 12 per cent is accounted for by wine.[21] With strong support from canvas, paper, glass and small-wares from Rouen worth over £20,000, wine gave France a share of imports of 22 per cent. It also contributed to Spain's 11 per cent and, through the Rhenish wine staple at Dordrecht, the seven per cent share of Holland. As the importance of these countries rose, that of Antwerp fell to 37 per cent. In all probability, however, her position would have been greatly strengthened by the inclusion of alien imports. It can only be surmised that Antwerp was at least as important in supplying the Italian and other alien merchants with imports as it was in marketing their cloths. If so, Antwerp's share of London's import trade would rise to a figure not far short of that for exports.

If Antwerp's importance in providing goods for the metropolitan market must remain in some doubt, the remarkable variety of wares the Adventurers bought there is not. As both entrepôt and a centre of distribution for local products the city

21. Tonnage was paid on the following wines: French 3504 tuns plus 92 from Holland; Spanish 1155½ tuns; Mediterranean—entered on the licence of the Italian Benedict Spinola and properly speaking to the alien account—1191 tuns 263 caroteels; Rhenish 1638 *aams*. The wine has been valued at the official rate of 10s. the *aam* Rhenish taking six *aams* to the tun. Cf. M. Morineau, *Jauges et Méthodes de Jauge Anciennes et Modernes* (Paris, 1966), p. 90 n. 2. It must be stressed that this procedure, which ignores price differentials within as well as between the various classes of wine and from one vintage to the next, can only produce the roughest approximation. Wholesale prices are difficult to establish though some for types of Rochelle wine are given in E. Trocmé and M. Delafosse, *Le Commerce Rochelais de la fin du XVe siècle au debut du XVIIe* (Paris, 1952), pp. 177–8.

offered almost every kind of commodity. Grain, wine and naval stores were the only notable exceptions. Foodstuffs were mainly transit-goods, especially spices. Of the costly silk, mixed fabrics and linens some were local manufactures, whilst others came from further afield with both quality and cost increasing with distance. Italy sent the most luxurious silks and fustians of the highest quality. Cheaper types of fustian were made at Ulm ('holmes'), Augsburg and Nuremberg; 'false' satins were fabricated at Bruges. Ticks were also a speciality of Bruges and of Turnhout ('Tournold' or 'Tourney'), which was the main centre of the Kempen tick-weaving industry. Oudenaarde was noted for tap-estries which were sold at the *Tapissierpand* in Antwerp's Nieuw-stad. More basic textiles were also manufactured close to Antwerp. The so-called 'Holland' cloths which often appear in the Adven-turers' consignments were in fact linens from Flanders and Bra-bant: they were merely bleached in the northern province. Similar cloths were made at Oudenaarde. Cheaper still were the 'Bar' or 'barrois' linen-canvases which were bought for wrapping the packs of broadcloth and thus found their way back to Ant-werp. If we add to this list of textiles the 'light draperies'—camlets, says and bombazines—and the threads of linen and worsted yarns or 'crewel', which are regarded here as semi-manufactures, the range available at Antwerp was truly remarkable. And there is still to be noted the metals which, as well as being shipped in the raw state, were imported in a wide range of manufactured goods: pins and wire, pots and pans, andirons and fire-dogs, swords and tools of all kinds.

Within any category of product the diversity of imports from Antwerp might thus be wide and complex. Any attempt at classification, as in Table 2, of the whole spectrum of wares from that source is bound to encounter difficulties. Commodities with more than one use could be assigned to two or more categories (fenugreek, for example, was a herb, medicine and dyestuff), while others have no clear application of any kind. Were 'catlins' a surgical knife, catgut for stringed instruments or neither? There is also the larger problem of distinguishing manufactures, semi-manufactures and raw materials. Some doubt must remain, for example, about the allocation of 'iron plates' and 'doubles' to metalware rather than metals. But such problems are not large enough seriously to affect the figures.

Table 2. Imports from Antwerp to London—English and Hanseatic—in 1567-8
(to the nearest £)

Manufactures and Semi-manufactures	£	Foodstuffs and Raw Materials	£
Linens	6744	For textiles (silk, wool, crewel, etc.)	1486
Mixed fabrics and woollens	8576	Furs and skins	590
Silks	11321	Metals	1002
Dressware	340	Dyestuffs	5744
Metalware	7410	Oils and chemicals	1197
Glassware	165	Groceries, drugs and spices	11966
Furniture and Smallware	165	Hops	1896
Unallocated	1223	Unallocated	448
Total	35944		24329

In the crisis years that opened Elizabeth's reign her secretary, Cecil, was pressed with advice and memoranda, some requested, others volunteered, on the state of English trade. One paper listed, according to no apparent criteria, 'necessary' and 'superfluous' imports.[22] Others drew the more obvious distinction between manufactures and raw materials in order to stress the country's costly dependence, economically and politically, on imports of the former. The figures in Table 2 give some measure of the relevance of such charges to the Antwerp trade. Goods wholly or partly manufactured comprised over half that trade and more than a quarter of all imports, wine excluded, in that year.[23] The cost of luxury fabrics for the adornment of the wealthy few (although the sumptuary laws imply that such conspicuous consumption was spreading) was clearly disturbing to the conservative and 'mercantilist' drift of the secretary's thought. Metalware had greater utility but, as the restrictive legislation of 1563 declared, imports curbed the growth of domestic manufactures.[24] And what was to be made of the spices, pepper especially, which added so much to the cost of foodstuffs? Many

22. Printed in H. Hall, *History of the Customs Revenue in England*, ii (1892), 236–42.
23. A classification of all imports in 1567/8 has not yet been attempted. In 1559/60 and 1564/5 manufactures and semi-manufactures were respectively 43 and 45 per cent of imports, wines excluded. These calculations are from contemporary lists printed in Dietz, op. cit., App. iii.
24. 5 Eliz., c. 7.

were necessary and few could be produced at home. But did Antwerp's effective monopoly sustain prices that were artificially high as well as naturally unstable? Lastly, manufactures included many articles which Clement Armstrong no doubt would have called 'strange merchandise and artificiall fantasies': tennis balls by the thousand, ear picks, perfumed soaps or 'washing balls', cap rosettes and so on. Such 'unnecessary trifflees', in Cecil's words, tended to obscure the import of necessary raw materials like oils and dyestuffs for the woollen industry, hemp for rope and flax for linen.

THE BALANCE OF TRADE

Antwerp, thus, had all the conveniences of a hyper-market for international buying and selling. A vast range of wares were offered in the one place at prices which were presumably, in so far as there were accessible alternative markets, competitive. For payment it accepted through a sophisticated mechanism of credit and exchange the cloths which were redistributed throughout Europe. There were, however, inconveniences in such a high degree of concentration, and in a memorandum drawn up probably during the restraint of 1564, and certainly in a mood of hostility towards the Low Countries, Cecil indicated some of them.[25] In his catalogue of complaints, however, on the crucial question of the balance of trade, which had never been far from his thoughts in recent years, Cecil was significantly hesitant and vague. The memoranda which had been submitted to him in those years included trade figures which purported to show an adverse balance for London.[26] Perhaps he referred to these when he observed that 'very lately the commodities carryed out of the realm . . . hath scantly answered the vallor of the merchandize brought in'. Yet, despite those figures and his dislike of Antwerp, he goes no further than the familiar criticism of the excess of 'unnecessary' wares and to predict that if trade in these continued 'but a whyle' money would flow out to pay for them. Thus, for Cecil the position was not clear; and given the nature of the problem and the state of the evidence, the historian is bound to share that uncertainty. If the record of the exchange of goods is discouragingly episodic and impressionistic, that of profit and services

25. *Tudor Economic Documents*, ii, 45–7.   26. Stone, op. cit., p. 36.

permits only the most uncertain conjectures. An intensive study of the exchanges and perhaps the level of mint supply (to continue that already made for the 1540s and 1550s) must also be a primary element in any such discussion.[27] However, the subject might merit some investigation, by way of conclusion, on the simple but hitherto undeveloped basis of the evidence of the port books and other customs accounts. On this can be built a series of arguments which inevitably contain much conjecture and inference. If the resulting structure is patently unsound it may serve at least to invite demolition.

Because of the limitations of the port books a retreat into 'statistical juggling' is unavoidable. As we have seen, they register exports for only half a year and imports for a full but different year, and then not for aliens. Even if the records were complete for one and the same year, it would clearly be dangerous to extrapolate trends from that year to others. The additional figures for poundage in Table 3 do, however, provide a framework within which the indications offered by our incomplete data can be amplified and so interpreted to permit a rough balance sheet to be drawn up for the two years. The first task, therefore, is to calculate cloth exports on the basis of the records for 1565. Assuming that the percentages of cloths shipped to Antwerp by denizen, alien and Hanse merchants were constant over the twelve months from September 1564 and allowing for the duty-free wrapper, we arrive at a total of about 90,000 cloths.[28] In the more settled year of 1567–8 when London's exports were presumably not less than 100,000 cloths, and assuming that Antwerp took the same proportion of those cloths as in 1564–5, shipments there have been estimated at about 63,500.[29] A notional value of £5 may be put on the shortcloth which, while it seriously oversimplifies a complex problem, seems to be a reasonably conservative estimate.[30] At this price exports would have been worth about £450,000 in

27. J. D. Gould, *The Great Debasement* (Oxford, 1970), esp. ch. 5.

28. From some date in 1559 one cloth in every pack of ten was allowed free of duty in London for denizens and for the Hanse the following year. Ramsay, op. cit., pp. 152, 175 n. 39. The allowance may not have been automatic and aliens may not have enjoyed the same concession. Willan, *Rates*, p. xvii.

29. An estimate from the triennial averages for cloth exports in F. J. Fisher, 'Commercial Trends and Policies in the Sixteenth-Century', *EcHR*, Ser. 2, 10 (1940), 2.

30. Based on price data in Willan, *Rates*, pp. xv–xvi, Smedt, *Engelse Natie*, ii, 350 and *Isham* (ed. Ramsay), pp. 52–3, 115, 138.

the boom year and £318,000 in 1567–8. Imports have been calculated on the basis of the port book and by assuming, first, that
alien imports did match their exports, and secondly, that for
1564–5 denizen imports from Antwerp were 36 per cent of their
total for that year, as in 1567–8. Thus, in the earlier year imports
were about £76,300 in the denizen account and £92,600 by
aliens. In 1567–8 the corresponding figures are £61,500 and
£66,000 with £300 credited to merchants of the Hanse. By these
estimates London emerges with a favourable balance of £280,000
in 1564–5 and £180,000 in 1567–8. The undervaluation of imports which has been noted would reduce these margins, but
against this can be set the value of London's other exports, however small.

Table 3. Valuations for Poundage of Imports into
London (to the nearest £)[31]

Year	Denizen	Alien	Hanse
	£	£	£
1564–5	206,095	118,579	—
1565–6	156,865	92,633	—
1566–7	141,072	97,681	—
1567–8	140,268	87,702	10,223

A strictly bilateral exchange of goods is of course a simplistic
model for trade balances. Triangular traffic certainly flowed between London, Antwerp and ports in France or Spain.[32] How important this was cannot be measured; nor can the profit and loss
on insurance and freight. But it is unlikely that multilateral
trading by the Adventurers was an important element in their
activities. When the Fellowship in 1579 condemned those members
who traded with Spain *via* the staple it did so on the grounds that
such traffic was opposed to the company's traditional bilateral
trade.[33] Similarly it is unlikely that the cost of insurance was ever
a significant item in the direct exchange. Risk was spread more
simply and directly by splitting consignments into small parcels in
several ships. In the *Lyon*, for example, which began to unload in
the Thames in March 1568, the cargo worth over £1000 was

31. E356/28. In the first three years Hanseatic merchants may have been
included in the denizen account.
32. Smedt, *Engelse Natie*, ii, 371, 392, 399, 424–6.
33. *Tudor Economic Documents*, ii, 53–8.

shared by fifty merchants. Individual cloth shipments were usually more valuable but the voyage itself was short and well conducted. Premiums at the Antwerp Bourse of two per cent rising to three in wartime were the lowest for any important route in Europe.[34] Moreover, if insurance was sought it could be taken up in Lombard Street where brokers and underwriters had the skills, resources and reputation to rival their counterparts in Antwerp.[35] Lastly, on the question of profit or loss on the transport account, some inferences may be drawn from the port books. These show that, as company policy required, the Adventurers' trade was largely confined to English ships. Licences were needed for shipments in foreign bottoms and, as one factor could testify, these were not granted lightly.[36] Foreigners were more likely to freight Dutch hoys and this was of some importance in the import trade. But it seems beyond doubt that English shipowners took at least half the transport profits and probably much more than that. The least that can be argued for both invisible items is that the distribution of profit between London and Antwerp could not have closed the gap in earnings from the commodity exchange.

A favourable balance overall would not preclude selective or temporary outflows of specie. Within the totality of the market served by Antwerp there were regions with which the terms of trade were probably unfavourable. Italy would be the most obvious of these. In 1565 the Antwerp magistrates asserted that the Adventurers shipped to England twice as many silks and fustians as they sent kerseys to Italy through the Low Countries.[37] Sharp falls in the exchange rate would also lead to short-term outflows, while a more persistent drain was presumably caused by the chronic imbalance in the alien trading account. Our evidence that their trade was import-led in both years lends support to the charges which were commonly made against foreign businessmen; and this despite the obstacles which were put in their way in remitting money to Antwerp by exchange. And so strong was the distrust of foreigners, especially the 'Caterpilleres the Bankeres of Antwerpe', that these essentially spasmodic or selective losses

34. Vasquez de Prada, *Lettres*, i, 243.

35. W. J. Jones, 'Elizabethan marine insurance: the judicial undergrowth', *Business History*, ii (1960). The Antwerp insurance market seems to have had a dubious reputation in the 1560s; cf. J. A. Goris, *Études sur les colonies marchandes etc* (Louvain, 1925), pp. 178ff.

36. SP46/13/133.　　　37. Smedt, *Engelse Natie*, ii, 387 n. 5.

could be magnified out of all proportion by special interest groups, not least the Adventurers themselves. If Cecil seemingly remained unimpressed, despite his distrust of foreigners, this may have been because he saw France as the principal drain on English gold, a belief the trade figures strongly support.[38] The Baltic trade also seems to have been import-led before the 1570s.[39] At Hamburg the exchange of goods was probably more in balance, but the trade in both directions was a virtual monopoly of the Hanse and of foreign ships. Moving to the periphery, Moroccan trade was an English concern, but the commodity exchange seems to have shown a loss.[40] Of London's main markets only Spain could be said with any confidence to have offered favourable terms of trade. A balance of the figures, on the lines adopted for Antwerp, would suggest this and support the observations of contemporaries.[41] Thus negative reasoning, as employed by Professor Brulez—though for the whole of England's trade with the Low Countries—supports a conclusion that is opposed to his, for London at least.[42]

December 1568 marked the end of an era in the structure of England's trade. In retrospect and in the long view the breach with Antwerp that Elizabeth caused by her uncharacteristically precipitate action forced changes in pattern and direction which, however disruptive and discomfiting the effects may have been in the short-term, proved to be both necessary and desirable. The closure of the hyper-market on the Scheldt dismayed merchants like Isham, but for others it was a spur to experiment and exploration in the face of the conservatism and complacency of generations of merchants who had built their fortunes inside Antwerp's secure and hospitable walls. By forcing them to seek alternative markets it helped to broaden the commercial base from which trans-oceanic trade and imperial enterprise developed. The closure also ended the 'triumph of the small ship' which had

---

38. *HMC* Hatfield, i, 162–5.   39. Zins, *Baltic*, ch. 9.
40. T. S. Willan, *Studies in Elizabethan Foreign Trade* (Manchester, 1959), pp. 107–112.
41. E.g. the 'direction for divers trades' in *Tudor Economic Documents*, iii, 199–210.
42. W. Brulez, 'Le commerce international des Pays Bas au XVIe siècle: essai d'appréciation quantitative', *Revue Belge de Philologie et d'Histoire*, xlvi (1968), 1205–21.

sufficed for the short, cross-Channel hauls and encouraged the building of larger vessels which were to serve as instruments of empire. In 1567–8 the average size of English ships entering the port of London was 56 tons. At the end of the century it had risen to 82 tons and the proportion of merchantmen of a hundred tons or more had grown from a mere six per cent to almost half.[43]

If the importance of these advances is not in doubt it should nevertheless be stressed how persistent some elements were in the evolving pattern of Elizabethan trade; and it may be argued, too, that the gains from the restructuring after 1568 were by no means unqualified. Continuing concentration in the sense of oligopoly and specialisation in goods and markets has been noted already. In addition and in spite of the widening and diversification of those markets the pattern of distribution shows remarkable continuity. In the late 1580s the Adventurers still provided 40 per cent of London's imports and in 1606 they shipped to Germany and the Low Countries almost exactly the same proportion of cloths as they did to Antwerp before its closure.[44] Trade thus remained essentially intra-European and within Europe it was narrowly confined to relatively short routes. Nor did the cloth markets, whether old or new, show convincing signs of sustained growth. Exports in 1606, a year of recovery from the slump at the turn of the century, were roughly of the same volume as in 1564–5. Demand for cloth was relatively inelastic and, as the century progressed, English textiles faced growing, if uneven, competition from foreign manufactures. Price movements, although difficult as ever to establish, seem to reflect these problems by rising slowly and slightly over the half-century.[45] When in the 1620s Gerard Malynes analysed trends in commerce in the previous seventy years, he concluded that the cost of imports had risen much faster than the price of English cloths. The cheapness of exports, he conceded, encouraged a 'lively trade' but one which

43. A comparison of the port book for 1567/8 with the record of incoming ships in 1599/1600 in E190/11/1.
44. A. M. Millard, 'The Import Trade of London 1600–1640' (London Univ. Ph.D. thesis, 1956), p. 71; Friis, *Cockayne's Project*, p. 61. The figures are 72 as against 71 per cent in 1565.
45. Prices are quoted in Lionel Cranfield's correspondence in *HMC* Sackville, ii; cf. also W. B. Stephens, 'Further observations on English Cloth exports, 1600–1640', *EcHR*, Ser. 2, 24 (1971), 254–6.

was adversely balanced.[46] An investigation of imports in that period reveals some encouraging features.[47] Linens seem to have fallen, along with metals and metalware, no doubt in response to the rise in domestic production and manufacture. But the import of wines, silks, mixed fabrics and some groceries had risen; and the aliens' share, after contracting during the recession of the late sixteenth century, had been restored when trade recovered after 1604. As in the 1560s, the Netherlands provided the bulk of their imports; most were manufactures (62 per cent in 1619–20) and 'transit-goods' were still prominent (43 per cent in the same year). In the searching debate on the state of trade which was occasioned by the crisis of the early 1620s the adverse balance, the aliens' persistence and strength, the continuing dependence on foreign manufactures and the expensive purchases of 'unnecessary' luxury goods were dominant themes, thus echoing the anxieties expressed by Cecil sixty years before and underlining the continuity of basic elements in metropolitan trade. And in the light of this debate the gains normally attributed to Antwerp's closure may not have seemed so obvious. If the diversification of markets had spread risks it had by no means eliminated them.

46. *Lex Mercatoria etc* (1636 edn), pp. 87–90.
47. Millard, op. cit., p. 37 and *passim*.

XI

Wealden Ironmasters in the Age of Elizabeth

J. J. GORING

In the age of Elizabeth most of England's iron was made in the Weald, that densely-wooded stretch of high ground, some sixty-five miles long and up to twenty-five miles wide, which straddles the northern part of Sussex and the adjoining parts of Surrey and Kent. The explanation of this pre-eminence is not hard to find: the region possessed an abundance of ore and timber, a large and growing labour force and, except in very dry seasons, a fairly adequate supply of water-power; it was close to northern France and southern Flanders, whence came the skilled technologists upon whom the industry at this period continued to depend; it was closer still to London, where there was generally a ready market for its products, and to the numerous ports and havens of the Sussex coast, from which iron could be shipped to more distant parts.[1] The demand for iron, particularly for military purposes, had grown considerably during the war-troubled years of Henry VIII's reign, and in the early part of Elizabeth's, although England was officially at peace, the trend continued. In the 1560s many new works were established in the Weald and by 1574 the number of furnaces and forges, which at mid-century had been around fifty, had passed the hundred mark.[2] Correspondingly there had been an increase in the number of men who devoted their energies to the business of iron manufacture—those enterprising 'iron-makers' or 'ironmasters' who are the subject of this essay.

Any study of the Wealden ironmasters in the Elizabethan period presents two initial difficulties. One is the problem of definition: what was an ironmaster? The term, which had no contemporary

---

1. Cf. G. F. Hammersley, 'The charcoal iron industry and its fuel', *EcHR*, Ser. 2, 26 (1973), 596.
2. H. R. Schubert, *History of the British Iron and Steel Industry* (1957), pp. 173–5.

currency, has sometimes been applied indiscriminately to almost anyone deriving financial benefit from the iron industry, including the landowner receiving rents from works established on his estates and, at the other extreme, the wage-earning clerk or manager who supervised ironworks on another's behalf. For the purposes of this essay a much narrower definition has been adopted—one that accords with this description of an early industrial entrepreneur: 'He is more than just a manager; he is a leader in business, an initiator, a policy-maker. He must either himself supply capital or have some control over the supply of it. He must also be a producer or developer and be personally involved in his enterprise, although not necessarily alone in it.'[3] In the following account, therefore, the word 'ironmaster' is not applied to people who were merely owners or managers of ironworks, but only to those who had a definite stake in the business of iron manufacture. The nature and size of the stake varied considerably from man to man, for the Wealden ironmasters were a very varied bunch of people—ranging from the small producer who personally supervised the daily operations of his forge or furnace to the great magnate who delegated most of the work to subordinates.

The second problem is that of identification: who were the Wealden ironmasters? For the Elizabethan period the only surviving lists of names which have any claim to completeness are those drawn up in 1574 when the privy council, deeply concerned about the illegal export of ordnance, summoned all those believed to be engaged in iron manufacture and ordered them to enter into certain recognisances.[4] But since these lists often include the names of owners as well as occupiers of ironworks, it is not always easy to discover who in fact were the ironmasters. Some men who look like ironmasters turn out on closer inspection to be merely landowners with forges or furnaces on their estates, while others, who appear at first sight merely to be landowners, turn out to be genuine entrepreneurs. However, after a certain

3. J. W. Gough, *The Rise of the Entrepreneur* (1969), p. 12.
4. See below p. 218. The most complete list of names is in SP12/95/20; printed, with amendments, E. Straker, 'Wealden ironworks in 1574', *Sussex Notes and Queries*, vii (1938), 97–103 (hereafter *SNQ*). Other lists of varying completeness and accuracy are in SP12/95/21, 61, 79; SP12/96 p. 199; SP12/117/39; BL, Stowe 570, f. 103. I am indebted to Mr C. S. Cattell for sight of the Ms. of his forthcoming article 'The 1574 lists of ironworks in the Weald'.

amount of adding and subtracting it is possible to identify sixty-one men who were almost certainly operating in the Weald in 1574, and it is upon an analysis of the activities of these men that this study is based.[5]

These sixty-one ironmasters can be divided into two categories—owner-occupiers and tenants. Tenants can be further sub-divided, as they are in one of the 1574 lists, into 'farmers', who held ironworks on leases for terms ranging from seven to forty years, and 'occupiers', who resembled tenants-at-will: one such was William Walpole, who occupied a forge and furnace in Petworth leased to his mother-in-law and held it 'during pleasure'. Too clear a distinction, however, should not be drawn between tenants and owner-occupiers: some ironmasters like John French, described in 1574 as owner-occupier of a forge in Chiddingly and as farmer (jointly with John Thorpe) of a forge and furnace in Worth, fell simultaneously into both categories.[6] Moreover, the nature and extent of their capital investment was often similar: contrary to what has sometimes been stated, tenants on occasion provided not only the 'working capital'—stock and raw materials —but also the 'fixed capital' in the form of plant, machinery and buildings. In 1562, for example, when William Relfe and Bartholomew Jefferay leased land in Waterdown Forest from Lord Abergavenny, they proceeded to erect, apparently at their own cost, all the necessary 'bayes, banckes, walles, hedes, dames, pondes, fludgates, sluces and trenches' and also 'lodges or cotages for ther colyers, worckmen and servauntes'.[7] Similarly in 1571, when Thomas Glyde and Simon Colman began to establish a furnace at Clippenham, all that the landlord provided was seven acres of marshy ground.[8]

The need to find large amounts of capital for the establishment of forges and furnaces provides one explanation of the tendency for tenant ironmasters to form partnerships. Partnerships had been unusual in the early Tudor period, but in the second half of the

5. For a list of their names see Table 1. The list is inevitably tentative and subject to revision.

6. SP12/95/79.

7. STAC5/A2/25; H. R. Schubert, 'A Tudor furnace in Waterdown Forest', *Journ. Iron and Steel Institute*, 169 (1951), 241–2. Waterdown Forest lay in the parishes of Rotherfield and Frant.

8. BL, Add. Ch. 30187. Clippenham, otherwise Batsford furnace lay on the boundary between the parishes of Warbleton and Herstmonceux.

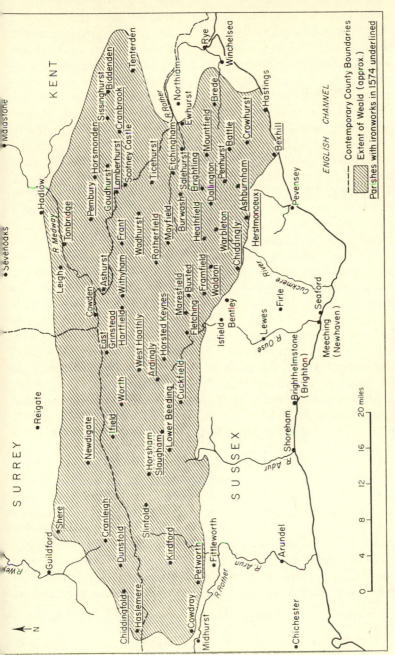

Map 3. Ironworks in the Weald in 1574

century they became increasingly common. Relfe and Jefferay's joint venture can be paralleled by many others throughout the Weald; indeed eighteen of the ironmasters under consideration were involved in partnerships at one time or another. Occasionally one man might belong to two partnerships at the same time: in 1574, for instance, John Duffield, in business on his own at East Grinstead, was associated with John Lambert at Cranleigh and with Thomas Smith at Kirdford.[9] There was, however, nothing very permanent about such arrangements: these loose personal associations depended for their survival upon the bonds of mutual trust and understanding, and these were sometimes rather fragile. The partnership of Thomas Glyde and Thomas Hay is a case in point. In 1579, when the two men became joint occupiers of a forge and furnace in Ashburnham, they agreed to keep 'jointe accoumptes, reckoninges, receites and other thinges' and to divide the profits of the enterprise equally between them. All went well for a time, but soon 'diuers controuersyes, variaunces and debates' arose between them over 'paymentes and receites of money, receites of woode, iron sowes and other thinges'. Each accused the other of underhand dealings: Hay alleged that Glyde had not kept true accounts, while Glyde claimed that Hay, who was much more familiar with the technicalities of book-keeping, had conspired with the clerk of the works to defraud him of his fair share of the profits.[10] Bad feelings between the two ironmasters persisted to the end: shortly before his death in 1590 Glyde complained that Hay, who had taken over his former partner's lease of Etchingham forge, had wrongfully deprived him of three tons of bar iron.[11]

One of the attractions of a partnership for Elizabethan ironmasters lay in the opportunity that it gave for a greater degree of vertical integration. Complete vertical integration, involving control over the supply of raw materials as well as the various stages of manufacture, was rare: only a few individual entrepreneurs like Sir Richard Baker, whose extensive estates throughout the Weald yielded an ample provision of timber and ore, could hope to achieve it. But on their own, many ironmasters failed to achieve even that minimum of integration provided by

9. Straker, SNQ, vii, 100; SP12/95/79. For other examples of partnership see Table 1.
10. STAC5/G4/28, H46/31.   11. REQ2/68/5c.

the possession of a furnace, in which to smelt ore into pig-iron, and a forge, in which to convert the pig into wrought iron bars. One who was in this situation in 1574 was Robert Woddy, who worked Benhall forge in Frant but seems to have had no furnace; he would therefore have been obliged to buy in pig-iron at a price which might be considerably higher than the cost of manufacture.[12] Woddy would probably have been attracted by the prospect of an association with other ironmasters that would ensure him an ample supply of low-price pig-iron; and this perhaps explains why in (or shortly before) 1578 he entered into partnership with Michael Weston and David Willard for the purpose of setting up a new furnace at Brede.[13] A partnership, moreover, might provide horizontal as well as vertical integration. The possession of a number of plants working in parallel offered a degree of flexibility denied to the individual entrepreneur operating on a smaller scale: in the 1560s Relfe and Jefferay, it has been suggested, were in a particularly strong position because they possessed a number of furnaces and forges 'between which they could switch as water or raw material shortages dictated'.[14]

Although partnership was becoming more common in the Elizabethan period, the most usual form of industrial organisation in the Weald was still the one-man business. Almost all the owner-occupiers and a majority of the tenant ironmasters carried on business on their own. While a few of these individual entrepreneurs, such as Henry Bowyer and Roger Gratwick, occupied several ironworking sites, most of them had but a single forge or furnace—or a forge and furnace in close juxtaposition.[15] Indeed the situation could hardly have been otherwise if the ironmaster was to exercise close supervision over his business. Many ironmasters, it seems, liked to live within a mile or two of their works: the house that Nicholas Fowle built at Riverhall near Wadhurst in 1591, for example, stands on the very edge of what was formerly the great pond of his ironworks.[16] Of course, not

12. Cf. D. W. Crossley, 'The management of a sixteenth-century ironworks', EcHR, Ser. 2, 19 (1966), 279–83.
13. E. Straker, Wealden Iron (1931), p. 341.
14. D. W. Crossley, 'A sixteenth century Wealden blast furnace', Post-Medieval Archaeology, vi (1972), 63.
15. See Table 1.
16. M. A. Lower, 'Ironworks in the county of Sussex', SAC, ii (1849), 218. For the location of the homes of the ironmasters see Table 1.

all ironmasters were able or willing to keep such a careful watch on their workmen. Sir Thomas Gresham, for instance, who paid infrequent visits to his house at Mayfield, would have been obliged to delegate to others the daily supervision of his gun foundry there.[17] Sir Richard Baker was in a similar position: in a survey of Kentish ironworks made in 1588 it was stated that he had in his own hands 'a fordge or hammer within one mile of his dwelling howse . . . called Sussingherst' and a furnace about four miles away, but that his founder was 'ouerseer of all Sir Rychard Baker's thinges and his onlie doer in his absence'.[18] Again Ralph Hogge, the Queen's gunfounder, whose official duties probably necessitated frequent absences in London, employed his brother-in-law as manager of his Buxted ironworks.[19]

Even if he did not employ a manager to run his works for him, an ironmaster often relied upon someone else to provide the technical expertise. It is well known that in the early part of the sixteenth century the Wealden industry had depended heavily upon foreign technologists—Frenchmen, Flemings and occasionally Germans—and this pattern persisted into the Elizabethan period. In 1571 four ironmasters in Rotherfield hundred—Alexander Fermor, John Carpenter, John Barham and John Porter—each had an alien 'servant' named in the subsidy roll.[20] Barham's man, one Pullen, may have been a kinsman of Charles Pullen, the Buxted founder whose engineering skill had earned him wide renown in the 1550s.[21] Another well-known family of alien artisans were the Pinions—Adrian, John and Gilbert: the last-named was probably an employee of Thomas Glyde, for whom he appeared as a witness in his lawsuit against Thomas Hay.[22] It is noticeable, however, that few aliens rose up out of the employee class to join the ranks of the ironmasters. One who may have done so was the otherwise unknown 'Quyntin' listed in 1574 as the occupier of a furnace in Cowden; he may have been a son of the 'Quinto, a Frencheman' who was taxed in the 'hundred of Robertsbridge' in 1524 and who was almost certainly an iron-

17. J. W. Burgon, *The Life and Times of Sir Thomas Gresham* (1839), ii. 425–6.
18. Staffordshire R.O., D593/S/4/28/3.
19. D. W. Crossley, 'Ralph Hogge's ironworks accounts, 1576–81', *SAC*, cxii (1974), 48.
20. E179/190/283, m. 18.
21. Schubert, *Hist. Brit. Iron and Steel Ind.*, p. 172.
22. E179/190/283, mm. 14–15; STAC5/G4/28.

worker.[23] Another is John Lambert, who used the more English-sounding alias of Gardiner and who may have been a relative of the John Lambert employed in ironworks at Hartfield in the 1540s.[24]

With these two possible exceptions all the ironmasters named in 1574 seem to have been true-born Englishmen. The great majority of them, moreover, hailed from south-east England; indeed it is likely that only four or five were not natives of Sussex, Kent or Surrey. One of the newcomers to Kent was Thomas Dyke, accredited by his descendants to 'a family long seated in that county', but who specifically referred in his will to Stoke Clare in Suffolk as the place 'where I was borne and brought vppe to schoole'.[25] In addition to first-generation immigrants there were some who, although born and bred in the Weald, belonged to families that had only recently settled there. Robert Whitfield's father, so it was reported in 1571, 'came out of the north 80 years past'; he had come in fact from Cumberland and in 1522, being taken for a Scot, had nearly suffered deportation as an alien.[26] Two others, Robert Hodgson and Ninian Burrell, may also have been of northern extraction.[27] But most ironmasters, it seems, were of solid Wealden stock; some indeed, like John Ashburnham, Roger and Thomas Gratwick, and possibly John Barham, were still living at or near the very spots from which in times gone by their forbears had derived their names.

While it is possible to determine the geographical origins of Wealden ironmasters, it is not always easy to be equally precise about their social origins. The ones who naturally present fewest problems are those at the top of the social pyramid—the peers and upper gentry, who may be described as 'magnate ironmasters'. Five out of the sixty-one clearly come into this category: Viscount Montague, Lord Abergavenny, Sir Thomas Gresham, Sir Richard Baker and Sir Alexander Culpepper. In addition there were two other men—John Ashburnham and Edward Elrington

23. Straker, *SNQ*, vii, 99; *Lay Subsidy Rolls for the County of Sussex, 1524–25*, ed. J. Cornwall (Sussex Rec. Soc., 56, 1956), p. 151.

24. Straker, *Wealden Iron*, p. 241. Straker confuses him with the John Gardiner employed by the Ashburnhams, ibid., pp. 371, 446.

25. *Burke's Peerage* (1959), p. 753; PROB11/125/20.

26. M. A. Lower, 'Notes on the family of Whitfield' (etc.), *SAC*, xix (1867), 84–6.

27. H. R. Hoare, 'Notes on the church of St Thomas à Becket, Framfield' (etc.), *SAC*, iv (1851), 302; J. H. Cooper, 'Cuckfield Families, iii', ibid., xliii (1900), 9n.

—who were heads of old-established armigerous families and were almost invariably accorded the status of 'esquire'. In some respects these seven were survivors from an age that had passed. At one time, it is clear, the Wealden industry had been largely in the hands of the peers and upper gentry, but by 1574 this was no longer the case: many of the big landowners, who had established ironworks on their estates in early Tudor times, had ceased to be entrepreneurs.[28] The best documented case is that of the Sidneys, who had once been among the most prominent of Sussex ironmasters: in 1573 Sir Henry Sidney severed his last direct link with the Wealden industry when he leased out his Robertsbridge works to Michael Weston.[29] And although in later years, when families such as the Pelhams and the Coverts took into their own hands some of the ironworks previously leased out to others, there may have been a reversal of this trend, there seems little doubt that in the Elizabethan period the magnate ironmaster was something of an anomaly.

In 1574 the great majority of the forges and furnaces in the Weald—over 80 per cent of them in fact—were in the hands of men below the magnate class for whom iron manufacture was not just a profitable side-line but a more or less full-time occupation.[30] These men belonged to that middle stratum of Tudor society which embraced both yeomanry and lesser gentry. The difficulty of drawing a clear line of demarcation between these two status groups is illustrated by the lists of 1574, where a man may appear in one place as a gentleman and in another as a yeoman; and even with those who were fairly consistently designated gentlemen it is not always easy to see what distinguished them from the rest. A few, like Anthony Morley, Nicholas Pope and John Wybarne, belonged to established armigerous families but then so also did Bartholomew Jefferay, described as 'a man well kinned, frended and alyed with the most part of the freeholders' in Sussex, but who never apparently enjoyed any higher status than that of yeoman.[31] Others were perhaps listed as gentlemen because, al-

28. Cf. L. Stone, *The Crisis of the Aristocracy, 1558–1641* (Oxford, 1965), p. 349. My conclusions differ from those of Professor Stone in a number of respects.

29. *Sidney Ironworks Accounts, 1541–1573*, ed. D. W. Crossley (CS, 4 ser., 15), p. 31. Robertsbridge is in Salehurst parish.

30. See Table 1.

31. M. A. Lower, 'Chiddingly—parochial history', *SAC*, xiv (1862), 219–20, Straker, *Wealden Iron*, p. 356.

though of yeoman stock, they had always been prosperous enough to maintain a 'generous' life-style: such were the second-generation ironmasters Henry Bowyer and Thomas and George May. On the other hand there were those like Roger Gratwick and Thomas and Stephen Collins, who were also the sons of wealthy ironmasters but who were invariably designated yeomen. It is surprising that such men, who evidently continued to prosper, never acquired (and never appear to have aspired to) a higher status. Gratwick, who added considerably to the extensive landed estate inherited from his father, ended his days as a yeoman; feeling himself slighted by some of the established Sussex gentry who, he maintained, regarded him as 'to meane a man' for them to associate with, he may have decided that nothing was to be gained from trying to keep up with the Coverts and the Carylls.[32] Similar considerations may have applied in the cases of Thomas Smith, who (if the 1571 subsidy assessments are any guide to comparative wealth) was the richest ironmaster in Sussex below the magnate class, and John French, another wealthy yeoman, who left cash bequests totalling over £1000: both men might have had difficulty in assuming the style and port of a gentleman since they could not even write their own names.[33]

Not all ironmasters, however, were willing to remain in the station of life into which they had been born. Alexander Fermor, designated yeoman in 1574, acquired a coat of arms in the following year, thus securing formal recognition of the status to which, as the owner of a fine new manor-house and of a prestigious new pew in Rotherfield church, he doubtless felt himself entitled.[34] Others, unwilling or unable to register a pedigree with the heralds, nonetheless adopted the rank of gentleman. One such was Thomas Stollion, who operated a chain of ironworks extending from Burwash to Waldron and by the 1590s had become sufficiently prosperous to purchase the great manor of Warbleton and rebuild the mansion-house there on a grand scale.[35] Not everyone,

32. J. Comber, 'The family of Gratwicke' (etc.), *SAC*, lx (1919), 42–3; STAC5/G3/6.

33. E179/190/283; PROB11/61/33; SP12/95/75; Lower, *SAC*, xiv, 228. The illiterate 'gentleman' was not unknown at this period, but he was becoming something of a rarity.

34. C. Pullein, *Rotherfield* (Tunbridge Wells, 1928), pp. 246–7, 348, 352.

35. *VCH Sussex*, ix, 206; T. W. Horsfield, *History of Sussex* (Lewes, 1835), i, 571.

however, recognised the newly-acquired status of this upstart ironmaster, who had begun his life in a comparatively humble home in a neighbouring parish: Oliver Cheney, heir to an estate in Warbleton which had belonged to his ancestors since the thirteenth century and of which, he maintained, Stollion was trying to get possession, pointedly referred to him as 'so welthye and wilfull a yeoman'.[36] For other wealthy and wilful yeomen with extravagant social ambitions the going was probably rather easier, because they set themselves up as gentlemen in places far removed from their native villages, where too many people would have been aware of their modest beginnings. Henry Bowyer, born at Hartfield, purchased an estate in Cuckfield (over fifteen miles away), where he built himself a magnificent mansion with an impressive gatehouse and endeavoured to play the squire; but his lordly behaviour was greatly resented by some of the local residents, including the vicar of Cuckfield and the cousins Ninian Burrell and Ninian Challenor, two prosperous ironmasters who were also grooming themselves for squiredom.[37] All three ironmasters eventually assumed the title of 'esquire', although only Burrell seems to have gained general recognition of his status; when nearly sixty years old he succeeded in marrying a niece of Sir Walter Covert and was thus able to claim cousinhood with some of the best families in the county.[38] But the most remarkable social ascent was that of Richard Leech, who seems to have started out in life with little more than the two cows, one pair of sheets, six napkins and the other odds and ends bequeathed to him by his mother, the widow of a small farmer of Smeeth in Kent, and who ended his days as lord of three Sussex manors and high sheriff of Sussex and Surrey. Leech's rise in the world was evidently assisted by Lord Buckhurst, whose ironworks he occupied at Fletching and whose generous patronage he acknowledged in his will.[39]

It would clearly be wrong to give the impression that at this period every Wealden ironmaster was prospering in business, for some men clearly were not. If the cash bequests in his will are any

36. REQ2/165/37.
37. J. H. Cooper, 'Cuckfield families, ii', *SAC*, xlii (1899), 36–8; R. B. (Manning, *Religion and Society in Elizabethan Sussex* (Leicester, 1969), pp. 113–21.
38. Cooper, *SAC*, xliii, 9–10.
39. Kent R.O., PRC/32/27, pp. 125–27; J. E. Mousley, 'Sussex Country Gentry in the reign of Elizabeth' (London Univ. Ph.D. thesis, 1956), pp. 346, 568–9.

guide to his wealth, Robert Woddy is an example of one who ended his days in rather straitened circumstances: he left only 20s. to his eldest son, 10s. to each of his younger sons and a mere 12d. to each of his unmarried daughters.[40] Clearer indications of business failure, however, are found in the cases of ironmasters dying heavily in debt. Bartholomew Jefferay, for instance, died in 1575, leaving behind him numerous debts 'as well in money as in yron', which George May and the other overseers of his will were to pay off over a five year period out of the profits of his forge in Bexhill.[41] Similarly Thomas Glyde directed that his executors were to sell all his stock of pig-iron, ore and charcoal, all his cattle, corn and implements of husbandry, 1000 cords of wood on his manor of Dixter in Northiam ('if so muche will there be had without spoyle of timber'), £150 worth of timber on his lands in Burwash and Etchingham and, if these sales did not realise enough money to discharge all his debts, the lease of his house at Ewhurst.[42] Of course in these cases the leaving of debts may not indicate a sensational 'business failure', but merely the normal situation that arose when an ironmaster working on borrowed capital died before he had paid back all his loans. In other instances, however, there is clear evidence of financial disaster on the grand scale. Anthony Morley, one of a small number of Wealden ironmasters who extended their operations into south Wales, overreached himself, went bankrupt and died owing (among other sums) over £1000 to the widow of his former associate William Relfe; he may also have owed money to the London ironmonger Giles Garton, with whom he had had extensive dealings.[43] Garton could be a hard taskmaster, as another unsuccessful ironmaster, John Ashburnham, was to discover. In 1572, being already deep in the ironmonger's debt, Ashburnham had been obliged to agree to the most stringent conditions regarding the manufacture and delivery of 120 tons of bar iron: the forge at Ashburnham was to be well and truly stocked with coals and iron sows so that 'she staye not when water will serve'; the iron was to be delivered in instalments at Bexhill sluice at the earliest possible date; and Ashburnham had to promise not to make iron for anyone else until this order had

40. PROB11/126/72.   41. East Sussex R.O., W/A6, ff. 321–3.
42. PROB11/77/1.
43. M. A. Lower, 'Ironworks in the county of Sussex', *SAC*, xviii (1866), 13; REQ2/242/14; *The Lavington Estate Archives*, ed. F. W. Steer (Chichester, 1964), pp. 110–11.

been completed.[44] Ashburnham, like Morley, died deeply in debt: long before his death in 1592 his creditors had evidently occupied his ironworks and were driving his wife and family to distraction.[45]

Why some men prospered in business and others failed to do so is a question that can never be satisfactorily answered. Iron manufacture was clearly a risky undertaking: success depended not only upon good management but also to a certain extent upon good luck. A succession of dry seasons could lead to a serious lack of water to power the furnaces and forges. The threat of enemy invasion could lead, in this vulnerable corner of southern England, to a temporary but serious shortage of materials: one ironmaster complained that, because he and his workmen had been 'imployed in the service of Her Majesty' throughout the 'troublesome somer' of 1588, they had been unable to get in sufficient supplies of charcoal and his furnace had subsequently 'stoodd still' for lack of fuel.[46] But more troublesome than Spaniards were the enemies that some manufacturers made within their own communities. Thomas Hay, riding one day along the road from Ashburnham to Dallington, was ambushed, assaulted and left 'in vtter dispaire of his lief' by a gang of men who were allegedly trying to gain possession of one of his ironworks. They were acting, he believed, on the instructions of another ironmaster, George May of Burwash, who seems to have had a name for such violent deeds.[47] May was also involved in a long drawn out dispute with Thomas Collins over some land which Collins's forbears had caused to be flooded for the establishment of Socknersh furnace (in Brightling). And although shortly before his death early in 1593 May was said to have advised his heirs to end the controversy, the advice was apparently not heeded; for on the night of 8 December in that year (so it was alleged) his widow and son assembled a posse of workmen who proceeded to dig up the dam of Socknersh furnace and let the water out of the pond. Collins claimed that he had spent much of the previous summer and a great part of his substance in stocking the furnace, which had been working for only a few days to his 'no greate profitt' when the water was drained from his pond; as a consequence the furnace had gone out, much

44. Ibid.. pp. 110–11.
45. STAC5/08/36; BL, Harl., 703 f. 2; Mousley, op. cit., pp. 221–2, 410.
46. C3/230/57.   47. STAC5/H27/23.

of his stock was lost, his workmen were unemployed and he himself was 'greatly impoverished'.[48] Incidents such as these, however,
were doubtless not very common and, when they did occur, it is
likely that the sufferers would greatly exaggerate their losses. For
most ironmasters a much commoner hazard was probably the
failure of customers to pay their debts. At the time of the Socknersh affray in fact Collins was endeavouring to recover 'divers
severall sommes of money' owed to him by 'divers persons
dwellinge towardes the north partes of this realme', including a
smith of Newark-on-Trent who owed him £11.11.0.; in May
1595, although the debts were over three years old and he had
'travelled to his said debtors for the receavinge . . . of the said
debtes', they still had not been paid.[49] His friend Thomas Isted
had recently experienced similar difficulties with a customer in
Nottingham to whom he had sold eight tons of iron bars in April
1588 and for which he was still awaiting payment in November
1592.[50] Collins and Isted were both prosperous men and such
small losses would not have ruined them, but these instances indicate one of the hazards that faced the Wealden ironmaster producing for a distant market.

It is likely, however, that the biggest risks were taken, and the
biggest profits made, by ironmasters who were producing for
more distant markets still—those who manufactured ordnance for
sale overseas. At one time the only man who was officially permitted to do so was Ralph Hogge of Buxted, the Queen's 'gun-
stone maker and gunfounder of iron', who in 1568 had secured
the exclusive right to export any guns and ammunition not
required by the Ordnance Office.[51] But this patent, as Hogge
complained to the privy council in 1573, had not prevented others
from participating in this lucrative trade: in addition to himself,
Robert Hodgson and Arthur Middleton, who (he reported) 'onlye
cast for the Tower', there were four others—Sir Thomas Gresham,
Nicholas Fowle, Alexander Fermor and Michael Weston—who
had recently begun to cast ordnance and, in some instances, to
sell it overseas.[52] If Gresham was selling ordnance overseas at this
date the transactions were probably wholly legitimate, for he had
received the Queen's licence to make a hundred 'hole culveringes

48. STAC5/C1/7, C25/10, C52/9.   49. C3/236/57.
50. C3/243/7.   51. Crossley, *SAC*, cxii, 49.
52. Straker, *Wealden Iron*, p. 150.

of caste iron' for the king of Denmark; but Fowle and Fermor, who were said to 'sell mytche alongest the coast at Lewys in Sussex', were almost certainly engaging in activities that were underhand and illegal.[53] Such activities, of course, were seen as a threat to the security of the realm, for it was feared that some of the ordnance exported to the Netherlands, Germany, France and elsewhere might come into the hands of England's potential enemies.[54] And in spite of the vigorous measures taken by the privy council in the early months of 1574, when Wealden ironmasters were required to enter into recognisances (each of £2000) not to manufacture guns without licence, the illicit traffic continued.[55] The Spaniards persisted in their efforts to secure supplies of English ordnance, and so apparently did the Barbary corsairs.[56] Gresham for one was not averse to doing business with such people: on one occasion in the spring of 1577 he sent a consignment of shot by night to the Isle of Wight *en route* for the Barbary coast.[57] By this time the number of known gunfounders in the Weald had risen to ten: Sir Alexander Culpepper, Henry Bowyer and David Willard had now joined the ranks of this exceptionally prosperous group of ironmasters.[58]

Just how profitable was the business of gunfounding, or of iron manufacture in general, can never be known with any certainty—even in those rare instances where fairly complete sets of accounts have survived.[59] Because one man died in affluence and another in comparative poverty it does not necessarily follow that the one was a success and the other a failure in business. Some ironmasters had other important sources of wealth—the revenues of inherited estates or the profits of some other commercial enterprise. Gresham was not the only one whose business interests extended far beyond the Weald: Thomas Dyke, for example, who had ironworks in Yorkshire as well as in Kent, stated in his will (made in 1614) that he had 'disbursed and layde out divers and sondrye somes of money in and aboute the adventures aboute the East Indies, Virginia and the Barmudoes'.[60] At least one ironmaster enriched himself by a fortunate marriage: after his wedding to a

---

53. Ibid., p. 150; SP12/95/62.   54. Straker, *Wealden Iron*, pp. 150–1.
55. Ibid., pp. 57–8.   56. C. M. Cipolla, *Guns and Sails* (1965), p. 35n.
57. S. T. Bindoff, *The Fame of Sir Thomas Gresham* (1973), pp. 16–17, and n. 21.
58. BL, Lands., 683, f. 21v.   59. Cf. *Sidney Ironworks Accts.*, p. 28.
60. STAC5/G14/27; PROB11/125/20.

wealthy widow of Slinfold it was alleged that Roger Gratwick had gained possession of her late husband's goods, chattels, rents and profits amounting to £2000 and had 'ymployed the same to his owen private gayne'.[61] Equally, with those who experienced severe financial setbacks, it is possible that the causes were sometimes quite unconnected with their business activities: John Ashburnham's difficulties may have been due not so much to the bad management of his ironworks as to the crippling burden of recusancy fines.[62]

Ashburnham was one of only three Wealden ironmasters known to have been recusants, the other two being Lord Montague and Sir Alexander Culpepper, whose ardent catholicism is well attested.[63] Two others may be regarded as at least sympathetic to the old religion—Christopher Darrell, who belonged to the prominent recusant family seated at Scotney castle, and John Fawkener, a servant, protégé and friend of the staunchly catholic Gages of Bentley and Firle and an active persecutor of protestants under Mary.[64] The rest, for want of evidence to the contrary, may be classified as protestants of one sort or another, and among them there were probably a fair number of that 'hotter sort' whom contemporaries dubbed 'puritans'. The identification of Elizabethan puritans is a notoriously difficult undertaking and it would be hazardous to try, on the evidence available, to separate the godly ironmasters from the rest. But if the language of their wills provides a pointer, some of the men under consideration seem to have been more than usually zealous in religion. Four of them— Ninian Burrell, John Eversfield, Richard Leech and Sir Richard Baker—expressed the hope that they might become partakers with the 'elect' in the joys of life everlasting; but this by itself cannot be taken as evidence of an uncommonly Calvinistic outlook, since the catholic Lord Montague recorded the same aspiration.[65] Clearer indications of puritanism are found in the wills of Nicholas

61. REQ2/42/13.
62. Cf. J. E. Mousley, 'The fortunes of some gentry families of Elizabethan Sussex', *EcHR*, Ser. 2, 11 (1959), 478–9.
63. C. Buckingham, 'The troubles of Sir Alexander Culpepper of Goudhurst', *Cantium*, ii (1970), 5–8.
64. BL, Add. Ch. 30277; PROB11/74/76; Foxe, viii, 337.
65. PROB11/81/22. 84/46, 86/42, 88/89, 126/50. Montague affirmed his belief in the redemptive work of Christ, 'by the which onlye I hope to be saved, and assuredlie truste to be one of his Elect', while at the same time 'protestinge to live and dye . . . a true member of and in the unitie of his catholicke churche'.

Fowle, Henry Bowyer and Thomas Dyke. Fowle trusted that his soul would be 'presented pure before the throne of God' and ordained that at his funeral there should be 'a sermon or godlie exhortation to admonish the hearers of a godly life'.[66] Bowyer, in the course of a two-hundred-word preamble, speculated upon the celestial prospects of 'vnworthie, vnfaiethefull and most vn-thanckfull' sinners like himself, requested 'no manner of pompe or glorye' at his funeral and, in a final parting shot, charged his son to 'imbrace the religion of the most glorius gospell of Jhesus Christe crusified'.[67] Dyke, with a more practical approach to evangelism, bequeathed £400 to endow a weekly lecture to be given by 'godly and religious preachers' in four named places in Kent, Sussex, Suffolk and Yorkshire.[68] In addition there were two ironmasters who, although they gave little hint of it in their wills, were nonetheless men of markedly puritan temper. Thomas and Stephen Collins were singled out in 1603 as two of the most active organisers of puritan petitions in the diocese of Chichester.[69] They may have inherited their fiery protestantism from their mother Julian, who (it was said) had been 'in great danger and perryll for religion in the tyme of the late Quene Marie'.[70] Thomas, anxious perhaps to perpetuate this pious tradition, was one of a number of Wealden ironmasters who adopted the peculiar puritan practice of branding his offspring with godly-sounding names: he called his younger ones Increased, Patience and Changed, while his friend Thomas Isted named one of his daughters Redeemed.[71]

If the majority of Wealden ironmasters were protestants (and a sizeable minority were puritans), did they show any signs of that 'charitable impulse' which, it has been contended, was character-istic of men of their class? Certainly, if their wills are anything to go by, there are few indications of any unusual concern for the poor. With the single exception of Ralph Hogge, who made no charitable bequests whatsoever, all those whose wills survive be-queathed the traditional funeral doles to the poor of the parishes where they had lived or carried on business; but these sums nor-mally constituted only a tiny fraction of their total wealth.

66. PROB11/96/67. 67. PROB11/74/74; Manning, op. cit., p. 124.
68. PROB11/125/20. 69. Manning, op. cit., p. 209n.
70. C3/105/16.
71. PROB11/89/35, 120/75; Parish Registers of Brightling (at Brightling), i, f. 29.

Thomas Hay and Ninian Burrell, for example, who each left legacies totalling over £3000 to their children, left £9 and £7 respectively to the poor.[72] Only one ironmaster, the childless Richard Leech, made a really substantial bequest to the poor: he left £200 to endow an annual distribution of money in Fletching, where he had lived and worked, and in Smeeth, where he had been born.[73] In addition one man left property to be used for philanthropic purposes: Nicholas Fowle bequeathed 'one litle house and a garden' in Wadhurst, with a provision of four loads of wood a year, for the use of the poor of the parish.[74] This, taken all in all, is not a very impressive record: the ironmasters' contribution to the relief of poverty was neither greater nor smaller than that of other Elizabethans of similar status and wealth. Nor apparently did they make much contribution to the relief of ignorance: some, like John Barham and Thomas Hay, made copious provision for the education of their own children,[75] but in this regard most appear to have been indifferent to the needs of others. The outstanding exception of course was Sir Thomas Gresham, but even he, it has recently been pointed out, gave less to his College than he did to his illegitimate children.[76] And in any case, although some of his money was made in Mayfield, Gresham cannot by any stretch of the imagination be regarded as a typical Wealden ironmaster.

If this essay, in concentrating attention upon a particular bunch of men with common industrial interests, has given the impression that they constituted a distinct and homogeneous group, the impression is not entirely false. There were families for whom ironmastering was, if not exactly a way of life, at least an established and continuing occupation. Certainly a dozen, and possibly a score, of the sixty-odd men in this sample were themselves the sons of ironmasters; and a few, like Thomas and Stephen Collins, represented the third generation of a family that had earned its living in this way. The tradition, moreover, continued: at least a quarter of those operating ironworks in 1574 were eventually to be succeeded in business by their heirs. And in addition to this

72. PROB11/69/7, 79/23, 126/50.   73. PROB11/88/89.
74. PROB11/96/67.
75. Barham left an endowment of £20 a year for the education of his three younger sons; Hay stated specifically that his younger sons were to be sent to university and to one of the inns of court. PROB 11/65/41, 79/23.
76. Bindoff, op. cit., p. 22.

continuity from generation to generation there were certain significant collateral inter-connections: a remarkable number of ironmasters appear to have been linked to other ironmasters not merely by partnerships and other trading associations but by the more lasting ties of kinship or friendship.[77] There were three pairs of brothers and several companies of cousins operating across the Weald. There was also much inter-marrying. The case of Nicholas Fowle is perhaps not atypical: he married a sister of Thomas Isted; his sister married Alexander Fermor; his brother's widow married Arthur Middleton; his daughter married Middleton's nephew and heir; his niece married a son of John French; and, to extend the ramifications still further, Fowle (in company with John Barham and Stephen Collins) was among the godfathers of John Porter's children.[78] Porter, too, was a brother-in-law of Isted, who in turn was a brother-in-law of Barham and John Baker, who in his turn was a brother-in-law of Thomas Hay.[79] And so perhaps the chain of connections could be continued if anyone had the time and inclination to pursue the genealogical quest. Unravelling the ties of friendship is a more formidable task, but it could be more revealing: the evidence of wills, deeds and other documents indicates a network of relationships that may have been more significant than ties of blood or marriage.

It would be wrong, however, to suggest that these Elizabethan ironmasters constituted some kind of industrial and commercial elite within the community of the Weald. Some of them, as has been seen, were not first and foremost industrial entrepreneurs: they were big landowners for whom iron manufacture was merely a lucrative sideline. And even for the great majority, who belonged to the lesser gentry or upper yeomanry, industrial activity was hardly a permanent vocation. While some men evidently continued to plough back their profits into their businesses and remained content to live and die as ironmasters, others were as anxious as merchants or manufacturers elsewhere in England to invest their new-found wealth in land, so that they, or at any rate their heirs, could move up into the ranks of the greater gentry. Some, such as the Mays, the Eversfields and the Hays, succeeded

77. See Table 1.

78. Pullein, op. cit., pp. 382–5; H. S. Eeles, *Frant, a Parish History* (Tunbridge Wells, 1947), p. 153.

79. *Visitation of Sussex, 1530, & 1633–34*, ed. W. B. Bannerman (Harleian Soc. liii, 1905), pp. 101, 169.

in so doing, and it was perhaps just as well for them that they did; for the industrial boom was not to last for ever. By the end of the seventeenth century, being unable to compete with the industries established in the midlands and north, most of the Wealden iron-works had fallen into disuse and many of the surviving iron-masters faced ruin. In the eighteenth century the Barhams, or at least those members of the family who had remained in the iron business, were reduced to poverty; and in the next century a direct descendant of the prosperous ironmaster of 1574 was re-ported to be working as a wheelwright under a walnut tree in Wadhurst.[80] Their neighbours, the Fowles, fared no better: Nicholas Fowle's great-great-grandson, obliged to leave the family mansion at Riverhall, kept the turnpike gate in Wadhurst; and in 1839 his grandson Nicholas, a day-labourer, emigrated to America, carrying with him (as evidence of his family's former status) the royal grant of free warren that had been given to them over two hundred years before.[81] *Sic transit gloria mundi.*[82]

80. R. Davids and A. A. Wace, *The Story of Wadhurst* (Tunbridge Wells, 1924), p. 78.

81. Lower, *SAC*, ii, 218.

82. I am grateful to Mr David Crossley and Dr Alan Davidson for their com-ments on an earlier draft of this essay.

THE IRONMASTERS OF THE WEALD

No.	I Name	II Status	III Home	IV Location of Ironworks
1	Abergavenny 6th Lord	Peer	Birling	Rotherfield*
2	Ashburnham, John	Esq.	Ashburnham	Ashburnham, Horsmonden, Penhurst*
3	Baker, John	Yeo.	Battle	Withyham
4	Baker, Sir Richard	Knt.	Sissinghurst	Biddenden, Cranbrook
5	Barham, John	Yeo.	Wadhurst	Frant
6	Blacket, John	Yeo.	W. Hoathly	W. Hoathly
7	Bowyer, Henry	Gent.	Cuckfield	Hartfield, Worth
8	Bullen, George	Gent.	Hartfield	Hartfield
9	Burrell, Ninian	Gent.	Cuckfield	Cuckfield
10	Carpenter, John	Yeo.	Frant	Frant
11	Challenor, Ninian	Gent.	Cuckfield	Ardingly, Cuckfield, Slaugham
12	Collins, John	Yeo.	Burwash	Burwash
13	Collins, Stephen	Yeo.	Lamberhurst	Lamberhurst
14	Collins, Thomas	Yeo.	Brightling	Brightling
15	Colman, Simon	Yeo.	Brightling	Warbleton*
16	Culpepper, Sir Alexander	Knt.	Goudhurst	Cranbrook
17	Darrell, Christopher	Gent.	London	Frant, Newdigate
18	Duffield, John	Yeo.	E. Grinstead	Cranleigh, E. Grinstead, Kirdford
19	Dyke, Thomas	Yeo.	Horsmonden	Goudhurst, Pembury
20	Ellis, Thomas	Yeo.	Mayfield	Mayfield
21	Elrington, Edward	Esq.	Harlesden	Shere
22	Eversfield, John	Gent.	Worth	Hartfield, Worth
23	Fawkener, John	Yeo.	Waldron	Maresfield
24	Fermor, Alexander	Yeo.	Rotherfield	Rotherfield
25	Fowle, Nicholas	Gent.	Wadhurst	Wadhurst
26	French, John	Yeo.	Chiddingly	Chiddingly, Worth
27	Glyde, Thomas	Yeo.	Burwash	Etchingham, Warbleton*
28	Gratwick, Roger	Yeo.	Horsham	Ifield, Lower Beeding
29	Gratwick, Thomas	Yeo.	Kirdford	Dunsfold
30	Greene, Richard	Yeo.	Winchelsea	Mayfield
31	Gresham, Sir Thomas	Knt.	London	Mayfield
32	Hay, Thomas	Yeo.	Hastings	Battle
33	Hodgson, Robert	Yeo.	Framfield	Framfield
34	Hogge, Ralph	Yeo.	Buxted	Buxted, Maresfield
35	Isted, Thomas	Yeo.	Mayfield	Mayfield
36	Jefferay, Bartholomew	Yeo.	Bexhill	Bexhill
37	Lambert, John	Yeo.	Cranleigh	Cranleigh
38	Leech, Richard	Gent.	Fletching	Fletching
39	May, George	Gent.	Burwash	Salehurst
40	May, Thomas	Gent.	Winchelsea	Ticehurst
41	Middleton, Arthur	Gent.	Rotherfield	Buxted, Mayfield, Rotherfield
42	Montague, 1st Viscount	Peer	Cowdray	Chiddingfold, Haslemere*
43	Morley, Anthony	Gent.	Isfield	Horsted Keynes
44	Paler, John	Yeo.	Rotherfield	Buxted
45	Pope, Nicholas	Gent.	Buxted	Maresfield*

| V(a) Owner | | V(b) Tenant | | VI | VII | |
Fn.	Fg.	Fn.	Fg.	Partners	Relations	
I	I					1
I	2	I				2
		I	I		32, 35 (b/l)	3
I	I					4
	I?				35 (b/l); 46 (f)	5
		I				6
		3?	2?			7
		I	I			8
I					11 (c)	9
			I			10
	I?	2?	I	(not in list)	9 (c)	11
	I				13, 14 (n)	12
	I				12 (u); 14 (b); 46 (f)	13
I					12 (u); 13 (b); 35 (f)	14
		½		27		15
I	I				42 (f)	16
I			I			17
		1½	2†	37, 51		18
	I	I				19
			I			20
	I					21
		2	3			22
		I	I	(26)	54 (f)	23
		I			25 (b/l)	24
I	I				24, 35 (b/l); 46 (f)	25
	I	½	½	54 (23)		26
		1½	I	15 (32)		27
		I	2		29 (c?)	28
			I		28 (c?)	29
			I			30
I						31
		I		(27)	3 (b/l)	32
I?						33
		2?				34
	I				3, 5, 25, 46 (b/l); 14 (f)	35
		I	I	(49)	39 (f)	36
			½	18		37
		I				38
			I		36 (f); 40 (b); 58 (c)	39
I					39 (b); 58 (c)	40
		2?	I	(not in list)		41
I?	I?	I?			16 (f)	42
	I	I		(49)		43
			I			44
I						45

No.	I Name	II Status	III Home	IV Location of Ironworks
46	Porter, John	Yeo.	Battle	Lamberhurst*
47	Quyntin, ——	?	?	Cowden*
48	Relfe, John	Yeo.	Crowhurst	Crowhurst
49	Relfe, William	Yeo.	Warbleton	Fletching, Heathfield
50	Reynolds, Robert	Yeo.	E. Grinstead	E. Grinstead
51	Smith, Thomas	Yeo.	Petworth	Hartfield, Kirdford
52	Stacie, John	Yeo.	Ashurst	Ashurst
53	Stollion, Thomas	Yeo.	Heathfield	Burwash*, Waldron, Warbleton
54	Thorpe, John	Yeo.	Worth	Worth
55	Walpole, William	Gent.	Fittleworth	Petworth
56	Weekes, Richard	Yeo.	Battle	Mountfield
57	Weston, Michael	Yeo.	Leigh	Cowden, Salehurst
58	Whitfield, Robert	Gent?	Worth	Worth
59	Willard, David	Yeo.	Hadlow	Tonbridge
60	Woddy, Robert	Yeo.	Frant	Frant
61	Wybarne, John	Gent.	Pembury	Frant

* and in adjacent parish (es)

V(a) Owner		V(b) Tenant		VI	VII	
Fn.	Fg.	Fn.	Fg.	Partners	Relations	
		I			5, 13, 25 (f); 35 (b/l)	46
	I					47
		I			49 (b)	48
I		I		(36, 43)	48 (b)	49
		I	I			50
	I	½	1½	18		51
		I	I			52
		I‡	1½	not known		53
		½	½	26	23 (f)	54
		I	I			55
		I	I			56
		I	2	(59, 60)		57
			I?		39, 40 (c)	58
		I	2	(57, 60)		59
			I	(57, 59)		60
			I			61

† I + ½ + ½   ‡ ½ + ½

The information in this table is derived from the official 1574 lists, the works of Schubert, Straker and Cattell, and numerous other sources cited in the footnotes of this essay.

Column II. This gives the status commonly accorded to the ironmaster in 1574; it takes no account of subsequent changes in status.

Column III. This names the place of the ironmaster's (principal) residence in 1574.

Column IV. This names the parishes (following the contemporary boundary divisions) in which the ironmaster's forges or furnaces were located in 1574.

Column V. This records the number of forges (Fg) and furnaces (Fn) occupied by the ironmaster either as owner (a) or as tenant (b). A '?' indicates that there is some uncertainty either about the number of forges and/or furnaces, or about the form of tenure. A '½' indicates a half share in an ironworks.

Column VI. This gives the list number of the ironmaster's partner or partners. The plain numbers refer to partnerships existing in 1574 and those in brackets to partnerships terminated before that year or entered into in subsequent years.

Column VII. This gives the list number of the ironmaster's brother (b), brother-in-law (b/l), uncle (u), nephew (n), first cousin (c) and friend (f).

The Historical Writings of S. T. Bindoff

I. BOOKS, ARTICLES AND LECTURES

1934   Great Britain and the Scheldt, 1814–1839, *BIHR*, xii, 60–3 (Summaries of theses, no. cxx).
British Diplomatic Representatives 1789–1852, ed. jointly with E. F. Malcolm Smith and C. K. Webster (Royal Hist. Soc., Camden Series 3rd Ser., 1).
Select Documents: Lord Palmerston and the Universities, *BIHR*, xii, 39–42.

1935   The Unreformed Diplomatic Service, 1812–60 (The Alexander Prize Essay), *TRHS*, 4th Ser., xviii, 143–72.

1936   Translation with the author, P. Geyl. *Geschiedenis van de Nederlandse Stam*, ii. *The Netherlands divided, 1609–48* (Williams and Norgate).

1942   A Bogus Envoy from James I, *History*, xxvii, 15–37.

1944   Contributions to *Belgium* and *Netherlands* (Geographical Handbook Series, ed. H. C. Darby).
Clement Armstrong and his 'Treatises of the Commonweal', *EcHR*, xiv, 64–73.

1945   The Stuarts and their Style, *EHR*, lx, 192–216.
The Scheldt Question to 1839 (Allen and Unwin).

1946   British Democracy, *British Book News* (Longmans for National Book League, 1948), pp. 96–105.

1947   Peace Making at Paris, *World Affairs*, new ser. i, 57–67.

1949   *Ket's Rebellion, 1549*. Historical Association pamphlet, general series G 12; reprinted 1971 and in *The Historical Association Book of the Tudors*, ed. J. Hurstfield (1973), pp. 72–102.
The Netherlands and England: the parting of the ways. Address delivered at the annual meeting of the Historisch Genootschap, Utrecht, 31 Oct. 1949. *Verslag Algemene Vergadering Historisch Genootschap*, pp. 61–74.

1950 *Tudor England* (Pelican Hist. of England, no. 5; Penguin Books, Harmondsworth).
Town Life and Commerce, *Life under the Tudors*, ed. J. E. Morpurgo (Falcon Educational Books), pp. 56–71.

1951 Four Deputies in search of an Agenda, *World Affairs*, new ser., pp. 263–73.

1952 1552–1952: the fourth Centenary of Liquor Licensing in England, *A Monthly Bulletin*, xxii, 147–9, 163–5.

1953 The Elizabethan Economic Scene, *F.B.I. Review*, No. xxxix (June) A Kingdom at Stake, 1553, *History Today*, iii, 642–8; reprinted in *Conflicts in Tudor and Stuart England*, ed. I. Roots (1967), pp. 38–52.

1955 The Marian Martyrs: Smithfield after 400 years, *Manchester Guardian*, 4 Feb.

1956 Geschichte Englands, 1485–1689, *Handbuch der Weltgeschichte*, ed. A. Randa (Otto Walter), ii, 1764–73, 1844–5.

1957 The Social and Political Background, 1500–1660, *Cambridge Bibliography of English Literature*, v, 190–200. Parliamentary History 1529–1688, *Victoria County History of Wiltshire*, v, 111–169.

1958 The Greatness of Antwerp, *New Cambridge Modern History*, 2 The Reformation, ed. G. R. Elton, 50–69.

1960 East End Delight. W. Besant, *All Sorts and Conditions of Men*. Re-readings: 4, *East London Papers*, iii, 31–40.

1961 The Making of the Statute of Artificers, *Elizabethan Government and Society: essays presented to Sir John Neale*, ed. S. T. Bindoff, J. Hurstfield and C. H. Williams (University of London The Athlone Press), pp. 56–95.

1962 Political History, *Approaches to History; a Symposium*, ed. H. P. R. Finberg, pp. 1–15 (Routledge and Kegan Paul; reprinted 1965).
Charles Kingsley Webster 1886–1961, *Proceedings of British Academy*, xlviii, 427–47.

1971 *Research in Progress in English and Historical Studies in the Universities of the British Isles*, ed. jointly with J. T. Boulton (London, St James Press and Chicago).

1973 *The Fame of Sir Thomas Gresham*. The Neale lecture, delivered at University College, London, 6 Dec. (Jonathan Cape).

1976 *Research in Progress in English and History in Britain, Ireland, Canada, Australia and New Zealand*, ed. jointly with J. T. Boulton (London, St James Press and New York, St Martin's Press).

REVIEWS

1935 J. C. Westermann, *The Netherlands and the United States: their relations at the beginning of the nineteenth century* (*EcHR*, vi, 128–9).

1942 W. S. Unger, *De Tol van Iersekeroord. Documenten en rekeningen 1321–1572* (*EcHR*, xii, 87–9). C. Wilson, *Anglo-Dutch Commerce and Finance in the eighteenth century* (ibid., pp. 89–90).

1950 R. H. Tawney, *Social History and Literature* (*Manchester Guardian*, 7 July).

1951 *Calendar of Antrobus Deeds before 1625*, ed. R. B. Pugh, Wilts. Arch. and Nat. Hist. Soc. Recs. Branch iii (*EHR*, lxvi, 187–8). *Bronnen tot geschiedenis van den handel met Engeland, Schotland en Ierland*, ed. H. J. Smit, tweede deel, 1485–1585; tweede stuk, 1558–1585, Rijks. Geschiedkundige Publicatien, 86, 91 (*EHR*, lxvi, 583–6). P. Caraman, transl. *John Gerard: an autobiography of an Elizabethan* (*Manchester Guardian*, 21 Sept.).

1952 A. J. Barnouw, *The Making of Modern Holland* (*History*, xxxvii, 262–3).
Sir Charles Webster, *The Foreign Policy of Palmerston, 1830–1841* (*Contemporary Review*, clxxxi, 26–7).
M. Waldman, *Queen Elizabeth* (*Manchester Guardian*, 1 April).
Sir A. S. MacNalty, *Henry VIII: a difficult Patient* (ibid., 8 April).
G. L. Hosking, *The Life and Times of Edward Alleyn* (ibid., 29 April).
J. D. Mackie, *The Earlier Tudors, 1485–1558* (ibid., 28 Oct.).
Ampleforth and its Origins, ed. P. J. McCann and C. Cary-Elwes (ibid., 20 May).

1953 J. A. Williamson, *The Tudor Age* (*History Today*, iii, 863).
G. Anstruther, *Vaux of Harrowden. A recusant Family* (*Manchester Guardian*, 10 Feb.).

1954 G. R. Elton, *The Tudor Revolution in Government* (*History Today*, iv, 279).
G. Connell-Smith, *Forerunners of Drake* (*Manchester Guardian*, 15 June).

1955 Barbara Winchester, *Tudor Family Portrait* (*The Listener*, 15 Sept.).

1955 *The Letters of James the Fourth, 1505–1513*, ed. R. L. Mackie (*Scottish Hist. Rev.*, xxxiv, 171–3).
C. Read, *Mr. Secretary Cecil and Queen Elizabeth* (*Manchester Guardian*, 20 May).

1962 G. R. Elton, *The Tudor Constitution* (*Archives*, v, 170–1).

1967 *English Historical Documents*, v (1485–1558), ed. C. H. Williams (*British Book News*, No. cccxvii, 969).

1969 T. F. Shirley, *Thomas Thirlby, Tudor Bishop* (*Journ. of Ecclesiastical Hist.*, xx, 177–8).

1970 M. Holmes, *Elizabethan London* (*East London Papers*, xii, 130).

1972 G. R. Elton, *Policy and Police: the enforcement of the Reformation in the age of Thomas Cromwell* (*Spectator*, 6 May).

1975 M. Green and A. White, *The Evening Standard Guide to London Pubs;* W. B. Hawkins, *Tavern Anecdotes* (*The London Journal*, i, 154–6).
London Topographical Record, vol. xxiii, ed. Marjorie B. Honeybourne (*ibid.*, i, 277–9).
P. Burke, *Venice and Amsterdam* (*ibid.*, pp. 281–5).
Ten Studies in Anglo-Dutch Relations, ed. J. van Dorsten (*Times Lit. Supp.*, 28 Nov.).

1976 Daphne du Maurier, *Golden Lads; A study of Anthony Bacon, Francis, and their friends* (*ibid.*, 12 March).

Index

Abbot, Charles, 73
Abel, Thomas, 106n
Abingdon, abbot of, 49
Alcock, John, bp. of Ely, 153
Allen, William, 190–1
Alsop, 32, 34
—, John, 34–5
Amboise, 120, 123–4
Anabaptism, 126n
Andrews, Lancelot, bp. of Ely, 164
Antwerp, 45, 186–203
Armstrong, Clement, 197
Arthur, prince of Wales, 33, 41, 157
Arundel, 16, 207
—, John, bp. of Coventry and Lichfield, 36
Arundell, Sir Thomas, 90
Ashwell, 138
Aske, Robert, 83, 84, 86
Audley, Thomas, baron Audley of Walden, 80, 159
Augsburg, 195
Axholme, prior of, 56n
Aylmer, John, bp. of London, 158

Bacon, Francis, 10, 21, 30
Baker, Robert, 169
Balsall (Temple Balsall), 27–30
Baltic, the, 188n, 189, 191, 201
Banbury, 49, 103; palace of, 149, 156, 159
Bancroft, John, bp. of Oxford, 163
Barbary Coast, 190, 218
Barcheston, 49
Barentine, family of, 63
Bargh, Richard, 37, 39, 40
Barlow, William, bp. of Bath and Wells, 158
Barnes, Richard, bp. of Durham, 156, 163, 165

—, Robert, 106n
Basle, 118
Bassett, family of, 33–5, 43; Eleanor, 33–5, 39; John, 59, 60; William, junior, 33; William, senior, 34
Bath and Wells, bp. of: see Barlow, Berkeley, Bourne, Godwin
—, see of, 128, 129n, 144, 158–61
Baynton, Andrew, 120n
Bayonne, bp. of: see Du Bellay
Beauchamp, family of, 102
— de, Richard, 13th earl of Warwick, 96
Beaufitz (Bevis), family of, 27, 41; John, 26–30; Thomas, 27n
Beaufort, family of, 97
Beaumont, William, 2nd viscount Beaumont, 8
Beccles, 25
Béda, Noël, 108, 113, 115–19
Bedford, earl of: see Russell, Tudor
Bedfordshire, 4, 5, 60, 150
Bedingfeld, family of, 10; Sir Edmund, 9, 10
Bellingham, Robert, 26–30
Benedictines, 45, 162
Bentham, Thomas, bp. of Coventry and Lichfield, 129n
Bentley, 207, 219
Bergavenny: see Neville
Bergen-op-Zoom, 193
Berkeley, Gilbert, bp. of Bath and Wells, 160, 163
— de, William, 2nd viscount Berkeley, 5–6, 12, 16
Berkshire, 49, 55n, 153
Berkswell, 26, 28
Bermuda, 218
Berne, 120n
Berquin, Louis de, 108–15